De Gavin le
_____ ae an
leo i Cepeed_____

Séamus

Tell Me Another

Tell Me Another

Séamus Mac Aogáin

Edited by Virginia Rodríguez Cerdá
Cover and design by Daniel García Pelillo

ISBN 978-15-1471-857-5

Dedicated to Noah

Contents

Prologue
John Liddy

The book opens with the writer outlining his reasons for leaving the place of his birth and boyhood. Thankfully, the leave-taking is prolonged as we are invited to travel back in time on a Superbroom, the ultimate 3D time machine, with Tess, the principal character, the writer himself and Annabel his first love.

This is an age-old story told anew of village life, the wily and wild ways of its people and the strange goings on that happen everywhere but few know or want to know about them. The writer's gift is to mix history and topography with folklore and superstition, to lay bare with copious doses of humour the small town contradictions and intrigues and to poke fun at officialdom and official church. Nobody is spared the sharpness of his pen but all is rescued in the honesty, clarity and directness of his writing.

From youth to maturity we follow Seamie into the magical world of Tess, his friend and mentor, who teaches him about the 'otherworld' and passes on such gems of wisdom and insight that we know there is a writer being formed and primed to fear nothing in the future.

TELL ME ANOTHER is a story that echoes Corkery's hidden Ireland and a plethora of other works such as 'Home Through the Fields' and 'The Farm by Lough Gur', albeit with darker tones reminiscent of The Valley of The Squinting Windows. Here too we learn about what it was like to grow up in a bygone time with its underworld in Lisnacreevagh, the ancestral home of the fairies and Leprechauns; Clonmacnoise and the monks (raised eyebrows here!), the majesty of the Shannon, the building of the canal that flows through the Midlands of Ireland today, the Black & Tans and the War of Independence, the Books of Ballynamanagh and Abbeyshrule; its drovers and cadgers, fishermen and poachers, shop keepers and publicans; its rivers and fields where youth learned to have its fling and where nature took its course.

All this is here in Séamus Mac Aogáin's second book, which is a fine achievement because of the writer's gift for storytelling and his ability to describe events with atmospheric mastery such as is found in The Long-legged Thief, A Mad Dash to the Midwife and the last paragraph of the last chapter Tempus Fugit.

There is merit also in its informative mixture of fact and fiction, its netting of the local vernacular "there's more adin in the cupboard than ad-out", its wry, matter of fact comment on everything he surveys and for the poems the writer has chosen to sprinkle the book with:

Above all it is a love story that the writer experienced and still displays for his people and place. In the chapter The Visit, Tess predicts the new born baby's future to his mother: "He has the mark in his hand from another land and that triangle there is without compare. The child is blessed and he'll build his nest where the eagles rest far away from here."

Séamus Mac Aogáin's heart and soul is in the right place. From where he currently lives he can observe his native land and his people with an eagle eye.

Tell Me Another

Time to Go

It was time to go. There was sweet feck all to keep him hanging around the village, or the parish either come to think of it. Begrudgery abounded on all sides. The rich got richer, the mean got meaner and the poor got poorer.

"Same as always," as Tess would say. Though not long reached puberty he had seen enough hardship and hard times to do him a lifetime. Time passed the place by and went on about its business. He'd have to do the same or become trapped in an endless cycle of scrabbling for a living and making do with hand-me-downs.

There was hope though. Hadn't he helped Tess manufacture the ultimate 3D Time Machine to take them to 'Abbeyopia' where only the bravest go? Hadn't they spent hours fine-tuning the 'Superbroom' that would make them the envy of all on broomstick highway? Countless hours poring over the blueprints were finally showing fruit. Little remained to do now except take her on her maiden voyage, but to do so would mean taking another maiden along too. The craft was ready, the crew almost. Just a little more adjusting of imagination and they'd be off on an adventure as good, if not better than the Bun's, when he found the entrance to the Underworld in Lisnacreevagh, the ancestral home of the Fairies and Leprechauns.

"That story needs to be told too Seamie," Tess said as she showed him how to switch over to star power if there was no moon.

"Just throw the handle on your brain a mhic, stir the embers at the back of your mind and you're there. Divil the bit more you'll need if you're to go where you want to go and see what only a handful have seen," she said as they readied the dining room for supper. That section of the house was always referred to as the 'dining room' because the solitary table and two stools there elevated it to that status. The supper could be anything from a mug of tea with a heel of a loaf toasted on the griddle, rasp reheated on the pan, green potato bread, or porridge made with goat's milk. It made little difference to either of them because hunger, they knew, was a great sauce and that it'd prolong the evening's entertainment anyway.

The library on the mantelpiece consisted of Rambles in Eireann by William Bulfin, 'Goldsmith Illustrated,' 'Recollections of an Irish Rebel' and Padraic Colum's 'Crossroads In Ireland' which she acquired at Canon McGivney's auction when she bid a thrupenny bit for the four of them.

"Apologies Tess," said Hanley the auctioneer. "Had the Canon known you had such an interest in literature he'd have donated his entire library to you I'm sure" brought raucous laughter from the assembly of gawkers, tyre kickers and piss artists. The few who could afford to buy anything examined their fingernails and kept a discreet silence.

"He couldn't take them with him or they'd be gone up in flames in Lucy's parlour by now," she sneered as she pointed to the marble fireplace. "Aye and the rest of ye who wouldn't know a sonnet from a linnet would be better off reciting your prayers than making little of decent people," she said as she sauntered through them with the books in her halter bag.

The area around the open hearth was the kitchen as anything remotely related to food preparation transpired there. Thin as a rake and not two hands higher than a duck she still ate like a sparrow to give the little she had to those who hadn't. Few called on her except the 'Bun,' a close relation, Maria McCrone if the lights were on, the Nugget and his son Rex from time to time, Nora occasionally and, of course, Seamie every chance he got. Fr. McCabe called as often as he could which was about every six months, and a few quare wans looking to have their palms read or their tealeaves pored over. 'And feck the much more' as she'd say herself. The majority peddled or strode smartly past by day or whistled through their teeth at night as they hurried about their business hoping she wouldn't spot them. She missed little though because if she didn't see them Billy did and kept her posted so she could see without being seen. For pure devilment she'd let out a blood-curdling screech from the bushes at the back of the house occasionally if someone she wasn't mad about dallied along the road by night. They didn't dally after that but flew past as if the place was haunted. Blessed with acute hearing she'd hear the grass growing and the breezes whispering if someone was about. Rather than engage in pointless pleasantries she'd disappear into the house or tend to her tiny garden and multitude of geraniums around the house. Diminutive in stature she had a presence about her that belied a natural intelligence beyond the realms of most of her peers. She didn't play on it though, preferring to choose those who chose her in a natural fashion.

The corner by the window was both the guest room and the planetary observation centre because of the settle bed and the tiny four-paned-window hidden from the outset by a blood-red geranium. From here mankind's movements were monitored as they approached the operations centre. A system of mirrors amplified the over-all view and, apart from Billy, there was another system of trip wires radiating round the exterior to keep her informed if anyone should darken her doorstep after the witching hour. It was so simple and effective in execution it never failed to impress those in the know, 'the Inner Circle' as she often referred to them. It was comprised of strategically positioned fishing line connected to empty Batchelor's beans and pea cans that, when disturbed, played a melodic note not unlike that of the corncrake. They weren't trip wires as such, more like underground cables as the 'Bun' once said. 'Ingenious nevertheless,' he added quickly.

The Aurora Borealis

"It was a rare kind of a morning," she told Seamie many moons later when they were chatting about children in general and a child born out of wedlock in particular.

"Every house has a story, a secret, something hidden or other," she started. "Everyone kinda knows what those secrets are but either pretends not to know or would prefer to say nothing in case the cat was let out of the bag and the Town Crier got hold of it. Not that it'd make a lot of difference mind you but a hint is as good as a nod to a blind man unless you're blessed like Ned Reilly who'd see the grass growing in a manner of speaking. Well, anyhow, none of us can talk because there's more adin in the cupboard than adout and no better place to find it than your own place. Sure the priests would be out to grass long ago if it weren't for us sinners. Look at all the money they'd lose and the chances they'd miss if they didn't hear it all adin in their box of secrets. Confession me elbow! How would the world know what was goin' on if it wasn't for the confession box? Didn't your uncle make a pure hoor out of it altogether when he went into the box for a kip one night before the missions and fell into a coma in a second. Being a boyo he was worn out with work and play and thought he'd have lots of time before the Missioners landed. The lads on the one knee by the back door knew he was adin and directed the ladies in from the short isle telling them the Missioner was adin and not to be surprised if he didn't answer them as he was supposed to be deaf and dumb. Spotting an opportunity, the best of the sinners used their privileged position to get what they could remember off their chests and nearly trampled each other in the process. As soon as they saw the Missioners coming over the bridge the boyos gathered up around the box and let him slip through them knowing they'd be filled in on the juicy bits later. Some of the oul wans nearly had a canary when they got wind of the word but sure they had nothing to tell anyway. The young wans didn't give a damn because they were on to him and either filled him full of lies so they'd draw him into their web or have the last laugh when he tried to make hay with their stories. It's a sight the way we let on to be listening to the priests and we mad for devilment every chance we get. But isn't that what makes life worth living? If we were to believe half of what we hear we'd have given up the ghost long ago. Heaven or hell is it! Make the most of it while you're here a mhic because unless the lads come in with their flying saucers and bring us away with them we'll have to make do with what's here.

I'm rambling a bit a mhic. What were we talking about? Ah yes, the young wan. The strange thing was she didn't even know she was pregnant. She had a bit of a heartburn alright but put it down to the bowl of gruel she had for breakfast. Anything else would have been better but there wasn't anything else.

"Half a heel is better nor no bread," her grandmother said as she sent her to the village to collect her pension. Feeling decidedly uncomfortable as she turned the corner by the graveyard she climbed over the stile and ran to the shelter of the abbey to relieve herself. What happened after that was a lot more than the poor girl expected! Out popped the grandest gossoon you'd meet on a month's march. With Nature taking over, as it usually does when looking after its own, the child was delivered without a bit of bother. Though a bit befuddled by the turn of events she managed to wrap the child in her shift before struggling home through the fields to her grandmother who didn't bat an eyelid, except to ask if she managed to collect the pension and the bit of tobacco before, or after the event. The answer not being to her liking she despatched one of the other ones with a sweep of the brush. As soon as she settled her head and shook herself she looked after both as only she could, no recriminations, no questions; the type of wisdom that only age can carry. She had seen it all before and saw God in it all.

Billy woke her up earlier than usual that remarkable morning she told Seamie. He was singing his little heart out and tapping at the window to wake her up. Something was stirring she felt sure because he was far too excited for this early hour. Suddenly, a brilliant flash of light flooded the bedroom area, which in winter shifted from the window to the fireplace or as close as possible without singeing the sugán, and woke her up the same as if there was a wogeous clap of thunder. Thinking it was lightning she shook the sleep from her and turned on the light under her cap. To any but her intimate friends this bundle of hand knit shawls and sheets made from flour bags was no more than they'd expect from such an extraordinarily eccentric individual.

Wide-awake now, she struggled to emerge from the depths of the old chair, as good as any cave in days gone by. She was well used to caves because, like her people before her, she had to hide out in them when the Black and Tans were scouring the country for those who didn't know how to lie down and die in front of them. Poorly equipped, these guerrilla fighters could only strike at night. This was fraught with danger however, because their houses were constantly under watch by the Tanners making their return home perilous. Despite that they soon learned how to beat them at their own game. After an exaggerated pretence of slipping in home they exited through a tunnel and joined their colleagues outside to trap the Tanners who had burst down the door, charged inside and got caught like flies in a bottle; an old trick perfected by Cromwell in Youghal and Drogheda when he ran the natives into cul-de-sacs and slaughtered them to a child. Big Joe however, turned the tables on his return from the Boer War. His intimate knowledge of guerrilla tactics and weaponry played havoc with the ill-trained Tanners not long out of prison and hospitals after the First World War.

'Hit and Run, hit and run' became the mantra of the IRA as they waylaid convoys of ill-trained Black and Tans escaping from jail and justice across the pond. Fearless in battle against the superior Boer forces he learned quickly and took his medals for bravery with humility and pride. The Boers had the Brits on the run initially with their guerrilla tactics but it was to play against them eventually as they were little match for the better organised and equipped British who had the devil-may-care, do-or-die Irish battalions who swept over them like Spring tides. Back home in Abbeyshrule he felt like a Neanderthal in a convent of nuns. Supping pints drove him to distraction until a passion for midnight sorties poaching salmon reawakened his inner being. Clever as he thought he was there were others watching him like hawks. It wasn't long until the knock came and his new life began. Supplied with a well-minded High Nelly and an old Lugar that was well past its sell-by date, he drank tea in every safe house in the parish. Within weeks he had the Nugget, the Potstick, the Horse, the Cuddy, the Bun and several others training around Lough Sheedon and Abbeyshrule bog. Not content with that he organised a group of influential ladies from the locality into a Cumann Na mBán women's group to provide backup, care and sustenance when necessary. And that they did as soon as they were fit to put a good leg under them or pull a trigger.

Survival became paramount as the Brits used every conceivable dirty trick to force confessions from the quietest of people. The last straw was the raiding of Ballynamanagh and the attempted violation of a decent woman who not only wouldn't utter a syllable, instead, blew the brains out of the bastard that ripped the clothes of her knowing she'd already signed her own death warrant. Just as the so-called captain was about to shoot, a four-pronged fork nailed him to the barn door. The rest were mown down before they knew what hit them. General Sean MacEoin just happened to be in the area and was quickly informed of the Tanners whereabouts. Using the shelter of Ballintubber lane he arrived in time to exact full revenge and that he did. It wasn't long until the writing was on the wall for the Tanners and they were forced to travel in larger groups around the bigger towns where MacEoin and his flying columns harassed them at every turn.

The final act that put the head sheaf on the farce was when the General and the Ballynamanagh crew ably assisted by Big Joe and Co. broke into the courthouse in Ballymahon just as an active group of the IRA were about to be sentenced to death by a Kangaroo court comprised of a bunch of Tans. MacEoin marched the sentries into the body of the court, forced the others to disarm and, bundling the so-called judge out into his own jeep, left the Nugget in charge until they were well gone. There was precious little the Tanners could do anyway as they were bound and gagged and weren't able to escape for hours because a local lad kept the few gawks at bay with an imitation gun. Realisation finally dawned on their superiors after the Battle of Balinalee (when General MacEoin and three hundred men forced over nine hundred British soldiers to withdraw after a solid week of intense fighting) that they were going nowhere with this raggle taggle of misfits. Finally, they were brought home by a government humiliated and whipped by Gandhi who had turned world opinion against a brutality he and his followers had experienced on several occasions.

As soon as the last ship had embarked a power struggle erupted in the Republic. Michael Collins had done his utmost for the best deal possible but DeValera was unconvinced. He somehow felt a better deal was possible when it patently wasn't; at a time when Britain was reorganising after the horrors of the First World War. Dev was also on a high after breaking out from Lincoln Jail and reappearing in the Phoenix Park to a tumultuous welcome from more than a million and a half followers who had packed trains, busses, tractor and cars as well as cycling and tramping from every corner of Ireland to hear what he had in mind. His opening sentence 'as I was saying before I was so rudely interrupted' won over the hardliners and endeared him to a nation ready for anything, even national suicide, rather than continue with the constant brutality being inflicted daily by a neighbouring country intend only on savagery in order to perpetuate their power and control over a colony. Their last throw of the dice failed miserably as the Black and Tans were forced to an ignominious exit.

The worst was yet to come as Dev and Collins fought for supremacy in a battle no one could win. It ended with Collins being murdered at Béal Na Bláth. The bloodletting that followed was savage and unremitting until De Valera ordered his men to down arms less than a year later. All very well of course if you were fighting the old enemy, but a different ball of twine altogether if it was your own flesh and blood. Common sense prevailed in the long run although there were vested interests hiding behind many a door, which kept the pot boiling at enormous cost to the fledgling republic.

The Visit

"Whist a ghrá," she said as she lifted the latch and let Billy land on the half door. "I'm sure, Imagine!" she said softly as he told her all about his early morning activities. Hopping onto her shoulder to retrieve the crust she had placed for him they looked a remarkable sight.

"Any wonder we're the talk of the parish," she smiled as he did his fainting trick, recovering his flight just before he hit the ground.

She knew that she often had the tongues wagging but delighted in being different. Though rarely seen along the roads, as she preferred the soft ground and green grass to the rough gravel, she often popped into The Shop to catch up on the latest scandal. Anyone lucky enough to be there when Tess and Maria McCrone from beyant in Arklone happened to be together, was left enthralled by their colourful speech and their even-more colourful costumes. The 'Twins', as they were commonly known, had a perspicacity to dress to impress with their brilliantly coloured bonnets, berets, shawls and homemade sandals. Having soldiered together when men were men they had huge respect for each other but that didn't stop them from bouncing of each other either. Neither of them having two washers to rub together, they were often the bane of Cody the postmaster who laboured in vain for their overdue accounts. Not that Tess owed much because she bought so little it wasn't worth worrying about, but being the man he was he had to have his pound of flesh.

Lights danced through the heavens like flocks of starlings as she gazed across the dew-covered fields to Colehill.

"He's landed Billy!" she said as she pulled the shawl tight over her shoulders and closed the front door behind her.

Rex was after filling a bag of turf in the shed and was flicking a match alight with his thumbnail when she lifted him out of his standing with her greeting.

"Cheeses Tess where did you spring from?" he stuttered as he stubbed the Sweet Afton out on an upturned bucket.

"Didn't I tell you I'd be here when Seamie arrived," she retorted. And no better day than this with the heavens telling us better nor the star beyant in Bethlehem."

"You did indeed Tess and I'm only after thinking of it. Go on up to see them because the nurse's work is done. I'll be in as soon as I fill another bag of turf."

"I will so," she said as she crossed the yard to the back door. A thought occurred to him as she lifted the latch on the door. Why hadn't he heard her and why didn't she make some kind of noise as she crossed the gravelled yard? It was if she was floating a couple of inches above the ground.

"What's up with you?" he asked Shep who was wagging his tail like a windmill. "How come you didn't hear her either?" He wasn't surprised that her shoes, if she was wearing any, made no sound on the ground. Nothing about this woman surprised him since he first met her as a boy going home from school. Unlike his friends he often stopped for a chat or sat on the bridge for a while as he related the day's events, and she in turn told him of her nocturnal wanderings. It wasn't long until he spent most of his free time with her. She was in her hay-day then and still unattached though many tried and failed to win her over. She had few friends then either but it was obvious to all she had a special grá for him.

As the door closed behind her it hit him that she had already named the child. It was Nora's idea to use the name Séamus if it were a boy and Sarah if it was a girl but he was positively sure neither he nor she had discussed this with anyone. Lying back against the jam of the door to ponder on her unexpected but welcome arrival, he felt proud to know her and considered himself to be mighty lucky to have learned so much from her.

Inside now, she called up from the kitchen to see if it was alright to come up to see mother and child.

"Is it yourself Tess? Come on up. I'm just feeding him," Nora called down as she readied herself and the child in the bed. A tap on the door as she entered brought a wan smile to the young mother worn out by her recent delivery. As they chatted away she noticed that the old lady was taking in everything about the child. Having examined him thoroughly and read his palm she then pronounced on him.

"He'll travel far before he finds his star Nora, but when he does he'll leave his mark for all to see," she said as she handed him back to her.

"He has the mark in his hand from another land and that trian-gle there is without compare. The child is blessed and he'll build his nest where the eagles rest far away from here," she intoned as she put a bright green stone in his tiny hand. As Nora went to hand it back to her the child's fingers closed on it. It would be much later before he'd let it go.

"It's for him anyway," the old lady smiled as she traced a cross on his forehead.

Remembering then that she had picked fresh herbs on the way up, she took them out of her shoulder bag and handed them to Nora saying they would help her over the travails of giving birth. Nora knew better than to enquire what might be in the bag so left it at that with a word of thanks and a warning not to leave without a mug of tea and some scones she made the previous evening. "Tell Mike I said you were to take a half dozen for yourself as well."

"I'll go away so Nora but you've done well girl. He'll be no bother to you at all at all." With that she bid farewell to the bemused young mother and closed the door gently after her.

"You'll have a mouthful Tess?" Rex asked as he slid the kettle over the blazing coals.

"I will so Mikeen," she nodded as she eased herself into the comfy chair by the fireside. Known as 'Rex' to most because of his dog Rex who followed him like a shadow throughout his youth, he was also referred to as Mikeen; it being an abbreviation of his proper Christian name Michael. He didn't much care what he was called except when some unfortunate idiot chose the wrong appendage and ended up with a warning or a headache.

As was her wont Nora had left nothing to chance knowing the well-wishers and nosebodys would arrive soon after the child was born.

"You'd swear the white smoke was after announcing Seamie's arrival," Tess laughed as she tore into the scones Nora made just before nature told her to take to the bed.

"You didn't need any white smoke," Rex remarked as he hinted at her early appearance.

"Pure mathematics Mikeen," she giggled as she kept her counsel.

Abbeyshrule and the Blue Sky over It

A pretty little village, it was neatly ensconced in a fertile valley of the River Inny. Big salmon and trout swam lazily in the deep pools while pike and bream lived in constant movement above them. A fisherman's paradise, it attracted followers of the fashion from far and near. Nor were the locals to be left out. The ones with a variable licence plied their hobby from bridge to weir while others less equipped hung back in careful watch or sought the comfort of the night to lay their lines. Both were equally successful, relying on years of austerity and long-learned lore to whip a big one from the depths. It was then the real battle began: how to get the prized fish home without being caught by the bailiff? A severe wetting was better than being up before the magistrate for poaching. This entailed a long march home through soggy fields rather than risk the road and the watchful gaze of a jealous neighbour or, even worse, the bailiff himself.

Being a lifetime student of the art, little went unknown to Rex. A good evening's fishing meant he could distribute a few nice trout on the way home which would bring a helpful hand when needed, or a shut mouth if the bailiff came a calling.

The smell of fish frying during the week brought out the worst and the best in some of the neighbours.

"You landed it Rex," was the quiet praise of a friend while 'is it Friday already?' meant one was not to be ignored when a trout was to spare. Either way, word would spread and he'd be watched like a hawk to see where his perch was, or what stretch of the river he was plucking such pickings from.

The Royal canal came to town around 1816 bringing a mini boom to the tiny hamlet of Abbeyshrule. As soon as the water started flowing under the new bridges the ghetto area known as the 'Mill Lane' soon filled up. These were originally mud or wood cabins where Gypsies and Tinkers had long settled with their women and kids. No one knew exactly when the Gypsies had arrived but it was thought they might have arrived from Spain around the time of the Spanish Inquisition when they were hounded from their homes with the Jews and the Moors. The Tinkers were probably the old Irish who had been consigned to hell or to Connaught by Cromwell but somehow managed to find a peaceful haven in the quiet backwater. They provided all kinds of services from shoe-making to pot mending, to barrel making, with the sharpening of knives, blades, cut throats and scythes a natural follow on. It wasn't long until a thriving trade in secondary services emerged, targeting the hard working, hard living canal workers. Some ladies of leisure plied their trade by night just off the banks of the canal, in their huts or under the bridge. The powers that be, namely Church and State, turned a blind eye as the mass offerings and purchase of provisions grew accordingly.

"It's an ill wind that doesn't blow someone some good," the PP remarked, as he heaved the ace of hearts.

"As long as it doesn't get out of hand or hit the headlines," the bishop replied as he slapped down the five of trumps.

The village itself would have been a good defensive position in the dim and distant past and this, no doubt, influenced the Cistercians in their quest for a peaceful retreat from the marauding Celts, Vikings and English. It didn't do them much good though as they attracted every hungry hoor that travelled the country over the centuries. Many of the monks were put to the sword for failing to comply with the unnatural desires of the savage invader. While the older nuns suffered horrendous abuse before being put out of their misery, the younger ones were raped and forced to be their personal playthings if lucky, and if not, they were forced to follow the foot soldiers through hell and back. Though the abbey was torched time after time it was rebuilt and restored to its former glory again and again until finally succumbing to the Saxon savages, as did Clonmacnoise. When the monks couldn't hide their precious chalices and patens from the rapacious hordes they flung them far into the murky depths of the Inny hoping to retrieve them later. That didn't happen until hundreds of years later when, as Quigley maintained, a new breed of whore came calling with metal detectors and frog suits to pluck the priceless treasure from the deep. Clonmacnoise succumbed to similar violation during the same era until finally the legal authorities got off their arses and passed a bylaw to at least prevent the booty disappearing across the Atlantic.

A fine chapel stood proudly in the lee of the canal bridge, evidence of the generosity of the same workers who built the canal between 1790 and 1817. Two bars, a Sheebeen by the graveyard, a post office and a few big houses belonging to the owners stood close to each other as a type of defense against trouble, which was probably the case in bygone days when the enemy could come from any corner. Generally of stout structure and usually well maintained, these houses stood the test of time and still stand proudly despite the hardships of time as Tess told Seamie. McGoeys being the bigger, partly thatched and partly slated, was the most frequented of the two bars. A couple of snugs for the ladies were discreetly positioned between the lounge and the 'Pauper's Bar' as Peter Dolan called it. One could spit and fart there without fear of invective he added. As well as catering for the daily needs of the rich and poor, most of the locals ran an account as they depended on the season's bounty to repay their domestic bills before the Christmas. This led to the odd puck in the gob and thick ear for some good for nothings who would drink Lough Iron dry if given half a chance. This was done discreetly of course as it wouldn't do to have a reputation for being hard men. Big Joe had an easy way about him but if asked to quietly put manners on someone he left them in no doubt where they stood. His time spent taking the Queen's Shilling against the Boers was enough to convince the foolhardy to change their ways. However, good husbandry, frugality and common sense being the norm for most decent folk, he was rarely called on to intervene. This changed dramatically however when he was asked to join the struggle and use his experience of guerilla warfare against the British, particularly during the short but viscous term of The Black and Tans.

The canal barges bringing beer and stout from St. James' Gate one way, and turf and timber on the return, provided some unique opportunities for the Go-Boys. Minor theft kept a rattle in the pocket of the night raiders who knew the odd barrel quietly removed from Mitchell or Cambell's charge in the dead of night wouldn't be missed, as it would be put down to natural wastage.

A few of the go-boys from the Bog Lane kept a close eye on local proceedings. Linking up with some ne'er-do-wells from Hellfire Terrace they swooped on selected barges during the night leaving nothing but veiled threats for the bargemen. Unscrupulous vintners, hoping to capitalize on the Christmas market, snapped up these barrels indifferent to their source. Many an ass and cart made its humble way with a reek of hay from Ballynacarrigy to Ballymahon without anyone being the wiser to a couple of kegs of porter lying snugly in the middle. Humble homesteaders living along the line kept the wheels of commerce turning by supplying the daily necessities of bread, butter, jam, fish, fowl, potatoes and vegetables while others waited patiently to empty loads of good quality turf into the holds at the harbours in Abbeyshrule, Brannigan and Ballinacarrigy.

The Ballynacarrigy brigade were, if anything, even more dangerous than the Ballymahon Boyos. In truth, they were a rare mix as more than seed potatoes were sown between the two down through the ages.

"Grand fresh mornin' lads," Rex remarked as he drew abreast of Hellfire Terrace on his way to Mullingar with twenty big bullocks from Knockagh.

"Will we turn dim inta the field for ya Rex?" the Gom called from the security of his garden.

"I'll turn your sister into an elephant if you're not careful," Rex laughed as he ushered his charges onwards.

"You mightn't be half as funny comin' back with your pockets full and your belly empty," reminded him to be careful on the way home. Renowned for his bargaining ability, he was given a free hand by the 'Duke of Antley' when it came to buying and selling. Now and again the Duke would turn up towards midday, but as trust was paramount and the Nugget was well got by one and all, there was never going to be any underhand dealings. Allowed the 'luck penny', as a reward for his industry and craft, he used his sharp wits and Quigley's teaching to keep him ahead of the pack money wise. Thereby lay the problem! The corner boys kept close watch on his every move on fair day knowing he was bound to have a bundle of money and a severe thirst on him by the time he got back to Ballinacarrigy.

Once he reached Sonna he lit a Sweet Afton because the fight was long gone from the animals by now and it was easy going from here to the canal bridge by the cathedral. Letting them graze the long acre he sat on the bridge a while thinking how best he'd cope with his busy life. He was in no great need for anything and few bothered him once he kept his head down and kept out of the firing line. That wasn't always easy either, because Rory Brady was pushing hard for complete independence from England and wasn't backwards in coming forward when he needed a job done or someone convinced that their path was the wrong one. To do that he needed strong men to do the convincing and there were times he'd rather not have had to be the one to carry out the command. Someone had to do it though and it might as well be him as anyone else he thought as he ushered the big bullocks forward.

"Get yourself and your bundle of bones out of my stand or I'll do time for you," convinced Spud Murphy to move his half-starved heifers to a safer location. The regulars knew their spots and knew instinctively when Rex would be along to claim his. Having dismissed the Spud he went nosing around leaving Muscles Macken, a drover from the goin'-in of Ballymahon whom he often broke bread with, in charge of the big beasts that were now munching away contentedly at the two bales of hay he secured for a sixpence.

Half way through the morning while the drovers and buyers were biding their time twiddling their thumbs and telling yarns, Rex spotted a couple of out-of-towners moving around asking questions. Handing a couple of coppers to Muscles he told him to tail the boys discreetly and find out what their business was. As he watched their reflection in the window he had a gut feeling he was about to be involved in some way. It didn't take Muscles long to find out what they were up to.

"They're looking for you Rex."

"I thought as much, thanks anyway. Stick around for a bit in case I might need you later."

"I'll be beyant the other side of the street. Just lift your blackthorn and I'll be with you in two shakes of a lamb's tail," he winked to show he could be relied on.

"Are you the Rex from Ballynamanagh?" the well-built one asked.

"Who wants to know?"

"We'll do the asking, you do the talking," the tall, skinny one warned as he parted his gabardine sufficiently to show his holstered pistol.

"You don't fucking know me if that's all you know," he bit back, showing a recklessness they weren't accustomed to. His aggression caught them off guard as they were used to a more servile reaction since the war started. While Hitler was advancing rapidly into France and Churchill was trying to involve Ireland in the struggle, strange forces were afoot. Secret agents roamed the land as Ireland fought to establish the Republic and the Old Enemy sought to keep a lid on the dissidents.

Dev's insistence on neutrality drove the warmongers to distraction, as his famous riposte to Churchill's threat to invade Ireland if they didn't join the fight, was echoed around the world.

"Invade Ireland and we'll open every port to the Germans," soon settled that debate. Dev's later urging to the Nation to 'burn everything British except their coal' didn't sit well with most, but it caught the imagination of a Nation keen to break the fetters of eight hundred years of tyranny from a bellicose neighbor.

"Sorry Rex we meant no harm but it's vital you get this package to your father who'll get it to Rory Brady as soon as possible."

"I didn't say what my name was."

"You're better known than a buck goat" brought smiles all round as he dropped his guard a little.

What's in the bag?" he asked.

"Better you don't know just in case you're followed," made the hair stand on the back of his neck but he knew his duty and wasn't going to shirk it now. It wasn't the first time he had acted as runner for Brady and company who had long led the struggle against the common foe. The intensity of the civil war and the aftermath of bloodletting did little to settle the fears of the locals who had seen far too much of it. Despite Dev's best intentions the enemy was still within and spies kept them well informed. Little did he know as he stood talking to them that he was being set up so that the real movers and fixers could get their dangerous work done?

"We'll scout around for a while in case anyone is watching us," Skinny said as they slipped quietly away. Beckoning Muscles over, Rex flashed the fags, lit two and handed him one as they settled themselves on the windowsill for a chat. Muscles said he had a lift home with George Vance but Rex wasn't sure as yet if the Bull would be in town or not.

Fending off a few tire kickers he waited patiently for Melvin, the Dublin buyer who usually bought whatever he had on offer. Sure enough it wasn't long until he spotted him skirting the smaller lots while making a beeline to him. There was little need for wrangling, Rex knew what he wanted, Melvin knew his market and five minutes later they were sitting on the high stool while the cattle were being taken care of by the Dublin crew. A couple of half ones and a Plough-man's Sandwich was enough to seal the deal. Handing over a wad of notes Melvin shook his hand and headed for the toilet before his long drive to Dublin to catch the Cattle Boat to Liverpool. It was as simple as that. Trust had been built up over the years so it was pointless wasting valuable time on chitchat.

Certain he'd have no difficulty getting a lift from one or other of the buyers he set out at a brisk walk towards Sonna. There wasn't a sinner to be seen on the road as the evening waned and twilight spread its shadow across the land. Thankful for a stout blackthorn and a fine pair of hobnailed boots courtesy of the FCA, he kept up a strong pace as far as the bridge of Sonna where he often shifted after a dance in the hall.

As he lazed a while chewing on a straw he saw a plume of smoke spiraling skywards from a small copse of beech nearby. Thinking someone had set fire to the thicket he decided to investigate. Following the riverbank he drew back behind a tree as a group of dark-skinned, dark-clothed people began keening and wailing as if at a wake. It struck him that they were most likely Tinkers and the flames that were spewing from one of the caravans was a ritual as old as time. Someone had died he was sure because that was their custom. Stepping into the open he wasn't surprised that they were already aware of his presence. They had been watching him too. Little went unknown to them because they were closer to nature than most and would hear the grass growing in the interests of self-preservation.

Ould Maggie drew herself to full height as he drew abreast of her. "It isn't everyone I'd walk into a camp at the dead of evening," she half warned, half praised him on his courage.

"You've nothing to fear from me," he returned.

"Tis well we know that a mhic, and your family the very wans who kept the death of hunger from us when ye had nearly nothin' for yerselves. But me poor heart is sore today after the pool there taking me man away from me, and he trying to sneak a salmon from the depths of it to keep body and soul together in the childer. Young Paddy nearly went with him but the others managed to get a hoult of him as he was goin' down for the third time God save us from all harm this blessed day," she keened as tears flowed freely from her anguished brow.

"We'll leave his bits and pieces to be burned as we've always done and tomorrow we'll bury him in the pauper's graveyard beyond the bog in Abbeyshrule. Tell Tess if you're passing her way because she'd like to know I'm sure," she asked.

Taking a fiver from his inside pocket he handed it to the old lady knowing words had no value in their sore need.

"Musha, Rex may you never have the likes of this on you the longest day you live," she prayed as she took from her neck a beautifully crafted leather necklace with a strange symbol etched on a silver medallion. "May the gods guide every step you take until you can take no more," she intoned as she clasped it firmly around his neck. Bidding farewell he wished them well as they in turn blessed him and all belonging to him.

The long day, the excitement and the tiredness eventually caught up on him. Manfully, he kept up the pace till he could go no further. Without further ado he flattened a bed of nettles in a cutting off the road, threw a few bundles of dockins on top, lay back and was asleep in seconds. An art form he had learned from his father, he put it to good use whenever the need arose. Angels and demons chased him along the road as he sought solace in sleep from the mental and physical weariness of a too-long day.

The rumble of a cattle truck woke him up but it was too late to do anything about it. Shaking himself with annoyance, he set off after it in a foul mood. Thoughts of the odd time he had helped himself to a bicycle along the way entered his head but that was before the war. It was much harder to find one lying around now with all kinds of shortages and cutbacks. It occurred to him then that he mightn't even get a pint in Ballinacarrigy.

"The divil sweep the lot of them," he cursed as he cut the miles between him and his next port of call. He felt the weight in his small backpack and wondered if he was doing the right thing or not. What if it were to contain a pistol or ammunition he wondered? The thought of dropping it into the river appealed to him but he decided against it. They'd find out one way or the other he felt sure so he dismissed the thought and kept going as fast as he could.

Tired from the long haul and thirsty to boot his thoughts were on little more than the high stool in Murtaghs as he drew abreast of Hellfire Terrace once more. Keeping to the centre of the road due to the failing light he sensed more than heard a furtive sound. Years of living close to nature had honed his senses to that of a wild animal and it stood to him now as he prepared himself for some kind of attack. Something heavy landed in the bushes beside him but he knew instinctively it wasn't an animal, just a ruse to distract him.

Ducking low and swinging round with his blackthorn fully extended, he caught Mahon flush in the face shooting blood in all directions. Jumping wide like a cat he dodged the half-hearted charge of the other two who sprung from a hiding place under the bushes. Seeing the element of surprise had swung against them they took to their heels after Mahon, but not before Maguire had been buckled with a well-connected trip.

"Ah Jaysus Rex we were only messin'. Can't you take a joke?" he cried as Rex's size ten flattened his nose to breaking point. The others were tearing down the back of the hedge by now trying to put a bit of distance between themselves and disaster. Holding the blackthorn an inch from Maguire's eyes he forced the truth out of him. It transpired they were hoping to catch him unawares and rob him knowing he'd be carrying a fair bundle. Asked what they were going to do with it then he confessed it was to buy guns and to rob post offices and the like knowing it'd be blamed on the Provos. He felt relieved. Had it been the IRA he'd have been in trouble as he'd be reported and probably punished, but as it was only half-hearted gangsters it was unlikely they'd bother him again knowing he was well connected. As Maguire slunk away he got the father and mother of a root in the hole to remind him and the others not to cross him again.

"Tell your sister to meet me below in Murtaghs or I'll swing for the three of ye," he threw back as he beat lumps out of the bushes for effect. A double-thirst on him now he hurried past Dan Keenan's corner and in the road to the village.

Elated at his success in routing his would-be assailants he was ready for anything, half a dozen pints, another fight, a ride even, if his luck held. It was a long shot but 'nothing ventured, nothing gained' he thought as he strode straight down the centre of the street knowing his every move was being monitored from behind the peeping curtains. Raising his cap in mock salute he couldn't help thinking of

Brinsley McNamara's celebrated masterpiece 'The Valley of the Squint-ing Windows' which he had recently read.

He fancied young Mary ever since her mother entertained him a few years earlier. They had been getting on famously until she took ill suddenly and passed away in the blink of an eye. The doctor said it was the dreaded TB. Though whisked away to a Sanatorium it was too late to save her. Mary's older sister Margaret had taken on the task of rearing her but it wasn't a big job because she was a natural with kids and looked after Margaret's own three while she went about her duties and earned a few shillings looking after the old protestant couple in nearby Kilixy Manor.

Though welcome in the house, he was well aware of clacking tongues and only dropped in now and again as he passed home from the market. Rumour had it that young Mary was blossoming like a rose but her brothers kept too close an eye on her to verify it. Like a hunter coming home from battle he was game for anything that sported a skirt, especially Mary if fortune favoured him.

He wasn't surprised to see the two bars closed. Had he not been delayed by the clowns at Hellfire Terrace he might have made it but things weren't looking good now.

"Never mind," he thought to himself as he tapped on the window of the Shebeen known locally as 'The Divil's Own.' A den of iniquity he rarely frequented, he decided to chance it as hunger and thirst were beginning to get the better of him.

A corner of the curtain fell into place as the bolt was slid back to let him in.

"God bless all here," he said as he headed for the high stool at the end of the bar.

"Get up ya cunt and let a decent man sit down," Ledwith spat at

Pender who, reading his mind and knowing he might get a pint for his trouble, quickly gave ground. Throwing his cap on the peg Rex eased back against the wall to survey the scene. Facing the front door and the side street he was able to keep one eye on the back door to his left and a half snug where a hush had grown around a small group as a youngster from Hellfire ran in with the news. Pretending not to pass a blind bit of heed he placed the blackthorn where it'd be seen, fished out a fag, flicked a match alight with his thumb and surveyed the scene casually.

He knew he wasn't very popular around Hellfire since he dipped his wick a couple of years earlier but the average five eight put it down to youth and thought no more of it. 'A casualty of love' was the phrase most often used. Some said it was a habit he should get out of but the women never complained, at least not the ones he knew.

Pete threw down a mat before settling a creamy pint on it.

"Wonders never cease Rex. You're a sight for sore eyes. The last night you were in here was the time you turned the tables on the boy-os and cleaned them out at the poker. Some of them had to sell "the family jewels to survive after that," he laughed. "That's on the house," he grinned. "I just heard your man's nose is broken and the other eejit doesn't know what hit him," he winked. "Don't pass a bit a blind bit a heed on the lads here. Most of them are as sound as yourself and any-way, I have what'll take care of the rest if there's any trouble," he said as he pointed to a metal box which probably contained a shotgun or something equally lethal.

"Enough said so," Rex replied as he licked the froth from his bone-dry lips. Asking if there might be a bit of grub to be got, his mouth began to water when two wedges of a loaf appeared soon after with a handful of rashers and sausages making it fit for a king. About to tuck in he felt rather than saw someone by his side.

"I suppose you'll eat all that yourself?"

"Cheeses Mary, where did you spring outta?"

"I was told to come," she grinned. "I let on I didn't want to but they made me and here I am," she smiled as she moved closer.

"A more welcome sight I've never seen girl. What'll you have?"

"I'll have a soda so," she said.

"You will in your arse," he said as he pulled up a stool for her.

"A soda cake for Mary so," he laughed as he played on her words.

"What'll it be Mary?" Pete asked as she looked for guidance from Rex.

"Ah give her a drink for Christ's sake Pete. It's not often we meet," he winked as he left the decision to him knowing he'd pull out his best for the occasion.

"Will that do Mary?" he smiled as he poured a generous measure of vodka into one of the few decent glasses he had in the house.

"Are you hungry?" Rex asked.

"I'd eat the lamb a Jaysus," she laughed as she put her hand on his leg well above the knee to balance herself before snuggling into him. Wise to the ways of the world she knew what was what and knew what she liked as well. The thought of spending a lifetime around a one horse town held little appeal for her and she'd buy or sell herself out of the place come hell or high water.

As Pete handed him his change he whispered a warning about the two trench coated strangers who had slipped in the back door as Slevin headed for home.

"Fuck it," Rex swore as he saw them in the mirror. "I should have known."

"Leave it to me," Pete advised as he advanced on them to take their order. Being a big man, his broad shoulders blocked their view allowing Rex and Mary to ease back behind the divider before they were spotted. A few curs (mongrel dogs) circled around their feet as they worked out their escape. The "Hairy" threw crumbs in the air to make the dogs jump ever higher. Not taking any chances, Rex placed his sambo on a ledge just out of their reach, or so he thought! An almost perfect standing leap saw the black soaring for the sandwich. It had reckoned without Abbeyshrule survival tactics however, because, just as it neared the feast its nose was flattened by a sucker punch leaving it spread-eagled on the sawdust-strewn floor. True to Nature the other two curs tore into it. Heavy hob-nailed boots soon sorted them but not before the leader of the pack sunk his teeth into the 'Hairy' who nearly had a canary trying to kick the shite out of it.

"Quieten down for fuck sake ya shower of knackers," Pete shouted above the din. "D'ye want the Guards to close me down or what?" he glared at the owners of the mongrels. As he reached up for the Hurley stick and made for the dogs, Rex grabbed Mary and the sandwich and bolted out the back door as fast as they could go. The Trench coats couldn't budge as Pete had blocked the door pretending to be mad at everyone.

"Where do you ladies think you're going?" he demanded as they tried to get past him. He was doing fine until a pistol was stuck in his ribs convincing him they meant business.

"Go right ahead ladies," he invited with an expansive gesture. Realising it was an elaborate hoax to let Rex make good his escape, they burst from the bar, leaped into their car and gunned it out the road to Empor as if their arses were on fire. By now Rex and Mary had reached the harbour where Troy kept a small punt for crossing the canal just below the bridge. Keeping low they poled their way along the canal bank until they cleared the town. The vast waste of bog land would keep them far from the road and all the way to Abbeyshrule after that if they had a mind to.

The curlew was plaintively calling as they eased into the reeds well out of harm's way. The surfeit of excitement had driven them crazy for each other. After taking on all-comers and proving himself worthy of her, she wasn't going to be found wanting in showing her appreciation either. As they beat down the reeds to make a comfortable bower under the light of a full moon their passion knew no bounds as they surrendered to Nature's inviolable ways.

The Dawn Chorus had already begun when she stirred him awake.

"Are you going to sleep all day or what?" she teased as she eased onto him.

"I wouldn't mind at all if you were with me but we'd better make headway just in case," he laughed.

"I'll tip back home by the canal and no one'll be the wiser," she smiled as she gave him everything she'd got. "I suppose it'll be the last I'll see of you but if you're around the place again I'll be here for you," she smiled as she held him like a winch. Don't leave it too long though because a girl needs company," she teased as she hugged him passionately.

"I'll be back for sure," he promised. "It's no distance and I'll do it in half an hour on my old reliable. "Sure, it'll only give me an appetite," he said as he found her again.

The faint light of dawn was casting pale streaks across the heavens as they eased apart and readied themselves for their respective journeys.

"Don't fall into it now" he laughed as he handed her the pole and pushed her away from the reeds.

"Didn't I fall for you wasn't that enough?" she waved as she started on her way. Watching her go he wondered if the war and his work would ever let them meet again.

Stuck in the Porridge Pot

"Did you ever hear of anyone sleeping in a skillet pot Seamie?" Tess asked one evening as she swished her besom at Ginger who was trying to steal the potato bread from the pan at the side of the fire.

"I didn't Tess. How could you sleep in a pot?"

"Oh it can be done a mhic. Didn't Pat Carrigy do it the night he left here after the Céilí. The cocks were crowing and he going home. He was starving for they wouldn't let him eat a bite in case he'd break the playing and everyone ready for anything. They used to slip in the front door when me back was turned and have a bit of a court beyant there on the settle bed. Shure they had the best of fun. You'd hear the laughs of them beyant in Tashinny. You couldn't keep in to them. There was more use made of that little bed than I ever made of it. Anyway, Carrigy went home and slipped in through the crack in the gable end so he wouldn't wake anyone. Seeing the skillet pot on the hob he knew it'd be full of porridge for the childer but he knew too that if he touched it he was dead. He'd never hear the end of it if he left them short. Lucky enough the other pot had a few spoonful's left after the supper, which he proceeded to lick clean until his head swelled and he couldn't get the pot of it. When he stood up to see where he was going he banged his head on the mantelpiece."

"Who's that?" Biddy demanded.

"It's only me I fell outta the bed," he muffled as he tried to dislodge the pot from his head.

"Go lang ya ludermaun," she laughed as she put her leg over her man for want of a better place to put it.

"What do you think happened then Seamie?"

"God, I don't know Tess. Did he complain about her leg?"

"Will you go away outta that. Are you not following the story or what?" she asked in a kind of a vexed voice.

"Only messing Tess, keep your cap on," he urged.

"Carrigy wasn't in the bed. He couldn't see where he was going so he sat down with his back to the hob and feel into a deep sleep with the fairies dancing round him."

"With the pot on his head?"

"Shure he couldn't get it off be himself, could he? Anyway, Biddy climbed over her ould man and came down to rake the fire. What did she see but Carrigy fast asleep adin in the pot and him snoring like Courtney's ass? What could she do but knock on the pot to see if she could wake him up? Not a bit of it. He'd be snoring still if her man hadn't lifted him and the pot out of the hearth."

"What's he doing with the pot on his head Biddy?" he asked.

"Don't ask me. I only came down to get the children's breakfast. He was here when I came down."

"Is that you in there Pat?" asked John. You couldn't make out a word he was saying but it sounded like he'd prefer if the pot were off his head. What did Johnny do then but march him out to the shed and put him sitting on the ground with his back to the wall. Before Carrigy knew what day it was he was roaring like a bull when Johnny split the pot open with the big hammer.

"Will ye look at me pot you pair of feckin eejits?" Biddy cried as she glared at the two of them.

"We'll have to get a bigger pot for him so," was all Johnny could think of saying. Carrigy had a lump on his head the size of a double-yoked duck egg. Putting a bandage on it and wrapping the rest of it around under his neck in case he was hurt she ordered him off to bed. Would you believe that Seamie?" she said as she nearly fell into the fire laughing.

"Go way out of that Tess. You're always pulling my leg," he laughed as he helped her back onto her sugán chair.

"That's what happened. Biddy told me that herself above in the Shop the same day".

"Was Carrigy all right?" Seamie asked.

"There wasn't a bother on him after a week but he wouldn't eat the porridge now even if he was to go hungry," said Tess as tears ran down her cheeks.

It was almost dark as Seamie left. This wasn't unusual for him as he often came in later than the others. Nora called him 'a night owl' because, even when he was much younger, he'd wander down the Long Avenue to where the tinkers were camped. Mrs O'Leary, or "Jessie" as she was affectionately known, kept a close eye on him in case her own would turn on him. That was the Tinker's way.

'Look out for yourselves first and mind each other from the settled people' was a mantra to protect their young. Jessie always maintained that Nora and her gossoon were different from the other settled people. She seemed almost like one of them and gave if she had it. Jessie felt honoured that Nora's child would pass the other houses to play with her little ones. There were times when the children tired playing and fell asleep in the long grass or on bits of canvas or potato bags which were drying out in the sun. Sometimes she'd put him lying down in her caravan with her two girls, Jenny and Jessie.

"Sure there's not a bother on him Ma'am," she'd laugh as Nora looked in on them. His mop of blonde curls was thought to be a lucky omen by the jet-black O'Leary's. Pat often asked for one of his curls for a laugh knowing that the child would allow no one but the girls to have one.

Drowned

Pinkeens and rasp were like bread and butter to Tess. Few if any thought much of them she said but it hadn't been that long since they kept the wolf from the door in many a poor man's cabin. She remembered Rex catching a fine salmon under the waterfall years earlier. He had an eye like a hawk and spotted the movement in the pool when he was passing one day. In he came running for a graipe but he might as well have been looking for a sirloin steak on Good Friday because the last time Tess had seen a graipe was when his father had threatened to use one when young Angie became pregnant and the reluctant father needed convincing. The graipe did the trick and they're living happily together since. But that was then and he needed something to nab the salmon right now. Spotting the creel in the corner he emptied the few sods out of it and was out the half door while you'd be blessing yourself. Well, it must have been a wise fish because it nearly drowned him with all the lepping. She hadn't seen such a hullaballoo since the Missions. What with Rex swinging and the salmon lepping she didn't know whether to laugh or cry with the excitement as she stood watching the carry on from the bridge.

"Will you hould on to him for fecks sake. Is he hot or what?" fairly annoyed Rex as the buck leaps of the salmon wet him from head to toe. The next thing wasn't the salmon out of the pool and off under the bridge like a torpedo. It didn't get too far because it got trapped in the pool below the garden. He whipped it out in a flash and that was that and I had to put down a rasper of a fire to dry him off before he went on over to Abbeyshrule to meet your mother. They weren't long going out together at that time but everyone knew it'd be a match even though he was a bit of a boyo and had a rag on every bush so to speak. If anyone were to settle him it'd be that little woman because even though she was only a handful like meself she had the power. Well anyway, he dried himself off there by the hearth and was raring to go with all the excitement and all. 'I'll call in for a bit of it tomorrow evening,' he said as he was putting on his coat. 'Call in on the way home and it'll taste nicer," she advised knowing he'd be late back because it was a Saturday night and there'd no hurry on him.

She was in another battle royal with the same salmon when his knock on the window woke her out of her dream in the middle of the night. The smell of porter off him would knock a double door down she said. As well as that he was wet to the skin having had to ride home from Abbeyshrule in a downpour, the kind of blustery rain that'd leave ya sittin' on your arse in the middle of the Plantin, or stuck adin in a heap of nettles if you weren't careful. Fitzie's was lepping too when he arrived with Nora on the crossbar he told her. Mattie Nevin would make a cat cry with his Jews harp while Pat Sammon was making fine music with a hair rake using tissue paper from a pack of Woodbines.

"I thought there was one left in that pack," Teague said as he scratched his head when Sammon slipped it up his sleeve like a professional. "It'd be like you all right," Sammon said by way of covering up his subterfuge.

Sammon was singing 'I'll take you home again Kathleen' but had his shite as Kathleen said. He'd have to do better than that she laughed when Nora asked her if she was going home with him. It was bucketing rain and only a few eejits chanced it. Fitzy set the tone by saying he'd give a drink at half price to anyone who performed. That started it. McCormack's Road Show wouldn't hold a candle to Fitzie's that night. He even sang himself even though the only note he had was out of the till. It eventually let up enough to get the women home safely but anyone outside the Pale was doomed to the father and mother of a drowning. The steam was rising from him when he knocked on the door at the dead of night.

"Will ya come in for cheeses sake," she told him when she lifted the latch and saw him standing there like a drowned rat. Between them they had the fire spitting sparks in no time. Handing him a sheet fashioned from flour bags she told him to strip off and dry himself. If he hadn't known her as well as he did he might have had reservations but he did as he was bid knowing he'd suffer otherwise. While he was at that she was reheating the salmon. It didn't take long as she had already done most of the cooking knowing he'd be in on his way home. Letting his lugs back at it then he nearly ate it all on his own.

Finding Tess

She'd never forget the day he stumbled into her little mansion she told him as she poked life into the log at the back of the hearth sending sparks flying like fairies up the pitch black chimney.

"I was adout be the side of the house pegging ashes on the rose bed when I saw you out of the corner of me eye. You were standing looking into the river and wondering' I suppose, how you were going to cross it. And that's no easy task either as you well know because it's neither narrow or shallow there. I watched you quietly from behind the boultree bush (bourtree) to see if you'd need help but divil the bit of it. I knew in a minute there'd never be a bother on you 'cause you figured it out for yourself whilst others would be scratching their arses. Picking up the oul plank I use for lying on when tickling for a trout you slid it over to the stone in the middle of the stream and then, as lively as a kitten, you hopped across it the same as if you were doing it every day. Well, in you came and down you sat on the three-legged stool there and started giving out the guff as if we were oul segoshias. And sure mebbe we were in another time.

I let you ramble on to your heart's content knowing full well when you were done you'd let me get a word in edgeways. Sure enough that's what happened.

Aye, I had seen you around the Crossroads with Nora alright but apart from passing the time of day I didn't let on I was paying a blind bit of heed to you. But I was. I learned long ago that if you give childer and animals enough time they'll eat out of your hands and follow you to the far winds. Oh I'd have run away with you all right but I knew the fairies wouldn't let me because they had big plans for you from the word go. Better to stay on the right side of those magicians or they'd turn you into a gold sovereign while you'd be looking around you.

I'd say you gave your mother a fair fright though because the poor woman was running demented from house to house looking for you until I sent word with the Bun that you were here.

I knew she'd land soon after that because she had the Crossroads in a tizzy with anxiety. Damn the likes of it he'd ever seen the Bun said later as they chatted over the whole fiasco. The Postmaster took down the double barrel, the Cowboy had his 'High Nelly' faced to the four winds and Bappy had every hewer of wood sentenced to several lives. Dolly was adin in the school with Mrs McGoey reciting the Sorrowful Mysteries in case of the worst, and as for meself, I had the kittle dancing on the hob to settle her knowing she'd be up to ninety when she landed. Sure enough it was no time before I heard the rattle of the mudguard as she hammered down be the Bull field. Her ould bike nearly had to park itself because she was off it the same as your man in Duffy's Circus that used to ride it backwards. Up she stood adout at the bridge there shouting in for you to come out as if we were after breaking the Ten Commandments. Bedad I knew her dander was up because she was nearly frothing at the mouth. It never knocked a fonc out of you at all. You took it in your stride the same as a walk on a windy day. You were only after telling me the story about the pound note she gave you to get a few things from the shop and how you somehow managed to lose it on the crossroads. Any wonder you came down to me with her ready to half kill you. Out we went together and when she saw you she was ready to tear your blonde curls out wan be wan as she made for the stile like a woman possessed. Ah but she was dealing with the wrong woman this time because I let her have it hot and heavy before she knew where she was. I'm not a woman to fight or to lose me timper but I knew she'd have to be put in her place straight away or there'd be no standing her.

"Hould your ground there now Nora," I said as she tried to get past me. I let her have it goodo until she sat down on the bridge and cried her eyes out the poor little woman; a saint if ever there was one. There was a lot more bothering her than I thought but a mug a tay did the trick and pacified her. I even read the tay leaves for her telling her the best of news she'd heard in a gay while. Bedad if she didn't have you above on her knee after that. Wasn't your father after arriving that blessed minute with Ginger on the carrier behind him! That bloody cat is not right because she knows what road he's coming home every evening and if he doesn't let her up she'll go into a huff for a week. In he came anyway with a small army of Job's Comforters behind him wringing their miserable hands and offering advice on how you shouldn't be let near me at all at all. I left the three of ye and out I went to run the rest of them that were adout. You wouldn't see the most of them except'n there was a wake or a wedding.

'Be off with yis ye shower of knackers,' I shouted as I waved me blackthorn at them. Well you wouldn't see them for dust as they took to their heels. I didn't get me reputation for nothing and well they knew it. All's well that ends well so after a few mugs of tay was drank I let ye all home knowing you wouldn't suffer for being another Livingstone when Stanley hit on him after wandering around Africa for ages looking for him.

I had a right go at your father as well the next time I saw him.

'Time to put an end to your gallivanting and gambling Rex,' I said. He never answered me but I knew it cut him to the quick. That finished it. Sure they were like young wans after that. Me own man was the same. You'd have to get him at the right time, sit him down and let him have it between the two eyes without him even knowing it. Sure we wimmin are deadly at that. And wouldn't we want to be with the way we rear you lads; spoiling ye awful thinking it'd make men out of ye but worse it makes ye altogether. But sure, we'll never learn. It's all to do with the Church as well because, as far as it's concerned, only the men count. It's high time they were taken down of their high horses. Ah sure, never mind, that's for another day.

It wasn't long after that I discovered your secret path down be the quick. You knew they'd be watching out for you and, no more than meself, you preferred to keep your business to yerself, so down the fields you came keeping the quick between you and the road. It wasn't long until you had a path like a pheasant's beaten the whole way down. Many's the time too you brought me a string of cupeens of mushrooms you'd gather on your way.

'D'you drink tay a mhic?' I asked.

'I do,' you said and nothing more. That set me thinking all right so I just got on with it. I had only the wan enamel mug at the time but you wouldn't drink outta anythin' else. I used the jam jar I kept for the Bun for meself but all you wanted was that mug.

'That's the very same mug you drink outta still,' she told him as she threw a few slices of a loaf on the griddle. "A little stale they were," she said, because it'd take her a week to eat a whole loaf if she hadn't help.

"You happened on a similar mug at home soon after and hopped it up on the ledge there saying it was for me. It was as good a present as ever I got, and coming from yourself it meant more than a good night's sleep or a twirl around on my broomstick on a moonlit night. When not in use they were left there in the recess be the hob. It kept them warm, if dusty, and sure feck the harm a bit a dust did," she laughed as a rub of her sleeve soon solved that. "Weren't they always saying that 'dust thou art and to dust thou shalt return'?" she laughed as she quoted the reverends. "As the kettle began to whistle 'The Stacks of Barley' he tossed a small fist of tealeaves into the teapot like a seasoned professional. Whatever it was that leapt up between them that day took batin'," she remarked as she winked at him. He learned quicker than the Tinkers she told him and if he wasn't careful he'd be on the road with them before the cat drank all the milk.

"What milk?" he asked knowing they had as much chance of getting a saucer of milk as he had of mounting her broomstick before he got his license. Changing the subject in case she lost him she said she had shown his mother how to read the tealeaves and she'd show him now if he was interested.

"What happens if I only see tea leaves?" he laughed. "Don't worry I know you'll see more than you think," she said as he poured the tea for her. He had heard his mother talking to Mags about the people who came from far and near to have their hands read and their tea cups too if she had any tea. A tradition arose whereby those in the know would advise the unwise on what to do for a good reading and that's when things started to look up a little for the 'Witch in the Ditch' as the begrudgers called her. Rather than call on her openly, messages were sent with Jim the postman who'd often stop for a chat and to find out two things: when she might be able to do a reading and to screen anyone who might be after more?

This arose out of an incident many moons before when she, as a much younger woman, had to use all her innate intelligence to outwit an unwelcome late night caller who had more on his mind than was good for him, or her!

"The full moon was peeping in the little window and sending a yard or two of light through the open door," she told Seamie one night when they were alone and she was reminiscing. It looked so good she let it shine on when normally she'd have it shut and the cats out for the night. Sipping a mug of tea while she was reading the last few embers in the hearth, the soft timble of the bean can alerted her and a shadow on the floor caught her eye. As she looked around she saw a half stranger leaning against the jam of the door.

"Grand night Tess," he said in a drunken slur.

"Tis surely," she answered as she gathered her wits about her.

"You'd hardly have a drop of the cratur for a thirsty man," he half laughed, half sneered as he strode across the floor and sat on the stool in front of her.

"What would I be doing with the like?" she asked as she tried to figure how far he was prepared to go for what he wanted.

"Well, whatever ya like Tess but a man has needs and if there isn't wan thing another will do," left her in no doubt as to his intentions. Stepping lightly past him she went to the corner where she had a bottle of poteen hidden behind some delftware she bought for a song at one of the annual Bring & Buy Bazaars. Pretending to be overcome with nerves she knocked over a few glasses while slipping Jack's cutthroat into the pocket of her bib. Seeing her produce a bottle of the quare stuff he sat back down again. As she attempted to pour a small measure he grabbed the bottle and her as well.

"Sit down on me knee woman and we'll see what rises between us," he leered as he took a mouthful of the potent brew.

"Jaysus that's great stuff," he said as he wiped the drool from his mouth with the sleeve of her cardigan. Fumbling at her blouse he ripped the buttons off as he thrust his big paw under and started mauling her breasts. Pleading with him to let her go only made him worse as he started tearing at the rest of her clothes. The smell of his breath and his unwashed body repulsed her but she knew she had to keep calm somehow.

"Look, if you want it that bad there's no point in making me suffer as well."

"What do ya mean?" said as he ripped the knickers off her.

"Stop, stop, I mean I'll let you have your way, and more besides if you take it easy and go your way afterwards."

"Now you're talking," he grinned as he held her at arm's length while he unbuckled his belt and released a boyo that'd make a jackass proud.

Weak at the knees she slumped to the floor in a swoon, her free arm falling listlessly behind her.

"What's up with you now?" he growled releasing her as he got a bit of a fright. That was her opportunity and she took it. Swinging with every ounce of power in her being she met him straight between the two eyes with the bottle. Temporarily blinded he fell back into the corner roaring like a bull. Seizing the moment she dashed for the door and made for the stile screaming for help, but knowing it was saothar in aisce (labour in vain) as it was unlikely anyone would be abroad at this ungodly hour. Nevertheless, she tried to put some distance between her and what she felt might now be her murderer. The screams died in her throat as she glanced back and saw him scrambling across the stile wielding the full of the fire of a stick. Try as she might she couldn't raise a whisper as her throat dried to a crisp with fright. Her worst nightmare came to haunt her as her legs started to give from under her. Diving into a bed of nettles in the middle of the bushes she begged the gods to come to her aid. She knew instinctively that he'd have to kill her now because the situation had gotten out of control and life imprisonment at best awaited him. Rolling into a ball she held the cutthroat close and awaited the worst.

"Come out ya witch. I know where ya are," he wheezed as he beat the bushes knowing she had to be in there somewhere. Frenzy and the fear of her escaping drove him on like a madman. If she got away he was doomed he knew but the poteen was working wonders now and he could almost see her naked in the long grass.

Fortune favoured her because her old friend Rex was on his way home from Abbeyshrule, and recognising her voice through her heartrending screams, tore down by the bull field in time to see her being pulled from the clump of nettles by the 'Humper', a ne'er-do-well from beyond Carrickboy Bog. Aiming the bike straight at him he pushed Tess back into the nettles before colliding full-force with the brute, sending the stick flying as well. With the wheels spinning madly in the middle of the road he pulled him to his feet and head butted him with the power of a buck goat sending more blood flying from his burst eyebrow. As he staggered back he hit him a hay-maker knocking him over the bridge into the river, now in spate after a week of summer rains. Clearing the wall like a ten-year old he landed on top of him, grabbed his mop of black hair and forced him under the water until he was breathless. By now Tess had the spade in her hand but was pleading with Rex not to kill him knowing it would destroy them both. She knew some people would say she had invited it on herself by leaving the door open late at night with such strange forces afoot in a young and troubled republic. Grabbing the spade from her he forced him to strip off before he lay into him mercilessly with the handle. On his knees now and gibbering like a monkey he begged for mercy promising all the gods that ever were he'd never darken her door again. Dragging him to his feet by the hair of the head he marshalled him across the stile leaving welts as big as bunions on his back and legs as he ran for his life. Not letting up until they reached the bullfield gate he told him he'd kill him if he ever came round the place again.

"I won't, I won't, I promise on me mother's grave," he cried as the face of the spade landed full on his arse as he clambered over the wrought iron gate. Rattling it for effect Rex pretended to follow him, but by now, severely bruised, the Humper was going flat out in the general direction of Carrickboy. He never looked back until he had put two fields between himself and the disaster that had befallen him. Lying against the gate to get his breath back Rex lit a butt to settle himself. It maddened him that such whore's bastards were walking the roads at the dead of night but he knew he wouldn't be seen next or near the place as long as he or Tess lived. The thought of his old friend being subjected to such base abuse spurred him back to her. Though badly shaken she had changed her torn blouse and skirt and had the kettle boiling by the time he appeared in a lather of sweat.

"I doubt he'll ever trouble you again Tess," he said as he steadied himself by the mantelpiece. Distraught by the sudden turn of events the poor woman was in the throes of blaming herself for it all. Despite that she was trying to express her gratitude to her dear friend and neighbour. Words failed her as he wrapped his arms around her like many a time before and let her cry it all away.

The Apparition

Jogging up the field at the back of Larkin's hedge on his way home he stopped for a moment to water the flowers. Happening to glance back towards the cottage he could have sworn he saw something move near the bridge but put it down to a trick of the moonlight or the branches of the poplar swaying in the light breeze. The soft glow of the candle by the window was no longer visible telling him she would be dozing off in her easy chair by now. He often wished that he could stay with her but that'd pose too many problems and set more tongues wagging. His parents had gotten over it but some of the locals thought the old lady shouldn't be encouraging the youth so much. Some said he was already a bit of a dreamer and her strange ways might not be good for him.

As he was about to continue home he saw it again. This time it wasn't a trick of the light. What he had seen earlier morphed into a semi-transparent female form which began moving slowly just above the water, her long light clothes fluttering in the night air as she turned and faced him. Translucent, transparent even, he was sure he could see the little cottage straight through her. A bunch of blood-red roses clutched close to her heart stood in stark contrast to the paleness of her skin and her snow-white dress. As she hovered inches above the stream he imagined he saw her enter the water by the bridge and exit from the pool under the waterfall as if to tell him what had happened long ago. Then, rising higher, she crossed the bridge towards the cottage. Completely bewitched, he followed her gaze to the cottage now enveloped in an eerie mist that seemed to lift it off the ground while surrounding it with twinkling fairy lights. A heavenly smile akin to The Mona Lisa lit her pale face as she moved away towards Bosque. He didn't feel in the least frightened despite the obvious implications. In fact, he felt at peace. She was at peace too it seemed. He even responded to her gentle wave as she melted away into the darkness. How he wished she wouldn't go. He had never experienced such beauty. It reminded him of Bernini's famous sculpture of Saint Theresa of Avila in ecstasy of which his mother had a painting in her bedroom. Looking back to the cottage he could just about make out its shape that had by now lost the mystic glow. He wanted to run back to tell Tess but it was already very late and he had enough excitement for one day. Mother would be waiting anxiously for him undoubtedly. She had long given up remonstrating with him whenever he was late home from his visits to the old lady. That there was a strange bond between the two despite the huge disparity in years was obvious. Though a little concerned for the child initially there was no point in making an issue of it because her heart told her Tess was more than a class act; more like an act of God if the truth be known.

A couple of evenings later on his way home from counting he was surprised to see her sitting on the bridge waiting for him.

"Anything wrong Tess?"

"Ah shure divil a thing a mhic," she smiled as he sat beside her. The warmth of her embrace as she put her arm around him settled his nerves. He wasn't used to that from his mother and thought it might be because Tess had no kids and didn't have to spread her love among many. Feeling this was as good a time as any he broached the subject of his encounter with the apparition. Her answer nearly floored him.

"It was her daughter," she said as she wiped tears from her eyes with a corner of her shawl. From that awful day when the waters took her she had blamed herself for her passing. Her grief knew no bounds because she blamed herself for taking her eye off the child for a minute. As time passed her nearness to nature helped her overcome the loss. Nevertheless, she knew the child hadn't yet reached her destination and she prayed to the old gods that one day she would, or that they'd take her instead and let the child reach the Promised Land. Her brother had passed away since then and she missed him a lot. Blame didn't enter into it. It happened. He was on the run at the time, had few friends, which was safer, but he needed a shoulder to lie on and cry on during the dark nights when dogs hunted him like a fox. She was his only friend when he lay low in Knockagh or hid in the byres and barns of those who sought to nail him.

"Better to be within the Pale than be without," she often told him when he'd tap on her window in the dead of night. The constant hardship finally claimed him as pneumonia set in after he almost drowned crossing the Inny escaping the dogs and his pursuers. Time passed but the vision kept coming back to haunt her. Now that Seamie had hit on the truth she knew all was well. She had spoken with Fr. McCabe only the previous evening as he spotted her sitting on the bridge. Unlike other priests who swept past her humble home he made a point of calling whenever he could. He never asked if she wanted confession or communion, only that she'd feel free to talk if she wanted to. He, in turn, was more at ease with her than those who thought they were closer to the Truth. He saw hypocrisy at every side and hated it. His only escape was to visit a few like Tess. There weren't many but if he had a bit of spare time he'd head for Lough Sheedon and the Mass Rock where he could commune with nature and those who had been murdered for their faith. Now, as he awaited the hypocrites jostling for communion he hated their perfidy yet knew it wasn't their fault; it was the fault of an organisation that sought to rob them of their very being. As he lay awake at night he cursed his calling at times, cursed those who used him, the ones who poured money into the coffers just to be seen to be above their neighbours. He cursed the colleagues who eased into their respective parishes knowing they could play their followers like a fine-tuned fiddle and cared as little for their calling as they did for those they used and abused.

She could never have done that before or she'd be read from the altar and sent packing like many another. That he was different from the rest of them, a true saint of the people, especially the Tinkers who'd swear by him, was obvious. They'd sooner bring a sick or delicate child to him than to a doctor. True, he could be tough when it was necessary but he usually found another way round a problem without the whole world having to know about it.

She had felt the force when he stood praying on the bridge and a strange peace came over her as he sent his blessing floating to the water like a leaf falling from the old poplar. Like the shadow of an angel her daughter rose out of the water, turned towards them, and with a hint of a smile floated away towards Bosque. Released from her watery grave at last her child was no longer lost. She didn't even notice the priest slip away. Not even the sound of the car disturbed her concentration as she dwelt on the astonishing turn of events. Another miracle to be chalked down to the people's priest she was convinced.

Talking about miracles brought up the story of Mikey's narrow escape from the next world. It was the time he was forcefully taken from the County Hospital when Rex lost the plot after finding lice swarming on his hat that had fallen onto the floor. Seamie didn't know the full story because he had only heard bits of it through listening at the landing at the top of the stairs and the whispers that followed him as he went his way around the parish. Knowing he was uncomfortable with half-truths and lies Tess decided to fill him in on the full story.

Picking the child out of the cot despite Nora's fears of what the authorities might do or say Rex made for the door and home. A nurse who had been keeping an eye on proceedings ran for Higgins the head doctor who appeared out of nowhere blocking the main door of the children's ward. With all the authority he could muster he ordered Rex to put the child back in the cot and to get out of the hospital before he called the police. Handing the child to Nora Rex whipped off his coat and told the doctor he'd do life for him if he didn't get the fuck out of his way that very instant. With the blood draining from his face as if he'd just seen a vision of the next life, he disappeared as fast as he arrived leaving them to get on with their task. Not another word was said until they reached Carrickboy where Nora dismounted panting for breath. Realising he was after pushing hard all the way from the Black Bridge he dismounted too and put his arm on her shoulder by way of apology. The simple gesture was enough to bring tears to her eyes because he wasn't prone to ostentation especially in public. Still up to the nineties he told her he'd sooner let the child die at home than in that excuse for a hospital. Agreeing with him she nevertheless advised caution. As they neared the crossroads Fr. Mc-Cabe was getting out of his car. Enquiring if everything was all right brought a well of tears to Norah's eyes as she blurted out what had just happened. Taking a quick look at the child he waved them on home saying there wouldn't be a bother on the child in a day or two.

After giving him a thorough washing and burying his clothes in the back of the fire, they took turns watching him through the night. It was near morning when a faint sound woke her watch and on looking up she saw the child smiling out through the bars of the cot at her. Nudging Rex gently in case she should frighten the infant after his enforced absence from home they spoke quietly as the child pulled itself upright and started belting out a litany of words at them. They couldn't keep up to him for the rest of the day as he rediscovered his appetite for life and food. A spoon of this and a spoon of that with boiled skimmed milk soon had the colour back in his face and, on taking him out to change his clothes, she nearly fell into a faint. There wasn't a sign of the eczema on any part of his body. On their knees they thanked all the saints they knew but put it all down to the power of the little priest from Fenagh. As word spread during the day the neighbours came rushing in to see the miracle for themselves and to marvel at how one man could harness such power.

"Common sense" was Tess's theory as Seamie asked her how it was done. Reminding him of his schooling and of the all the people who had demonstrated amazing gifts down through the centuries since Christ was a boy, she reminded him that Nature throws up extraordinary individuals every so often. She was sure the priest was endowed with the power to cure just as Leonardo da Vinci, Michelangelo, Luis Pasteur and even Goldsmith himself were all blessed with their own singular powers. She told him of old Tom Morris from Clonbrin who had the power to cure ringworm by muttering some incantation or other and rubbing the three copper pennies given him by the infected person. They weren't to know that a short while later he'd be cured by the same man after being infected by one of the animals around the farm. That led to the natural and herbal cures she herself possessed and to the many holy wells dotted around the country where people travelled huge distances to seek a cure for this and that. It was well known that the font created by a hollow in the stone over the bishop's grave in Abbeyshrule held a cure for warts and scabies and that St. Sinneach's well was revered far and wide for all kinds of cures, especially those related to stomach and heart problems. And if that wasn't enough they rounded it up by chatting about the seventh son of a seventh son and the cures they invariably possessed. In the event of such an occurrence a live worm was placed in the seventh son's palm as soon as possible after birth. If the worm shrivelled up and died then that child had the power and it was just a case of finding out what the power was. It soon became evident where it lay as word spread and his ability to cure illnesses was narrowed down. Asking if the seventh daughter of a seventh daughter had the same kind of gift she was unable to tell him but doubted it was the case though she'd explore further to see if there were any instances of it happening. She agreed it didn't make sense that it should be left to male children only because, without the female, the male wouldn't exist, and that was another miracle. Seizing the opportunity she filled him in on how a child came to be born and the marvels bestowed on mankind by Nature herself.

Acting the Blackguard

It was Halloween and the lads around the Crossroads were planning devilment. They had gotten into trouble the previous year when Guard Fay caught them trying to take Larkin's gate off the hinges. He took their names and warned them that if he heard another word he'd do a lot more about it. He had never summonsed any of them before and they didn't think he'd do so now because he was soon moving to Longford with the whole family, cow and all. Nevertheless, they'd have to be careful. The hollow road was selected, as there was less likelihood of being caught there even though there was a full moon.

'Appleblossom's' was their first port of call and probably the easiest as she'd be in bed by now. Potch would be studying, or reading by the Tilly lamp, while her brothers would either be playing cards or reading the newspaper by the fire. They watched anxiously as Doherty crawled along the corrugated iron rooftop and put a big scraw on the top of the chimney. His heart was in his mouth as he tiptoed back and jumped down into the cabbage garden where the lads were waiting.

"You just missed the shite," Bullwire laughed as they whacked him with the kale stalks they had pulled up while they were waiting for him.

Mullin's neatly thatched farmhouse was next. Doc had taken a small can of tvo, a mixture of kerosene, petrol and diesel oil, from the Bull's tractor in Knockagh the previous evening. Pouring it on a crumpled copy of The Leader he stuffed it under the thatch at the lower end of the house in case anyone came out and cut him off at the pass. As soon as the thatch caught fire they high-tailed it out through the haggard banging the gate as they went to raise the alarm in case it got out of hand. Pat was out in seconds, and spotting the flames, started shouting for the girls to grab buckets of water, while swearing vengeance on the blackguards who did such a dastardly deed. It was quenched in minutes. The pranksters were happy to see the flames being brought under control as the last thing they wanted to do was endanger anyone, least of all their neighbours. Content that matters were under control they moved on to their next assignment; Barney Flower's farmhouse.

A frequent visitor to Barney and his sister, Seamie often delivered their groceries, rarely leaving without something worthwhile, a book, a magazine about the wonders of the world, or a Macaroon bar at worst. Their old dog Shep loved to see him coming as he usually brought biscuits for him. Peryl, a neighbour who lived down the Abbeyshrule road, used to give him a small packet of Marietta biscuits for bringing the milk from Byrne's Creamery. He took such a dislike to them that he couldn't eat another one, trading them off instead to his friends for sweets and comics. Peryl's dog Ludo was another of his pet hates. The mongrel nipped him on the heel one evening as he mounted his bike outside her gate. The same dog would lie in wait as he heard the bike coming down the road from the crossroads, tearing out at the last moment in another attempt to bite him. The fact that he used to put a piece of leather between the spokes to annoy it didn't endear him to the dog either. On learning the mongrel had bitten his friend Veronica as well, he decided enough was enough. Splitting sticks for the cold winter nights was one of his duties so he thought a fist-sized wedge would do the trick nicely. It was one of the chores he liked best because he always got praise from his father for a job well done. He also felt it was toughening him up for the football and felt it was time well spent.

Selecting a good sharp wedge he wrapped it in a piece of cloth and put it on the carrier of his bike. As he would be serving mass the following evening he reckoned it would be as good a time as any to carry out his plan. Whistling loudly, with the leather making a high-pitched sound, he approached Peryl's at a brisk rate. Sure enough out came Ludo at the last moment. Waiting until the cur was almost at his side he hopped the sharp wedge on its nose sending it yelping like a mad thing into the gate where it got caught up in the chicken wire. Not waiting for the inquest he disappeared as fast as he could pedal knowing Paddy or Peryl would be out like a flash. Delighted that his plan had worked so well he knew Ludo would never trouble him again.

He also knew he could easily silence Shep with a few whispered words. He had a few biscuits in his jacket pocket for the old dog and went into Barney's yard talking quietly all the time as he did so. Shep took the biscuits without barking as Seamie gave his owl call to give the all clear. Barney and his sister were invariably in bed before ten as they were accustomed to rising early for the milking. As the old tractor was hard started he used to leave it at the top of the fall at the back of the house. Used to Hewart's Ferguson, a similar model, Seamie slipped it out of gear and let off the brake. Jumping clear, he took to his heels as it gathered momentum and started to wobble on the incline before crashing into the duck pond that Barney built onto the stream that came down from Ballintubber bog. The lads looked on in awe from the safety of the little copse, barely able to make out the top of the tractor as it settled deep into the mud in the pond. Barking furiously Shep was almost pointing to where the lads lay low as Barney emerged with a big flashlight and a cocked shotgun.

"Cheeses," said Bullwire as he burst away from the group who had no option but to break for it too. The rattle of the gate as Bullwire fell over it alerted Barney. Shouting that he'd shoot if they didn't stop, he let of a shot in the general direction of the gate. Seamie stumbled, grabbed Smiler's jacket and fell into the damp grass like a log.

"He got me lads, I'm done for. Save yourselves, don't wait for me," he whispered as the lads bent over him in a blind panic.

"Where did he get you Seamie?" Smiler whispered panic stricken as the youth rolled over again and kicked like a mule.

"He got me in the bollocks lads. Ye'll have to look after June for me. I'm done for."

"Always the feckin' same," said Doc as he whipped off his jacket and put into under Seamie's head. "There he is dying on us and he can't get sex out of his brain." They nearly shit themselves with fear when they heard Barney opening the haggard gate.

"We're done for lads. We might as well surrender before we're all killed," Smiler cried as he knelt beside Seamie who had gone deadly quiet. They were about to call out to Barney not to shoot any more of them when Seamie sprang to his feet and ran like a redshank in the direction of the Crossroads.

"Ya feckin' cunt," Smiler gasped as he realised they were after being hoodwinked.

"Run lads," he whispered as he took flight. The others were already clearing the hedge, making a beeline for the hollow opposite Stewart's hay shed, not stopping until they saw Seamie rolling around the middle of the Crossroads kicking like he had just done above at Barney's. He was laughing his head off as they tumbled down beside him.

"You're a bastard Seamie. You could have had us all killed," Smiler laughed as they pretended to rough him up. Although they had gotten a right fright they revelled in the madness of it all and agreed to a man that it had put the head sheaf on an unforgettable evening.

"Cheeses lads that was brilliant. You should be on the stage Seamie. You got us good there ya fecker," Smiler spoke for all of them as he threw his arms around him.

You Can See if You Want

"How's Ned?" he shouted as he drew abreast of the blind man's cottage.

"Not a bother Seamie," he answered as though he had seen him as clear as day. Ned was known to have acute hearing which compensated for his blindness, a bacterial virus that had struck him early in life. There wasn't a more fervent supporter of the football team than he, nor did he miss a match if at all possible. Often accompanied by one or other of his kids, he'd cheer and cajole with the best of them. No one ever queried his understanding of the game or the fashion in which he enjoyed it as his girls gave a highly colourful commentary of every move and player on the field.

St. Sinneachs were being stretched on the rack in Munis's Field and the young curate knew it. Legan were lording it in centre field with Andy Flood catching every ball over the lads heads and whipping them in to Eddiejoe who converted points from every angle. Fr. Chris knew their goose was cooked unless he pulled a rabbit out of the hat. Substituting 'Poperty' with Bilsheen whom he had warned to lie low, he struck panic in the Legan defence. The world and its mother had heard Bilsheen had been caught sowing his wild oats and knew he'd be dropped from the team as soon as the housekeeper had a word in the curate's ear. With him gone, Legan knew the game was theirs for the taking and played accordingly, spreading balls like rumours around the field. Bilsheen's teammates weren't a bit happy about it because without his high fielding and accurate kicking they were always going to be struggling. Tony Mitchell was fielding great balls despite the sun showers, but prone to inaccuracy, most went as wide as a haggard gate. Somebody saw the curate beckoning to Bilsheen, taking his coat from him and handing it to Johnjoe. The place erupted like Mount Etna. As he burst on the field a cheer went up that'd do Mick O' Connell proud. The comparison was richly deserved because, in another time, in another place on a team like Kerry he would have stood shoulder to shoulder with the legend from Valentia Island. But each parish has its heroes and the Reillys, especially Bilsheen, Mickey and JP had few equals in any of the surrounding seven parishes. The slip of paper safely delivered to Leo meant Bilsheen was free to roam, and that he did. Fresh as a young bull he went high over the lads to field Jim Mullin's long kick out single-handed, turned on a sixpence, jinked left, then right before making a beeline for the goal. Poetry in motion, he soloed twice before burying it in the back of the net, barely looking up as he did so. The crowd went wild. Johnjoe nearly had a canary relating the move to Ned who saw it as clear as daylight though he was as blind as Cody's Corner.

"JP has it. He's after pulling it out of the air with one hand. He's gone on a solo. He's after giving it to Bilsheen. He's heading for the goal. The Legan's are bouncing off him, he's nearly in," Bernadette gushed.

"I see him, I see him," Ned shouted. "Bury it Bilsheen, bury it," he roared as the ball hit the back of the net and the place went wild. It was like trying to mark a furl blast after that as he jumped and leapt in the air picking balls single-handedly out of the clouds as if they were apples on a tree. Even Tony's shooting improved with the excitement as he pointed balls that'd keep Tony McTeague happy. Big Kelly tried to buckle Bilsheen a while later but didn't spot Murray until it was too late! Eamonn's duty was to mind the good players and keep them injury free. It was a role he revelled in as it brought out the savage in him even though he was as placid as Lough Sheedon normally. Many's the forward wished he hadn't attempted an underhand punch or a dirty tackle when Eamonn was around because his peripheral vision and innate cunning left many scratching their heads in wonder at how he could deliver a sucker punch without even the referee witnessing it. Spread-eagled on the ground in front of the referee Kelly looked a sorry sight. Not even his own had much sympathy for him knowing full well what he was up to.

"Did ya see that Ned," roared John Joe as he threw his cap as high as the crossbar.

"A course I saw it. D'ya think I'm deaf or something?"

"Blow the feckin whistle, Leo, or did you lose your friggin' watch?" they shouted in unison. Leo blew it up soon after knowing the game was over as a competition. Nothing would hold Sinneachs now. The smell of the Sunday roast was almost physical and would be spoilt if he didn't get home soon.

"That's the best bloody finish I ever saw," said Ned as Bernadette linked him towards the road gate.

"There's a County footballer if ever I saw one," was one of a chorus of compliments directed towards him as even the Legan supporters shook his hand warmly.

"There's no harm in being bet by a better team but to be bet by one man is hard on the stomach," said the 'Duck' as he slapped Ned on the shoulder.

"Sure every dog has his day," were his words of comfort as he accepted a lift from Frank Kenny who would be passing his house on the way home.

"A man's game boys," was his answer when quizzed by EddieJoe afterwards. It was left at that for another time but even Eamonn knew he'd have to be middling wary the next time they'd meet.

Trooping off the field behind the curate the players were surrounded in seconds by friends from every corner of the parish as they strove to change in whatever shelter they could find. There wasn't even the pretence of a hut to afford them the minimum of privacy but they were well used to that by now. As clever as a jailor, Mulvey was beside the PP who was engaged in friendly banter with 'Red' Lennon pretending not to notice the girls milling around the boys who were trying to arrange a get-together without parent or priest being any the wiser.

"See you in Sandy's after the devotions," was as clear a signal to one as it was to the other. Johnjo was trying to get the better of Doreen but had his work cut out for him this time. Standing round in groups and chatting like old women the rest of the team were making whatever arrangements they could. Innocence prevailed on the way to the devotions but you'd want eyes in the back of your head on the way home when Costello would eliminate competition with a lump of a scraw that'd have your ear aching for a week. No mercy asked or given in the battle of the budgeens, one had to be able to look after oneself or be on the right side. Speed, good reflexes and the ability to see in the dark kept Mullin and Costello under control, but smart as they were, they couldn't cope with the ability of a tinker to look after himself.

Growing up Fast

Doory Gates had been the meeting point the previous Sunday and most of the regulars turned up as there was no game on and time was their own. Chatting like a haggard of sparrows they whipped off their surplus clothes and hid them in the outhouse at the back of Doory Hall until they were coming back. It was a beautiful day with the sun beating down on them as they dallied along the laneway that led to the back of Carrickedmond and into Clonfide. Someone spotted a lone walker ahead who appeared to be looking for bird's nests or something.

"It's Annabel!" Kate whispered, as she was the first to identify her.

"Ask her to join us Kate," Seamie whispered as they quickened their pace to join her.

"Hi Annabel, would you like to join us?"

"All right so but I can't stay too long because my father will be collecting me later. He's over checking mearings or something with Pat Farrell," she added as she fell in with the group. It didn't take long to become acquainted as they mingled along as naturally as a flock of starlings. Her natural reserve soon gave way to uninhibited joy as the excitement of the new group of friends swept her along like a leaf on a stream.

The Clonfide River temporally checked their progress as they sought a safe wading point, or better still, a jumping point. Her local knowledge soon brought them to Ganlys where the river deepened and narrowed through a small ravine cut through a series of rocks. It was perfect for the challenge needed to make a day memorable. The older lads would check the distances first and then showboat as a sign of their march to manhood. Allowances were made for the girls of course and a helping hand proffered if it was obvious the challenge was too great or too risky, but it was also a time for them to show their pluck and fitness. Safely over with the lads Seamie turned to encourage Annabel.

Not waiting to be asked, she stepped back a few paces, struck the pose of an Olympic athlete for the gas of it and took off with her short skirt flying and her pink knickers flashing like a lighthouse. A hush fell as she almost made it. Though a valiant effort, her momentum was not enough to take her all the way across. Seamie, who was holding on to an overhanging branch, grabbed her outstretched arm and pulled for all his might. Her sheer devilry and his heroics brought shrieks of laughter as the weight of the two proved too much for the sapling which bent under their combined weight and left them in the middle of the river with a mighty splash. Spluttering and splashing they rose to the surface still holding on to each other. Striking out for all his might he held on to her as they kicked hard for the bank. Devil-me-care now, they struck out together knowing they were safe.

A reluctant hero, the long-armed Bullwire was leaning out with one leg wrapped around a sound stump of an ash to pull the pair to safety. Strong as a bull, he was nevertheless wary of water since he had been accidently pushed into the deep end of the dam the previous summer. Some of the alikadoos, jealous of his height and strength, used rib him about being afraid to wash his teeth in case he'd drown and then run in case he took offense but he never did. Not being the warring type he could take a joke as well as give one. Playing cowboys and Indians shortly afterwards, his brother Kevin nearly took Seamie's eye out with an improvised arrow but having good bone structure the arrow skidded past with minimal damage. Roughing up the brother for effect, Bullwire drew up a code of conduct and was sheriff-like in maintaining it, especially if the rough and tumble tended to get out of hand. A shout or even a dirty look was enough to keep order as he often refereed the crossroad derbys where the girls could tackle as hard as the boys and even harder in a clinch in the haggard afterwards as dusk descended.

Back at the river with heart beating a mile a minute Seamie could only apologise for failing her. Though somewhat bemused she threw her arms around him and kissed him full on the lips. Astonished, he asked what that was for.

"For giving me the thrill of my life," she replied. "The others might have thought I was too big for my boots but we're all the same now," she smiled.

Bullwire had retreated to allow some privacy and to keep the others at bay while they were organising themselves somehow.

While thinking he was the unluckiest person alive he was amazed at her reaction.

"Very different!" he thought as they squeeze-dried their clothes in the sanctuary of the thicket alongside the river. Not that it was a big job, because, being a beautiful Summer's day, they were wearing the absolute minimum, much less than their parents would approve of if they could only see them. As she stood wide-legged in front of him he couldn't help but notice her firm breasts through her wet t-shirt. She noticed he noticed and without warning took his hands and placed them firmly on them. A shock like that of an electric fence passed through him almost bowling him over but the fact that he didn't was due to another picture flashing through his brain just then. An image of an incident the previous summer burst through his consciousness saving his composure and his blushes.

Laughing gaily as they crossed Mullins' field on a glorious summer's evening the three friends, Carol, June and himself were delighted to be away from the rest of the gang who used follow them like Christ's disciples. It had taken a lot of subterfuge to shake off a battery of suitors led by Bullwire, but by pretending to meet them at Costello's river later they managed to give them the slip and have the dam on Tess's River all to themselves. He vividly remembered June asking him to tie back the top of her bikini prior to a swim and the way the two of them laughed when she deliberately let it fall. Embarrassed at first, he threw caution to the wind as she turned and gave him a full frontal. He was sure it was Tess who had prepared him for this moment and smiled as June dared him to go naked. Discarding the top of her colourful bra she prepared to dive in. Without a second thought he launched himself from the high bank in his birthday suit. She was beside him in a flash with Carol immediately after. Though done in fun it was enough to wise him up and stood to him now as this new challenge tested his resolve. They melted into each other as naturally as two ice creams on a sunny day.

Bullwire shouting, "Come on you two. What are you up to?" dragged them apart for now but both knew it was only a matter of time until they bonded again. The flames had been lit and it would take many moons and fierce tempests to drive them apart.

The job wasn't finished though. The other girls were not quite as feisty and were anxiously awaiting developments on the opposite bank. Bullwire had everything under control by now and his long reach made it easier for the others to cross. Safely over and high on an adrenalin flow they were chattering like a haggard of sparrows as they milled around Annabel. Her courage and bravado had endeared her to all placing her at the top of the pecking order with Kate, a task that would normally take ages to achieve.

Rarely apart after that she became the heroine of their many escapades as they wandered far and wide in search of adventure and experience. The experience they sought was that of maturity which didn't come easy. The Church forbade that knowledge except to the chosen few. Tess had other ideas though. Wise to the ways of the world and wiser still to the laws of nature she used her knowledge of life to protect her protégés. Though it was early days and she hadn't as yet met Annabel, she kept a close eye on Seamie as they grew closer and closer. She knew it wouldn't be long until their exploration of the countryside turned to exploring their intimacy. Ready for that too, she wasted no time in filling them in on how to enjoy their youth without the fear of being destroyed by it.

Practise Makes Perfect

Football practise was a must during the week, hail, rain or snow. Much the better if the sun shone and the girls came wandering by! It was a chance to catch up on the news and to find out who was going to join in the Sunday walks to the butt end of the parish. The girls quizzed the lads as soon as they got home as there was no way they were going to miss out on the fun and games. Any attempt at hiding the truth meant they could look after themselves, which usually meant no clean shoes, shirt ironed or trousers pressed. That would be a disaster for those looking forward to the monthly hop in St. Sinneach's or 'The Aurora Hall' in Legan where you'd be fairly sure of a decent return on a soft drink investment. The worst one could hope to get would be a shift, maybe even a full-blooded court or, if very lucky the 'Real McCoy' if you promised to be gone before the crack of dawn. Despite the Church's threats of damnation the natural order prevailed allowing the young to enjoy life without losing the run of themselves. Some lost out of course by overcooking the bacon but many got the best out of their youth with only the inner circles being party to their abandon. Contraceptive devices were for the privileged few but there were other means of avoiding undesirable consequences and these were widely practised from an early age. Knockagh and the Commons were firm favourites, though Doory Hall and Clonfide were gaining in popularity because the lassies from the back of the parish, being a bit wilder and daring than the Abbeyshrule contingent, often joined them. This was no idle statement and far from uncomplimentary. Their passion and fiery tempers were like magnets to those who attended Colehill School. Firstly, they were different, if anything, more natural and less inhibited than their counterparts from the east of the parish. They could curse like troopers but laugh like hyenas as they got stuck in and jumped ditches and drains every bit as good as the lads.

"It's the water!" Tess laughed when Seamie asked her about the sexuality of the Clonfide girls.

"Ah don't be daft Tess," he shook his head in disbelief at her jocular treatment of what he perceived as a series subject.

"Only joking a mhic, lighten up and I'll give you my opinion," she said as she gestured to the three-legged-stool by the hob which was his favourite and where he often fell into dreamland as she wove her magic on him with her treasure throve of madness, invention and home-grown philosophy.

"I often read palms as you know Seamie but I can tell you there's a big difference between The Carrikebwens and the Shrulers. You see, the good land is here and the bog land is beyant Abbeyshrule around Clonbrin where they came across those bronze shields and ornaments belonging to the long ago. Tis said there's an awful lot more of that in places like Taghsionnad, Lough Sheedon and Mornin Castle but that remains to be seen. You'd have to go on over the Inny to Castlewilder or Williamstown to hit on better land nor here," she said.

"Now here's the thing a mhic, it's hard to hould on to anything that's good or even fairly middling. Wimmin would be a good example for you. If they're better than middling, there's men as would love to be with them and the ones they're with don't see that. First chance they get they're gone, if only for an hour, but sometimes for good as well. And who's to know the differ? Now the Carrick wimmin are all there and if their men don't see that then they're not there. They're gone rambling to Maggie Farrell's or Mary Glennon's where it's all sorted and everyone is happy. Wasn't it the same beyant in Clonmacnoise when the monks serviced the young wans who were married to auld fellas because they had a bit of land and feck all else. Síle Na Gigs me eye! It was Nature looking after its own. The auld fellas believed it was a miracle, the women who travelled with the young wans got looked after by the nuns, and the monks were only doing the work of God. What more could you ask for?" she tittered as she slapped her knee at the good of it.

Her infectious laughter rolled over them as they jumped up, slapped hands and danced around the table with tears rolling down their cheeks. "Round the house and mind the dresser," they said in unison as they completed their little jig.

"That's the best yet Tess," he giggled as they courtsied regally.

"You'll enjoy the rasp all the better for it now," she said as she heaped it on to his plate. That done he escorted her to her easy chair by the hearth and poured the tea into their enamel mugs.

"I'll read your palm in a minute and show you how to do it as soon as you've let that into you," she said as he tidied around her.

The Long-legged Thief

Used to catching bigger fish with his father, he would never have thought of eating pinkeens were it not for Tess. She produced them one night he was rambling, and not one to quibble at her fine fare he ate his fill before asking what type of fish it was. That started another of her games as, not only did he have to guess what it was, but where she caught it as well. It took him a while but once she mentioned Bosque he had it.

"Pinkeens," he said jubilantly.

"That's right a mhic and you didn't turn up your nose at them either."

He knew because he used catch them there himself but they were for fishing and great bait for a big salmon or trout if there were a few of them on the hook. He used to channel them into a little pond and then whisk them out with a big jam jar before transferring them to a water-filled hollow in the centre of the Rath where they'd be safe until needed. At least he thought so until one evening he was surprised to see there were only a few remaining in the holding pool. Perplexed, he went fishing once more with his jar and soon had the pool lively again. Thinking it might be a mink that was decimating his stock he decided to partially cover the pool with branches from the nearby hazel wood. As soon as he was satisfied he had done a reasonable job he left it be for the moment. Returning the following day he wasn't surprised to see his man-made pool almost empty once again. Annoyed now, he repeated the action before withdrawing to the sanctuary of a little copse close by. While loading his catapult for action he kept a close eye on the sunken Rath and his live bait.

Within minutes the king of all herons swept low along the river before alighting by the sardine-filled pool. It didn't take it long to access lunch as it promptly picked at the leafy cover throwing branches hither and thither as it did so. So intent was it on its lunch it failed to see Seamie slipping from bush to bush. Close enough, he took careful aim and let fly. The first shot whizzed past, but the second caught it fairly on the wing forcing it to flap away in pain. With a flying dive, reminiscent of Mike Gibson in his heyday, he landed on top of the big bird and held on tight. The poor thing got such a fright it just lay there waiting for its fate to be decided.

"Now what do I do?" the young hunter thought as he tied her legs together with his bootlace. "Will it make a dinner or would it be better to let it go, hoping it might have learned its lesson? He decided to let it go after examining its wing to see if anything was broken. It didn't appear so. Surprised at its size and strength he was just about able to keep it subdued until he had untied the knot and shooed it away while he walked in the opposite direction. Looking back he was astonished to see it following him. Sitting by the well he waited to see if it would attack. The bucket was at hand if it did, but he felt something else was happening. Stopping a few yards short of him it just plopped down as if it were about to have a nap. He waited. Sure enough it stretched its long neck back under its wing and appeared to nod off. Afraid to move away in case he disturbed it, he sat back on the rock and fell into a deep sleep.

Standing in the witness box in the middle of the Rath, with, herons flying in from near and far to witness the trial, he felt he was in for it. Two sour looking bastards stood each side of him, their dark suits filling him with fear as the long-necked lawyer for the prosecution approached him gobbling in Gaelic while brandishing a catapult and a fistful of pebbles.

"Will the injured party take the box," spoke the honourable King of the Herons. Sitting erect and gazing straight at her attacker, Helena Heron listened as the case was brought for the prosecution. As always, there was the usual flapping of wings and rustling of feathers from the gaggle of lawyers and barristers preening themselves as they swanned around the body of the court. A big-beaked broad outlined the case for the judge before the prosecutor started firing questions to the delight of the surrounding eloquence of lawyers.

"Are these the instruments of torture you employed against a defenceless woman?" a hump-backed heron asked.

"Defending my possessions," he answered defiantly.

"Your possessions, your possessions!" the prosecutor snapped as he turned on him.

"Your Honour we should be charging this youth for stealing food from our stores as well as physical abuse," he gobbled at the discovery of the new charge.

"Objection, Objection! You cannot add a new charge at this point," the long-legged lawyer for the accused argued as he mopped his brow with a feather.

"Miss Helena, why would a renowned pacifist like you be attacked?" he asked after beating round the bush more for effect than anything else.

"I was about to organise lunch when I saw a take-away right beside me. Not being one to quibble with Nature's bounty I decided to help myself. I realise now I was raiding this boy's booty when he nailed me goodo," she replied in all honesty.

"Case dismissed," the King spluttered as he brought his gavel down in disgust at such inordinate abuse of his valuable time. With that he rose into the sky and flew away over the Crossroads towards Abbeyshrule bog, closely followed by his entire retinue.

Awaking with a start he was amazed to see the bird wide awake and nestling beside his outstretched feet as if keeping guard. Edging slowly past he was surprised when she rose and waddled after him.

"I guess we're friends so," he laughed as he stroked her head. "Let's see what Tess says when we get home," he said as he filled the bucket and took the longer route home feeling the stile might pose an insurmountable obstacle, at least until she felt fit to fly again. Still beside him as he opened Larkin's gate she slipped through on his urging. Tess was leaning over the half door, beside herself with mirth as the two of them crossed the river, he by the stepping stones and Helena plopping in and out of the water as if she were used to the spot.

"Well that's the best ever," she grinned as the two stood side by side at the half door. "Are ye comin' in or what?"

"I could do with a mug of tea and maybe a crust for Helena here," he nodded towards his new-found-friend.

"Do ya think it'll come in?" she asked.

"Ask her yourself," he grinned. "I only met her a while ago. Her wing is a bit hurt where I hit her with a stone but I think she'll be fine after a while. Let's see what she does."

Opening the door the big bird followed them into the cool interior and plopped down on the turf bag in the corner.

"That's it so. We're stuck with another mouth to feed," he laughed as he hung the kettle over the coals.

"Well, that beats Banagher and Banagher bet the devil," she said as she handed him a hot scone with a spoonful of blackberry jam in the middle.

"I'd better not say anything at home or they'll think I'm away with the Fairies altogether."

"Well, you are now," she laughed as she slapped her knee with delight. "Damn the likes of it I ever saw and I've seen quare things in me time. You have the power a mhic and that's for shure. God knows what you'll bring in next; a Protestant or something!" Helpless with laughter the two of them could be heard in Abbeyshrule, but not even that disturbed Helena who seemed to be at home with these two oddities in their equally strange habitat.

Exploring

By the time they had reached the fairy fort they were in a lather of sweat, giggling and laughing as they threw themselves on a bed of moss in the middle of the enchanted circle. Thick clumps of hazel and whitethorn guarded the ancient fort like a troop of giant warriors, leaving them completely secluded from the outside world. The warm summer sun shone softly on their skin as they rolled around on their bed of lichen. The excitement of being alone in such a wondrous paradise swept over them raising subliminal passions as before at Clonfide River. Their flimsy summer clothes barely kept their excitement from boiling over as they explored virgin territory. Their unwritten pact of reasonable restraint allowed them to savour the moment without spoiling the enjoyment, thus allowing the fever to subside as every fibre in their body absorbed the tempest. Words were unnecessary as they gently eased apart. They had committed to each other entirely but had no intention of spoiling the fun with stupidity. Allison had prepared her well for such a situation but could hardly have expected her to bloom so quickly, or to meet temptation so soon in the form of Seamie whom Tess had also prepared in her own inimitable, roundabout way, sufficiently graphic to spare no blushes.

Laughing heartedly, they talked about the way adults tried to explain what was as obvious as an erection. Weren't they forever seeing animals giving it the holly around the farmyard? They'd want to be stupid not to know these things they agreed, though the in-depth analogies by Allison left little to the imagination. Their enjoyment they knew had to be more discreet, intimate and honourable if it was to continue the way they both wanted it to.

Keen to show his secret world he took her hand and led her to the sandy area beyond the well where he often cooled off when he hadn't time to join his gang by the big pool in the Inny. It was perfect for frolicking as the raised banks forced the water faster and deeper through the sandy channel. It was Tess who told him of it though he'd most likely have found it himself as he wandered the fields doing the counting or after rabbits. She said it was the only place she ever went to have a bit of a swim and a wash away from prying eyes. It didn't surprise him because it was so secluded that anyone approaching would have to know the pathway intimately and would undoubtedly be heard long before being seen.

Stripping off before he had time to say anything she was in the water in a flash, just like that fateful day they met beyond in Doory he thought as he threw caution to the winds and was in after her with a flamboyant buck leap. Swimming towards him with a radiant smile she threw her arms wide and wrapped herself around him before pulling him under where the soft sand caressed their skins like satin. Used to her games by now after the thrills and spills of the Turlough, he stayed down with her until survival kicked in forcing them to the surface spluttering and splashing in a frenzy of happiness.

Hadn't their friendship come a long way since she first filled his fists with her breasts at Doory he remarked as they cuddled on the sand bank where the river divided in two? They knew their love was different from what people thought but weren't in the least concerned because Tess and Allison had prepared them well leaving nothing to chance. Nevertheless, they weren't prepared to run the risk of prying eyes or public criticism.

Though it seemed only minutes since they left the house they knew they were ages gone and didn't wish to leave their dear old friend fretting in any way.

Checking first that the coast was clear they dried each other off before dressing quickly and crossing back to the well for the water and the watercress; an essential ingredient in Tess's exotic salads.

They mightn't have worried for she was sitting waiting on the stone she called 'Eithna's Throne' in memory of the Goddess, who, according to legend, was drowned in the Inny at Tenelick. She had told him the tale and Quigley had backed it up by giving him a fascinating book that he often pored through. He distinctly remembered the lurid details of the death of the goddess by the Inny and had even shown it to Tim.

The motif of the divine lady drowned in the river is fain in the story of the goddess Eithne, whose name is eponymous of the two rivers called Inny, an Eithne in Irish. The major one flows from Lough Sheelan and joins the River Shannon at Lough Reed in the centre of Ireland (Co. Westmeath and Longford) and the smaller one flows in the peninsula of Iveragh (Co. Kerry). Eithne's name is derived from the Irish word ét, 'envy' and means 'She who causes Envy'. A legend, contained in an early text in Old Irish, entitled Ferchuitred Medba, recounts that Eithne was drowned in the stream of Bearramhain while she was pregnant by the mythical King Conchobhar mac Neasa. Their son Furbaidhe was cut from her womb and the river was called after her:

'7 Eithne ingen Echach Fedlig, ben aili don Concobur cetna, mathair Forbaidi mic Concubuir 7 is aire atbertha Forbaidi dhe .i. a forbud .i. a gerrad do roinduib (sic) a broinn a mathar iarna bathad a nGlais Berramain frissa raiter Eithne indíu 7 is uaithi sloindter ind aband .i. Eithni.

And Eithne, the daughter of Eochaid Feidhleach, another wife of the same Conchobhar, the mother of Furbaidhe son of Conchobhar, and the reason why he was called Furbaidhe i.e. he was hacked i.e. he was cut with spear-heads from the womb of his mother after she was drowned in the stream of Bearramhain, which is called today the Eithne, and it is from her that the river is named, i.e. Eithne.

Another poem, entitled Carn Furbaide ['The Carn of Furbaide'], contained in the Metrical Dindshenchas, offers a slightly different story. It tells that Eithne was the wife of Conchobhar and Lugaid drowned her while she was expecting Furbaidhe in a river which now bears her name:

'Atá sund Carn uí Chathbath fors'rimred arm imathlam, lechtán láechda laích col-lí, fertán fráechda Furbaidi. Furbaide Fer Benn, ba brass, mac do Chonchobar chomdass: Ethne a máthair, moltait raind, siur do Meidb is do Chlothrainn. Luid Ethne sin cóiced cain co m-báe h-i fail Chonchobair: dia m-bátar and immalle de dorónad Furbaide. Iarsin mostic Ethne anair dia h-assait i Cruachan-maig: dolluid Lugaid ara cend co bun síd-maige Silend. Sáeb-écht doróni

110

Lugaid for mnaí Conchobair chubaid: tuc am-mac tria tóeb immach iarna bádud balc-thorrach.Is uaithi ainmnichther de ind abann dian ainm Eithne, ó mnaí, ní scél cleithe cruind, atá Eithne arin abaind. [...]

Here stands the Carn of Cathbad's grandson against whom a nimble weapon was wielded; Furbaide's heath-clad grave, martial monument of a glorious soldier. Huge was Furbaide, surnamed Fer Benn, son to comely Conchobar: Ethne, whom verses extol, was his mother, the sister of Medb and Clothru. Ethne came to the pleasant province and made her home with Conchobar: when they lived together there Furbaide was begotten by him. Presently Ethne journeys from the east to be delivered in Mag Cruachan: Lugaid came to meet her at the fairy plain of Bun Silenn. Lugaid committed a foul crime upon shapely Conchobar's wife: he drew her son forth from her side after drowning her in ripe pregnancy. [From her is named thenceforth the river that is called Ethne; from the woman—'tis no grudging secret—the river bears the name of Ethne.]

Aware that they were swimming in the sandy run below the well she left them in peace and waited until they came laughing along with the canisters of water and bunches of watercress. Her heart swelled with happiness as she saw a visible aura of joy around them.

"Blessed they surely are," she thought as she glanced into the fairy fort to thank her other little friends for the great joy they brought her in her declining years. Looking back through her long life brought little sadness in truth. Yes, there were hard times, difficult decisions to make, long hours worked for sweet feck all and, of course, the loss of her one and only and so on but, that said, there was little to complain about in truth. There were many more much worse off if the truth were known. Illness rarely knocked on her door through the years though few lived as primitively as she did. Perhaps that was the secret!

'Eat when you're hungry, drink when you're dry and if the divil doesn't catch you you'll live 'till you die' was an ould refrain her grandfather used use when he hadn't what'd jingle on a tombstone.

"I thought ye might be a while so I came for a walk to pass the time," she said as they drew alongside. Annabel, blushing beautifully knew Tess knew and could read them like a book, knew also they had been as intimate as one could dare under the circumstances. Her body, still tingling with excitement despite the freshness of the fast-flowing stream, must surely have been a dead give-away if her youthful blushes weren't.

Tess didn't show it, being much too wise to act like some of the parish hypocrites who's every thought and act was governed by Church and State. As soon as she saw them coming out of the fort she knew there was a job to be done. Rarely had she seen such an aura of joy around two people, and she had seen some in her time. The joy was palpable, vibrant and natural. Her mind shot back through the decades to a young girl bursting out of herself with the mad exuberance of first love. Already gone from home and school at just twelve tender years, she had settled nicely into her first real job as a maid to the mistress of Killeigh Park, an Elizabethian Manor near Mount Temple. Her mother had served her time there too and was highly thought of by the owners and their many visitors from across the pond. It wasn't the least surprising that the young blood from Uisneach took an instant shine to her, although he could give her a few years and then some. As the early sunshine bathed the mistresses' bedroom a thunder of hooves echoed in the long driveway. Throwing clean sheets on the expansive bed, often referred to as 'the Bull Ring' she ran to the window to see who it might be. Dismounting as the big stallion reined in to the side gate, the tall youth cleared the high gate as if it were a low perimeter fence. Rushing down the stairs to get the door she made it to the bottom step in time to be swept off her feet by the flamboyant youth.

"Put me down this minute or I'll call Miss Maye," she ordered as he whirled her around in the hallway.

"They're gone to town Tess. I met them at the main road just a short while ago. We have the place to ourselves. Her protests were lost on deaf ears as her carried her up the stairs to the big bedroom where a few hours earlier Miss Maye had entertained the Captain whose wife was away visiting her sister in London. Barely able to sleep for the noise, Tess's neat little nest in the attic above them amplified the sounds like an echo chamber. Now as they lay on the big bed Ultan covered her in kisses as he held her close. Though deliriously happy she had no intention of surrendering to his amourous advances. Her mother's words of warning rung like a clarion in her ears.

"Don't dirty your bib child and keep your knees together until it's worth your while to do otherwise." Though unsure of her meaning then, she had no doubts now. In fairness to the young man he respected her honour saying he'd wait until she was ready. The rules of engagement clearly defined they could now enjoy their intimacy without the attendant risks.

As they fell in alongside her their exuberance washed over her and she was young again. It hadn't occurred to her that she might have to bring them down to earth so soon but there was no time to be lost if she was to do what she knew she should do.

Deep in thought she barely heard them as they chattered away. Delving deep into the recesses of her mind she found the answer she wanted etched in stone. By the time she lifted the latch on the front door her anxiety had given way to relief, the relief of knowing she wouldn't fail her dearest friends in the entire world. Though donkey's years divided them they chatted like long-lost friends as they dallied back to her weird and wonderful haven by the river known only by her name. It was as if she shared their love for each other and wanted to be part of it. Though old to some she was anything but to her young friends who hung on her every word. The strange thing was, Seamie often thought, she actually seemed like a young girl at times as they chatted by the fire in the days before Annabel entered his life and changed it forever. It might have been the firelight or…? He didn't know or care because she had led him along the path to puberty and beyond, and now this strange new goddess was by his side. Could he cope with the two of them? He knew he could because the bond between them could only have been arranged in another time on another planet, the one she called 'Abbeyopia'.

"Life goes on like that from day to day in much the same way," she continued. "Neighbours who weren't fighting were making a go of it, and if there was an hour to spare they'd wander over the road for a chat and a cuppa. Little went unnoticed day or night because there was always someone on the move. Some were rambling, some gambling, some cheating and some taking liberties with other men's wives or property. It was no different from anywhere else in the wide world," she told her young friends.

The fact that she had never been out of the parish made no difference because she met many that had been halfway around the world and knew what they were talking about she told them one evening as they chatted around the hearth. Watching them growing rapidly from children to teenagers she never wearied of them and always had a new old story or a conundrum to test their ability. Though having to leave school at the age of twelve she spent her life learning and could impart her wisdom as good if not better than most. Her house was an open university for those who cared to learn. Most went quickly by for fear of being tainted by her 'madness' but those who came and stayed reaped the riches of her weird and wonderful ways.

Since she first met Seamie she had been on a rollercoaster with the two of them. Like him, she had fallen under Tess's spell and with an equally open imagination magic and miracles became commonplace after that.

"It was this time of year," their old friend would say, and she was off again on another extra-terrestrial adventure. Seamie sat back in the sugán with his hands full as Annabel lay into him as happy as the day is long. They had just eaten a couple of pans of rasp and were in the mood for an evening of her weird and wonderful stories. It often happened that they ended up in her place. It was safe, they were safe, and she kept them safe by leading them gently along the path of life where they could enjoy their youthful exploration without the fear of God or Church. She'd often slip into a deep sleep in her sugán chair as they cuddled on the settle bed under the little window. The essence of discretion as always, she'd exhale loudly indicating she was awaking thus allowing them sufficient time to compose themselves after their personal voyages of discovery. Not needing to be told Seamie slipped the kettle over the coals while Annabel organised the enamel mugs for the three of them knowing the tea would set her mind a wandering once more.

"The birds were singing in the bushes, the cattle were chewing the cud, the priests were playing with the boys and girls, the men were after the women; better someone else's woman if possible, and brother was playing with sister. All in all a lovely happy time in the parish," she explained as the two of them looked at her in amazement.

"Look at how happy they are above on the bog road; living on their wits half the time, off hunting rabbits, pheasants and the like as well as putting out night lines or helping themselves to anything that wasn't tied down. Others on the breadline are afraid to admit it and would sooner suffer than do the necessary. The Church and the rich have us moidered about accepting what the good God gives us or doesn't give us but ye can be sure they won't go hungry or cold. They rob and steal in a thousand ways but woe beside the rest of us poor unfortunates if we take a turnip from them. The rich make the laws and the Church and State help them keep them. I learned long ago that these laws have nothing to do with God and are just another way of pullin' the wool over our eyes. Of course you can't say that or you'd end up in Mountjoy Jail or the like. Them that have power got it by taking it by force or trickery and hold on to it in the same way. Look at your wan beyant in Buck and Ham Palace! Laughing at the good of it all she is. Her gang have been there since Christ was a boy and unless we cop on to ourselves she'll be there if he ever comes back though after the shock he got in the year one thousand I doubt He'll be in a hurry back. Did I tell ye about that one? No, well, He was due back to celebrate a thousand years and the boys came on before Him to pave the way- a bit like Johnny the Baptist himself. Well, the three boyos, Peter, James and John, flew in on a big cloud and landed beside the Lake of Galilee expecting a huge turnout. They had their Ballymahon because there was no one there at all except for a few fishermen out on the lake and a couple of women drawing water from the well on the far side. Humming and hawing for a while Peter asked if either of them brought any drink or was it still Lent?

James piped up that he still had a nice bottle of wine from the north of Spain if that'd do?"

"Not as good as a bottle of Kilbeggan but it'll do for now," said John. They were settling into it nicely when they heard a roll of thunder that'd waken the dead. A Flash of forked lightning decorated the heavens immediately after that and left Peter in no doubt as to what was going on.

"Put away the drink for Christ's sake or we'll all be bucked! Can't ye see He's landed! With that the luxury cloud parted and out stepped Himself looking every bit the proper dandy, hair down to His shoulders, long robe flowing in the wind, cowboy boots kicking up the dust and a cigar that'd do justice to Hemingway."

"Well boys, how's tricks?"

"Could be worse I suppose," said James trying to put a good face on it.

"Not many about, I see!"

"They'll likely be along shortly," said John. "Would you care to have a drop of wine while you're waiting?"

"Sure I might as well," He said holding out a copy of the Ardagh Chalice.

"Aren't we well equipped for a bit of a hooley," said Peter as he poured a good measure. "I suppose you have something up your sleeve to feed the multitude later," he laughed.

"Go lang ya bollocks," He said a little annoyed. "Just like ye to make a laugh after all I've done for ye."

"Ah no need to get all hot and bothered for Christ's sake. Sure you had a few great miracles that time. Which do you think was the best anyway?"

"I'll put money on it," said James, "that changing the water into wine would take beating even now."

"Not at all, feeding the multitude with only five loaves and three fishes was much better. Sure if you could do that again you'd win an Oscar," said John.

"I'll put my money where my mouth is and bet a grand that the time you walked on the water was by far the best," said Peter tongue in cheek.

"There's merit in what you say Peadar but I'll let ye decide."

"There's only one way to prove it and that's for you to do it again."

"Put down your bets so and I'll show you how it's done," said He taking off His robe.

"What're you taking the robe off for? It's not going to get wet is it?" laughed Peter.

"You have a point there I suppose," said He as the boys placed their bets. Stepping back a few paces He swished his robe like a bullfighter before making a little run at it. It was lucky it wasn't too deep because he went down like a ton of bricks after a handful of yards. As He rose to the surface spluttering and splashing the boys were laughing their heads off pointing to their hands and feet. It took Him a while to get it but He took it well in the long run and they went off on the next cloud saying there'd be white blackbirds before they'd bother their arses leaving the comfort of Abbeyopia for such an unthankful lot of hoors. Seeing how well her little audience received her somewhat irreverent story she explained that one could say what one liked as long as one meant no harm. They agreed wholeheartedly with her but wanted her to go on with the story about how people lived in the past and how hard times were then.

"There's people round this parish that have to run to Brady Brown every time a child is ready for communion or confirmation," she continued. "D'you think they could run to the parochial house for a handout? Not a bit of it childer. You might as well be looking for a leg of ham on Good Friday as that. The poor divils would sooner sell themselves, and some of them have to do just that to make ends meet. Most women are happy enough to look after their own men and some have no problem who they look after, but many would sooner die than do it with a stranger.

"Horses for courses, as they say nowadays," she suggested. "Those that do have nothing left to them, no other way to make ends meet or put a bit of grub on the table. Some have the good sense to go into the convent where the nuns give them what they can but, apart from the odd saintly priest like Fr. McCabe who delivers indirectly, the rest would sooner play the cards or humour the bishop when he comes calling with a vintage 10-year-old for a ten year old. Life's the same the world over. The rich get rich and the poor get poorer."

As soon as they got home they busied themselves organising a bite to eat. A nice bunch of dried sticks soon had the fire blazing and the black kettle singing. Sending Seamie for firewood in case the evening turned cold she was able to draw Annabel out in a roundabout way. It didn't take her long to find out that they were more than just friends and that they were wide awake when it came to minding themselves. It was obvious she loved Seamie more than anything or anyone. She had never met such an open-minded and trusting child and knew they'd die for each other. She imparted her deepest thoughts to the old lady knowing she understood completely and gave her Druidic blessing without question.

Content that all was well with the world the two new friends busied themselves preparing a bite to eat. Though humble in contrast to her normal fare Annabel never ceased to be amazed at the rich diversity on offer. Most of the menu came from natural ingredients. If it wasn't salmon it was trout or even pinkeens which were every bit as tasty when grilled. Failing that, it would be fresh rabbit, hare or pheasant with all kinds of wild herbs to season and embellish them. She had learned more from Tess about what nature had to offer than any of the cookery books used during domestic science class in the convent. And it wasn't just the ingredients either. It was the way the old lady prepared and cooked them that made all the difference. She had watched her prepare stuffing that would make your mouth water and your eyes brim with tears. Wild garlic mixed with mushrooms she had never heard of never mind seen were added to the pot kicking up a wealth of rich smells that'd make any chef proud to be called one. Potatoes done slowly in the hot ashes always tasted better than when boiled in the pot she was convinced. Apart from that it was the essence of everything around her way of life that was so simple but in other ways profound that drew her to the old lady. She had never met such a fascinating person in her young life even though she had many uncles and aunts that came visiting from time to time. She couldn't warm to them because they were always on the make or making things up. Though well-educated they were out of touch with nature and thereby out of touch with a decent way of life as far as she was concerned. Rarely staying in their company longer than was necessary to be polite and to comply with her parents' wishes she soon realised their gifts were to impress and meant little to her. They could keep their half crowns and florins because Tess's penny or tuppence to Seamie meant more to her than all the money in the mint. She already knew that he had his own secret supply from the bridge at Abbeyshrule as well as his other money-making schemes, but the light in his eyes on receiving as little as a few farthings struck right at her heart strings. How could one not appreciate such friendship she thought as she set the table in the 'dining room' for the three of them?

Soon after her first visit to Tess she was taken to Seamie's other secret pool. It lay on a bend in the river below in Lisnacreevagh but was something else as it was a sharp bend on the Tashinny River. The waters ran fast and deep as pressure forced it from the depths of Carrickboy bog to the Inny in Demsey's Bottoms. A sizeable pool signaled the force of the water but held little danger for either of them because they were well used to tricky waters in the Inny and the Turlough. Rumour had it that more than the fish went with it but Tess's version sounded more likely.

"It was no coincidence that some butchers had a surfeit of meat around that time of year," she told Seamie.

They took no chances as they checked the terrain thoroughly in case the midwife was about. Though time had passed since that particular story there was no knowing whether it might be repeated or not. It caused a mighty stir when the Ballynamanagh girls fell foul to the nurse's narrow-minded views of how they should disport themselves in the presence of the opposite sex. Were it not for Seamie and his brother Mikey their youthful forays might have been blighted forever? Mammy Fay took the reins and saw to it that innocence would reign where ugliness sought to prevail. Though chastened, the girls and boys continued to roam the fields around Knockagh and the Commons just as Seamie and Annabel were doing just now.

Checking the coast was clear they began to shed their clothes leaving just the minimum. Looking up, they laughed, threw discretion to the wind and, joining hands, dived into the clear pool now warmed by the heat of the late summer sun. Tumbling and rolling like dolphins they held hands as they kicked for the shelter of the long reeds where they enjoyed the sensual delights of their rapidly growing young bodies.

His free arm held her tight as she sat on the bar of his bike on the way back to Tess's.

Two buckets of clear water from Bosque stood on the little sideboard alongside a ponger of watercress they had taken home with them a while earlier. Normally, the few perishables such as milk and meat would keep safely in the dark corner away from heat and light but if it happened to be a kind or soft day she'd sit the milk in the little rivulet Seamie had cut out to divert a tiny flow of water towards the house where it served many purposes, mostly to keep food fresh.

As she lit the oil lamp a warm glow spread through the room as shadows lengthened on the wall and floated up into the rafters where Billy's pal Methuselah was getting ready for a night's hunt.

"Would you care for a wander before the night falls?" she asked as she threw a few cipíns over the coals.

"Yes please Tess, Annabel enthused at the thought of another magical mystery tour with her two very best friends. It was hard to imagine how her life had changed since she first met Seamie and his super soul mate but she knew it would never be the same again. Nor did she want it to be. She had already shaken off the chains of normality by associating with these two quare hawks and hadn't a single regret to go with it. She had hinted at her somewhat strange bedfellows to some of her best friends but decided to keep her private life to herself on seeing the strange looks she received. Allison advised her to ignore them, as her real friends were more important. Little did she realise her lovely daughter was already in another world where few ventured and none returned."

"Right so boys and girls fasten your seat belts and we'll head off for a bit of an ould adventure." Giggling happily, they lay into each other as the hum of the lunar-driven motor signalled another flight of fancy in her strange but wonderful time machine. As the little cottage capsule took off across the Commons and wheeled left towards Abbeyshrule they could clearly see the twilight movers at work and play. Sweeping down the Mill Lane they could hear Pierce's fiddle as he played 'The Blackbird in the Mill Lane' an old favourite he had composed with the Piper Dolan and Willie Reynolds many moons before. Though now hitting the twilight years there was music in them yet and lots of followers to enjoy their harmony and compositions. Tess told them she often wandered over the fields and sat by the hedge in darkness to savour the Piper's soulful music that floated across the fields to Tashinny and over the airfield to Abbeyshrule where Pierce would pick it up and play it to the living and the dead in the village.

Jimmy and the lads were letting the cows out of the byre after milking as they swept down the Inny and round by the big house. A heap of kids from the Bog Road and its environs were hanging around the Mill Lane waiting for the call to come and get the free milk. Fagin-like, Jimmy's mother was dishing out the milk making sure not to spill a drop, or overfill the canisters that would invariably be spilt on the way home anyway. Not renowned for her patience she would read the riot act if any of the waiting kids stepped over the pantry line before their time, or gave back guff as she called it.

A pounding of hooves registered high on the micro meter just then, and as they checked the console they saw Miley Nugent arriving at a bold gallop. Alighting from the piebald pony after a hot ride along the canal he changed over to a hotter one, commonly referred to as 'Red Biddy', a much more satisfying if demanding ride for the young jockey. It didn't take him long to get stuck in though as the more mature mare was game for a gallop. All the rest of the gang could do was marvel at his courage and wish they were in his shoes as they watched them hurry round the canal turn and disappear out of sight.

Watching from within the plantation young Paudgeen was beside himself with excitement until the ever-present 'Watcher' from the Avenue happened along, took him by the hand and led him quickly along the canal where the reeds grew tall and strong and his excitement could be harnessed. The dole and tax-free earnings from his nocturnal wanderings from Billy to Jack kept him flush, and fair game too if one was prepared to suffer the servicing quietly. Young men down on their luck or devil-may-care about their preferences could lead or drag him where they would if the price was right. Nurtured in the secretive halls of various institutions he brought his hard-learned trade to the bogs and boreens of the Inny valley. Though reluctant to expose her charges to such deviant activity Tess knew it was important for their on-going education and sure to save them from unsolicited advances in their future lives.

In the shade of the spreading chestnut tree Billy was doing his best with Chrissie but she was having none of it, certainly not for free, as she had already established a suitable fee with the Askabog Dog who, hung like a donkey, hit the accelerator whenever he had the necessary spondulics. If skint, he was still good for credit on the odd occasion providing he didn't abuse it or her. His was a hard act to follow unless one had the necessary equipment and was confident enough to employ it.

Above under the bridge, feathers of smoke rose like spirits as the lads smoked turf mould in dudeens in lieu of the real McCoy. Mac's idea was somewhat better with rushes stripped and dried giving a decent imitation of tobacco and a passable high when mixed with a few magic mushrooms from the high field where Jimmy flew his Tiger Moth and drew devil-may-care adventurers from far and near.

Having established Abbeyshrule as a centre of excellence for all things aerial it wasn't long until all kinds of light aircraft were following the canal from Dublin to the village. Being an outrageous extrovert and self-promoter, he drew high rollers around him like a Las Vegas casino. Very soon the plans were drawn up for an annual air extravaganza that brought thousands from near and far lining the pockets of the organisers in jig time.

The 'Three Amigos' left the scene and swung along the canal to see how Nugent and red Biddy were getting on. Job done, he was inhaling a woodbine like Bogart as the mare settled herself after the excitement. No explanation needed Tess sat back as the co-pilots followed her pointed finger to the high field.

Continuing their education for life she wanted to show them the good, the bad and the ugly, warning them that what they were about to see would pose more questions than answers.

Where Kindred Spirits Meet

A casual meeting on Doory Boreen the previous summer had brought an angel into his life and neither friend nor foe could tear them apart from that moment on. Their friendship had grown in leaps and bounds since then and now the moment of truth had arrived.

The unmistakable sound of Tim's jeep entered their consciousness as the black kettle began to purr like a kitten.

"She's landed," Tess smiled as Seamie jumped up like a scalded cat.

"Cheeses a mhic, settle yerself. It's not the Blessed Virgin that's arriving," she tittered as she busied herself tidying up the table and few chairs.

"Well, I know she's a virgin and for sure she's blessed!" he said, grinning as she looked sideways at him.

"Only codding with you Tess, sure how would I know?" he said as seriously as possible as she pretended to take the besom to him. Allowing the old lady to lead the way to the front door, he leaned over her shoulder as Annabel jumped out of the jeep, face flushed, skirts flying and an angelic smile radiating from her milk-white teeth and lightly-tanned features.

"God save all here," said Tim in his clipped West Brit accent as he eased across the style, his customary riding crop under his oxter as he dragged his reluctant leg over, the result of a rock fall in a copper mine in northern Chile.

"And all adout as well I'm thinking," said Tess as she laid her hand on Annabel's shoulder.

"You'll be having tay I presume?" she said warmly.

"We won't say no, Theresa," he nodded as he followed her into her little mansion. In truth he was as keen to see what all the fuss was about, because, since his lovely daughter had met these two he could hardly get sense out of her at all. He knew she was besotted by this wonderfully, weird, woman and her young protégée, and though not in the least fearful of the fatal attraction, he wished to know what the attraction was.

His enquiries about the possible age of her house led Tess to surmise it could have been built around the time of the famine, but she couldn't be sure because there were no records and no one alive could throw any light on it. Her father had left it to herself and her brother and it had served them well down through the years and during her marriage to Jack Maguire also. Though simple in construction, the walls were thick and strong, whereas the roof was in dire need of new rafters and a fresh thatching.

The dim interior reminded Tim of Velasquez's painting of 'Old Woman Cooking Eggs' and could have been from a different era and a different area. The bare essentials within; a sugán chair, a couple of stools, a small table, a settle bed, a dresser with a glass front and a mantelpiece on which a wood-surround mirror reflected the stile by the side of the stone bridge. Little moved unknownst to the old lady, and what did, was picked up by Billy, who watched the place like a hawk.

"Who'd want a goose or a dog?" she often said when asked if she was afraid living on her own. "Yer man would hear the grass growin'" she'd laugh.

Try as he might Tim couldn't force himself to eat the freshly-warmed rasp knowing his stomach would reject it immediately. A mug of tea would be just the biscuit he suggested by way of excusing himself. Annabel found herself in the same boat and was forced to use a similar lame excuse. Thanking the old lady sincerely she nevertheless declined knowing she'd need time to adjust to such rich fare. Seamie had no qualms however, having already overcome the initial stomach-churning revulsion when he first broke bread with the old lady. A veteran of her cooking by now he could let his lugs back at anything she threw at him, fish, fowl or fancy.

Having mentally taken note of every nut, nail and bolt, Tim made his apologies and stood up to leave requesting his daughter to follow suit. Seamie's face fell like a bad horse at Beecher's Brook. Tess however, was unperturbed.

"She'll be back child, relax," she advised as he peered through the jungle of geraniums surrounding the gaily painted little window.

"She's coming back!" he whispered as he ran to the stool pretending he was as cool as the old lady.

"Didn't I tell you or is there any edumacation in you at all at all," she winked as a soft knock sounded on the half door.

"Come in child or is it afraid of us you are," she laughed by way of welcome.

"Well, I'm not Theresa but father warned me to be on my best behaviour," she said as she opened the half door in front of her.

"We'll have less of the Theresa bit child. Your father is an edumacated man an all that but you're with your friends now and you must call me Tess the same as Seamie does."

"Very well Tess. It's an honour for me. Father said he was most impressed with your lovely house and told me to give these groceries to you," she said softly as she handed them to her.

"Father said he preferred practical things to ridiculous presents," she said as she sat on the three-legged stool Seamie offered.

"Maybe the girleen would prefer the chair with the back in it," Tess suggested.

"Not at all Theresa, sorry, Tess," she replied. "I'm perfectly happy here."

"Your father is a wild clivir man and I'll accept the groceries providing he doesn't make a habit of embarrassing a poor ould woman like meself," she smiled as her two young charges gravitated towards each other like magnets. Instinctively, Seamie pulled out the log he often sat on rather than sit on the chair that would put him above her and possibly leave her at a disadvantage. This didn't go unknown to Tess who was to commend him later on his thoughtfulness. Pretending to be busy doing nothing, it didn't take her long to spot the obvious magnetism between the two teens already itching to be on their way and on their own.

"Away over to Bosque with the two of ye or I'll get nothing done this blessed evening," she waved as she indicated the enamel bucket to Seamie. Needing no further encouragement they were up and out the door like hares chased by whippets.

"We'll get some watercress too," Annabel waved back as she grabbed the can hanging from the boultree by the gable end, and was gone skipping along the narrow path by the river.

Making a half-hearted effort at following them, the cats soon gave up and went off looking for field mice, leaving the two pals dancing along by the river to the hazel wood at the corner of Harry's Field.

Standing in out of the Rain

Commenting on how well Annie was looking, Nora enquired if there was any special occasion or if she was expecting anyone special? Hewart had asked her the same question she replied. It was alright for her to ask as they were friends for years but it was none of his business she laughed. She added sarcastically that it wasn't him she was expecting anyway. He wasn't a bit pleased as he had just given her a Sweet Afton and was sitting up on the counter for the long chat. She cut the boots of him, she said. Catch her to tell him anything. She might tell him about Dolly just to rise him though. Did he not notice that the Yank had a different smile on him these days? And did he not think it strange that he was spending a lot of time visiting his former lady friends? She could see that Hewart was raging because he got redder and redder as she dug the boot in.

"Wasn't it a good thing she could mind her own business?" Nanny continued: "Or there would be all kinds of stories doing the rounds."

"They'd have little to talk about if there wasn't a bit of scandal or something unusual going on around the crossroads," Nora laughed as she turned the soda cake on the griddle.

"Sweet mother of Jesus I'm out of here. Didn't Biddy read her well? I'll fly before she nabs me. You're well able to deal with her Nora, good luck."

"Thanks Annie, I'll remember you for this!"

"Was that herself I saw going over the road?" she enquired as she stepped into the kitchen.

"It was indeed Bappy. How strange! You just missed each other."

Commenting on the great times the woman had and that it might be better if she spent more time at home than running the road tormenting the men and the like, she was soon in full flow. Nora turned on her sharply reminding her that none of them could afford to talk. Though stung by the remark, she bit her lip and changed the subject, because Nora was the last person she wanted to offend for several reasons.

The ritual of life around the crossroads rarely changed. Though hers was always an open house it could be a bit of a bind at times. She knew her near neighbour kept a close eye on who was coming and going, but then, so did most of her neighbours, even herself! Generally speaking, it caused her no great pain except when Bappy, a serious story-carrier, even mischievous at times, talked about her friends. Nevertheless, she was a good neighbour and had looked after her fowl of late since she had been unable to do so herself.

Telling her to sit down and rest herself while she got on with the feeding of the turkeys, Babby headed for the various enclosures that protected the fowl from the wily fox. She moved quickly through the pens checking that all was well with Nora's large flock now almost ready for the rapidly approaching Christmas market. It was no easy task, as clean water, a dry run and a mixture of cereals and nuts was essential for their rapid growth. The water still had to be fetched in galvanised buckets from the well below in Bosque, a task that required no small amount of care.

An onerous task at the best of times as awkward fences and stiles had to be crossed and re-crossed, Bappy gave little thought to it as she headed off with the two buckets. The fences and stiles had been erected to keep the Bó Gáineamh (thieving cow) from breaking into their fields, an all-too-regular occurrence when good grass was scarce. Renowned for its pure water and unfailing spring even in the hottest summers, Bosque well brought people from far and near. The fact that it was situated beside the fairy fort and the giant's grave only added to the mystery surrounding it. The powerful spring could clearly be seen pushing up tiny pebbles as it burst from its source under the hill.

Nora had the tea ready when she returned in a lather of sweat. It was only then she realised that Bappy was pregnant. Shrugging it off by saying the exercise would be good for her, it struck Nora that she was unaware of her situation until then. Nothing new in that she thought! She had no idea she was pregnant herself until her older sister remarked on it.

The Duck loaf that Annie had given her earlier was already sliced and placed invitingly on the table near the front window. Mopping her brow with the tea towel before spreading generous amounts of Nora's newly made butter on several of the slices she tucked in with a relish. The rigours of the journey and the weight of the two buckets of water had put an edge on her hunger. Munching contentedly on the fresh bread she washed it down with copious amounts of well-sugared tea. Naturally, the conversation swung back to Nora's recent visitor as she hadn't failed to notice the new hairdo, or the fact that she had had her red dress on which normally indicated something special was happening or about to happen.

Nora's earlier rebuke, already forgotten like the winter snow, failed to deter her from airing her acerbic opinion. Aware of her failings when it came to gossip, Nora let her ramble away on this occasion due to her good deeds and the fact that she had just realised that she was pregnant even though she had no idea of it.

The lads nursing the shovels knew full well what was going on she suggested while watching out of the corner of her eye for Nora's reaction. You could do feck all with them because they were worse than the Tinkers with all the signs and things they use she said as she refilled the mug. It was highly likely he'd be calling for the cuppa that very day on account of her being all dolled-up she continued as she helped herself to another slice of the duck loaf.

"You can't beat the bit of tart and tay for tempting the men," Nora said with a wide grin.

She had to laugh at her next comment about it being a good job she minded her own business or she'd never hear the end of it. "The laugh of it all was," Bappy continued, "the ganger usually met Toddy, Annie's man, going the other direction whilst he was on the way to visit her. The poor man had to cycle to the far side of the county to be out of the way so that the two of them could have a chat in comfort. Annie didn't want him interrupting with nonsense about the weather and the like when she was more interested in what went on in the town. She was sick to death of hearing the same old tune every day. Clancy's accent was different, more refined, not the flat Midlands accent that she was used to. Some of the words he used went over her head but she liked that too and often wrote them down so she could look them up in the old dictionary she bought at Canon McGivney's auction.

It was amazing how that man got away with it," Bappy added as she mopped out the scullery. "Sending men here and there so he could act the lad and play the field was hardly good enough. Some men would go a long way for a cup of tea and a bit a cake! It was hard to credit but he actually got off the bike recently and started chatting to me! The bloody cheek of him!" She couldn't get away from him for ages because they were talking about this and that and everything.

"He's a fair hand to talk I know," Nora agreed.

"And a good sense of humour as well which I wasn't expecting from him."

He told her a story that same day about the time he cycled out from town to do his rounds. It started to rain at Carrickboy and was a virtual downpour by the time he neared the Blue Doors. A few women on their way to Carrickboy for the children's allowance had stepped in for shelter in the small porch at the old Quaker house. Wheeling in quickly he asked them if they'd mind him stepping inside as his brolly couldn't cope with the wind as well as the rain.

"Not at all," they echoed as they nudged each other. Clancy's reputation as a lady's man was well known but it didn't stunt his growth as the Cuddy once remarked.

"It would be a tight squeeze but if he didn't mind he was most welcome," Lily said as they squeezed together to let him into the middle of them. There was no way an opportunity like this was about to be passed up on.

"Divil the bit Ladies," he answered as he squeezed in through them. His umbrella would help to keep the rain off if he held it over them he suggested as the women moved closer. As there was no immediate sign of the rain to stop they began chatting about this and that, mostly about their men folk, some of who had temporary jobs on the Council. They would be most grateful they said if he could see his way to offer any employment due to the hard times that was in it. Promising to do his very best as always he slipped in nicely behind Lily.

"You'll never guess what he said to me then Nora?"

"I wouldn't have an idea girl."

Bappy was rising to her story now. She said he confessed to her that he had the devil of a job trying to contain himself because Lily kept leaning back into him. She kept wriggling about saying that she couldn't help it with the rain and the wind or she'd get drowned or blown away. Better that than getting wet he agreed. The next thing he knew she had her hand down his trousers giving him the works. What could he do only pretend nothing was happening until he wasn't able to hold out any more and began to take deep breaths as quietly as he could. Luckily the wind was strong so he managed to get by without the other women knowing what was happening, or so he thought!

Lily, an earthy woman if ever there was one, related the incident soon afterwards during a break in the bingo in St. Sinneach's hall.

"You'd think butter wouldn't melt in those women's mouths Nora, and they with a heap of kids and their own men as well."

"I suppose we're all human at times. We wouldn't be straying far from nature or from when we were playing the field ourselves."

"Could you credit that Nora?"

Nora knew she'd never hear another story from her if she stopped her now so she let her continue without interruption.

"Did you ever notice the suits he wears? You could shave yourself with the crease he puts on his trousers even after riding all the way out from the town," she said as she rinsed out the nappies she had washed earlier.

"Annie must air it out for him while they're having their tea and cake Nora suggested much to Bappy's amusement."

"That woman knows where her bread is buttered make no mistake about it."

The Written Word

Two great books written around the 12th century, 'Leabhar Báile Na Mánach' - The Book of Ballynamanagh - and 'Leabhar Mainstír Shrúthla' - The Book of Abbeyshrule - written in Ballynamanagh and the Abbey respectively, went missing from their previously secure hiding places in Knockagh and Doory during the Civil War and hadn't been seen since. Rumour had it that a certain cleric sequestered them for an American buyer and that they were in a private collection in New York. However, as rumour is not worth the paper it's written on it was pointless arguing the toss until the books come to light again as they undoubtedly would. It was said that the Book of Ballynamanagh outlined a huge network of man-made tunnels from one lís to another around South Longford. This network from Knockagh to Ballynamanagh included Lisnacreevagh, Killeendowd, Doory, Taghsionnad and two or three at the back of Carrickedmond, most of them joining the many monasteries and abbeys together before exiting on the Mountain near Moydow.

Tess could only verify the local ones as the others were outside her sphere of influence.

These tunnels and caves when well maintained, as they were in those dark and difficult days, offered more than places of refuge. Small bands of warriors led by 'a few hardy hoors' as the Nugget would say, led lightning raids against Cromwell's freebooting Roundheads then disappeared into the earth just as quickly. It was the type of hit and run guerrilla tactic that the English were unused to, and barely able to contain. They did take revenge in a savage way though by lining up any scapegoat they could find subjecting them to the most horrific torture to either force them to reveal the whereabouts of their compatriots or die for the cause. As death was a constant in their humble lives they chose to die rather than betray their own.

Tess told a strange story about one of her own whose knowledge of the tunnels was so complete that he could pop up anywhere when least expected. Known as the Double-Giant due to his ability to swivel his arms and feet like an octopus, he harried the Scottish mercenaries out of the Midlands by appearing ghost-like whenever they were about to burn his people's cabins to the ground or torture the women and children. Fearless, he swooped on the foe out of the thick mists taking no prisoners, just helmeted heads to scare the daylights out of their fellow countrymen. Chasing a small band of warriors, the Cromwellian foot were led a merry dance through Lisnacreevagh and into the dense wood of Tashinny where the Double-Giant was waiting to wreak havoc on them. Gouging out the eyes of the few survivors he had them led back to Ballymore by the only sighted one remaining. There they recounted the horror of the vengeance the Double-Giant had inflicted on them and the written threats he sent to warn them from returning. Though driven to distraction by anger the English had to up stick and go by forced march to Dublin where greater threats were being posed by the combined Irish forces who were attempting a last stand against the accursed invader.

Peace finally settled on the Midlands even if their lands had been stolen and divided amongst Cromwell's followers. Some of these had learned the hard lesson and managed to ingratiate themselves with the locals by offering a subsistence living through rough quarry work, stone breaking and the widespread erection of stone walls and boundaries. In return for this backbreaking work they received the absolute basics and no more. At least it was better than before because they could now hunt for food without the fear of being caught and murdered for it. Try as they might the new Planters were unable to locate the tunnels or caves due to a complex system of blockages and venting employed by the Double-Giant. Nevertheless, his family kept the secret safe for the future though few set foot in any but small sections that served other purposes down through the years.

The big oaks fell fast as boat building grew all over the Continent. Armies of Scottish and northern English woodcutters moved in to loot the fertile plains and ship their booty to the lowlands of Holland, Spain and Portugal as well as England. This done, they joined Cromwell's murdering mercenaries and, in lieu of monetary reward were granted swathes of mixed land throughout the country.

Two perfectly shaped Raths commanded the crossroads and would be there yet Tess said but for poor management by the County Council who ceded one of them to a local landowner who promptly levelled it. The other was given to the school to be used as a car park.

The stark Puritanical school built in 1895 resembled a Poor House on one side of the crossroads, while Cody's Victorian-style Manor on the corner of the Hollow and the Tashinny roads had a much more soothing effect. Though long converted into a Post Office, courtesy of Protestant privilege prior to the declaration of The Republic, it served the area well. Good husbandry and a shut mouth kept the wolves at bay before the political scenario eased from the bullet to the ballot.

It also held a pivotal role in the administration of the local civil service. It was the fulcrum for payment of the children's allowance, the dole, the old age and widow's pensions and the payment of fines for minor infractions. A brown telephone box with as much privacy as a toilet in the middle of a field stood inside the narrow double door.

Open plan shelves with everything from a safety pin to a tin of sardines covered the walls from floor to ceiling around the room. A glass-fronted meat fridge and cabinet acted as counter, display and storage where backs of bacon, rashers and sausages were laid out in rows alongside Killeshandra butter, Galtee and Mitchelstown cheeses, as well as Flynn's, Breaden's and McNamee's bread.

Big bags of Clarinda for turkeys, oats for the hens, nuts for the cattle and sheep, as well as porridge for the people were propped up under the yard window. Four stone bags of potatoes, oats and Indian meal were neatly lined up on pallets, which also served as seats during the Friday rush for the pensions.

The administrative section was behind the main counter in a closed off area where business could be conducted in private. Hewart could keep an eye on the driveway and the crossroads from this vantage point where little escaped his eagle eye. The Cuddy maintained he kept a life-size painting in the window whenever he was checking the perishables in the pantry with the maid or going through Nelly's inventory. The same Cuddy used to drive Nelly to distraction with the oft-quoted refrain attributed to the itinerant poet Francis Kendall Husband.

> *In Barry town of poor renown*
> *Where stands neither church nor steeple*
> *Behind every half door*
> *There stands a whore*
> *Making little of decent people.*

> *Along the line there stands a pine*
> *Where locals piss and scutter*
> *Be careful there for the cailíns fair*
> *Will melt your heart like butter.*

The majority saw the Cuddy's stories as being harmless, but it was hard to say if one were looking through a semi-frosted window.

The postal distract covered a huge area stretching to the outer limits of the parish, a defined ecclesiastical, if not geographical area. The Rex's neat two up, two down, stood at the head of the long Avenue and was formerly a gate house leading to Colonel King-Harmon's huge estate in Forgney on the Westmeath border. The two carved granite cups and saucers that once stood on the pillars of the gates had long been removed and placed in Cody's front lawn before King-Harmon sold out in 1920 prior to the arrival of the dreaded Black and Tans.

"There they stand, a memento to lost glory and greed," Quigley was wont to say. In truth they would have been destroyed by vandals long before had they not been moved. Few believed the old stories that they were the drinking cups used by the Giants of the Commons in ancient times, but stories were told, and enormous flat stones seemed to verify their authenticity, of wandering giants hiding out in the ancient oak forests of the Midlands. The Seanachaì told stories of them suddenly appearing to wreak havoc on invaders who came up the river Inny from the Shannon or down from the plains of Meath.

"If you listened hard," they said, "you could hear their howling during the depths of night or at the height of a storm."

Cromwell's arrival in Ireland in 1649 signalled dire times for the Midlands according to the Master. Although a brutal teacher, he differed little from most of the others who were given carte blanche to beat learning into their pupils. Though severe in his methodology, he was nevertheless, a brilliant teacher. He knew everything and forgot nothing. Not even the PP or the doctor could find a solitary error in his teaching. An enormous map of the world was wheeled out of the old press each day and was eagerly pored over by the kids who showed immense interest in World Geography, principally because Quigley left them alone while they looked up rivers, lakes and capitals. It was the highlight of every other day. Kids loved it, even asking questions of each other in the playground. If you didn't know the capital cities of most of the countries of the world, you were insignificant, even more insignificant than usual! Seamie quickly figured out that all you needed for this and most other subjects was a good memory, to pay attention, and you were up there with the smart arses, the really clever ones. They mightn't let you into their circle but you could hover around on the periphery without being given a thick ear. He felt he had had enough with thick ears. He'd force himself to remember the details by rhyming them off to himself as he beat a path to Byrnes's for the milk or daydreamed on his way to count the sheep or cattle for Hewart.

Once he got the hang of this there was no stopping him. Maths problems that used to make him the laughing stock of the other kids soon became a lot easier. His worst nightmare happened when Quigley set a tough task to all his charges. They had to figure out a difficult long division problem but they had as much time as was necessary to solve the equation. A doddle for some, it was a serious challenge for most, but one by one they walked to the master's desk and joined the elite. Sweat broke out on Seamie's forehead as the numbers dwindled alarmingly. He tried to focus but something was preventing him from grasping the answer. Try as he might the answer eluded him. He could get so far but no further. Suddenly, he heard a voice speaking clearly in his ear.

"Start at the beginning, find the pattern and follow it to the finish."

It was Tess. She had come to his rescue once again. He did as she said, and not surprisingly, the sequence was as obvious as the nose on Aodh Goo's face. "Saved by the bell," he thought as he beat Bertie the Butcher to the punch.

"Think, think," he'd urge himself as he brought the buckets of water from Bosque or cycled the lonely roads delivering telegrams to the far outposts of the parish. It wasn't long until people noticed the change coming over Seamie. The Master eased off his sudden and unprovoked attacks, occasionally even asking him to "tell that numskull the answer before I have to confess to serious injury to a fellow human. Tell him tell him, I beg you in the name of Jesus Christ."

"Yes sir, I will sir, the correct answer is..." Seamie couldn't believe it himself!

"I did it, I did it. It worked! I'll listen to every word the oul bastard says and I'll know the right answer every time. Nobody will beat the daylights out of me for not knowing the answers ever again," he promised himself as he counted the coppers that Tess and others had given him for the errands he ran for them.

Quigley could tell stories like the best of them and was at home with history. The minute he perched on the corner of the desk where young McGivney sat, the boys knew a story was coming. It meant a lull in the fighting, an armistice, and an uneasy peace. He'd start easy, crank up the engine and he was gone. They followed him on flights of fancy from Toowoomba to Timbuktu and back to Tenelick where he told them about the struggles against the Cromwellian genocide in Ireland.

Having been schooled by the younger Master many moons before, Rex had a heap of stories for Seamie. One evening as they played out their lines for a big salmon in Dempsey's Bottoms, he recalled the day the Master put himself, Cummins and Farrell standing up on the ledge of one of the big front windows. He had grown tired of their pleading to be let home to save the hay on account of the glorious day that was in it. It was unusual because it was customary to let the lads out if essential work had to be done or hay made while the sun shone. A half hour passed and still no sign of him to let them down from the ledge where passers-by would make faces at them knowing it was the reward for foolishness. Hatching a plan, the three lads waited until he was about to pass under them on one of his thousand walks around the room. Without warning they jumped him and pinned him to the ground. A sudden hush fell around the room as he struggled to get up but he hadn't a ghost with the three lads firmly planted on top of him. Realising he was likely to get an epileptic attack with the undue excitement he begged them to let him up as he wasn't feeling well. After forcing a quick promise that it'd go no further they helped him to his feet and walked out the door with most of the lads after them.

There was nothing for it but to dismiss the stragglers, lock the door and head into Miss Morris for a mug of tea. Silencing her with a savage look he picked up The Irish Press and started to read.

"Will I let the girls go too?" she asked nervously.

"You might as well because they'll be fit for nothing after seeing the boys racing across the crossroads. Despite falling foul of his violent temper the three lads were soon forgiven and had to promise him they'd lead the guard of honour when his time was up and he had cast off his mortal coil. They agreed because Rex knew his heart was in the right place and often quoted line and verse from Goldsmith's Deserted Village as proof of the Master's brilliant mind."

> *Beside yon straggling fence that skirts the way,*
> *With blossom'd furze, unprofitably gay,*
> *There in his noisy mansion, skill'd to rule,*
> *The village schoolmaster taught his little school.*
> *A man severe he was, and stern to view;*
> *I knew him well, and every truant knew:*
> *Well had the boding tremblers learn'd to trace*
> *The day's disasters in his morning face;*
> *Full well they laughed with counterfeited glee,*
> *At all his jokes, for many a joke had he;*
> *Full well the busy whisper, circling round,*
> *Convey'd the dismal tidings when he frown'd.*
> *Yet he was kind, or if severe in aught,*
> *The love he bore to learning was in fault.*
> *The village all declared how much he knew,*
> *'Twas certain he could write and cipher too;*
> *Lands he could measure, terms and tides presage,*

And e'en the story ran- that he could gauge:
In arguing, too, the parson own'd his skill,
For e'en though vanquish'd, he could argue still;
While words of learned length and thund'ring sound,
Amazed the gazing rustics ranged around;
And still they gazed, and still the wonder grew
That one small head could carry all he knew.

Waxing lyrical, he recounted local history in the area from the dawn of time until the present day and how a few families managed to survive Cromwell's purge by hiding in the oak forest near the Giant's Rocks in the Commons. A warren of caves interlinked underneath the enormous boulders he told the lads. These led away to vantage points on the side of the hill facing the Inny River some distance away. From here the hounded unfortunates could keep a watchful eye on Cromwell's hordes as they crossed the ford where the eel-weir now stands. The problem lay, invariably, with their immediate neighbours, who, when flushed out by Cromwell's murderers, were subject to such barbaric torture that their secrets were forced from them. Some great Saint or law of Nature kept a few of those hiding in the Commons safe. It may also have been the fact that the rivers and streams followed their own courses during this time and had not yet been channelled by mankind. Cromwell needed to move quickly to subdue the enemy in this tiresome land. The richer pastures of Meath and Westmeath offered better booty and the poorer land of Longford and Leitrim would pay his mercenaries for their murdering enthusiasm. Thatched houses were simply torched as Cromwell's hordes moved on, raping and pillaging as never before in the troubled history between such close and antagonistic neighbours. Quigley spared nothing about the death and destruction dealt out to the long-suffering Irish who tried to evade the Scottish mercenaries who made murder their middle name to achieve their reward.

Apart from the few protestant families who were granted land during the Plantation of Longford in 1619, the area was 95% Catholic, according to Quigley. He told them about the siege of Athlone where a few men risked life and limb to tear planks from the town bridge to keep King William of Orange from taking the castle in 1690. He even sang The Ballad of Athlone though he wasn't blessed with a voice like McCormack or Mikeen Keegan.

Does any man dream that a Gael can fear?
Of a thousand deeds let him learn but one!
The Shannon swept onwards broad and clear,
Between the leaguers and broad Athlone.

"Break down the bridge!" - Six warriors rushed
Through the storm of shot and the storm of shell;
With late but certain victory flushed,
The grim Dutch gunners eyed them well.

They wrench'd at the planks' mid a hail of fire;
They fell in death, their work half done;
The bridge stood fast; and nigh and nigher
The foe swarmed darkly, densely on.

"Oh, who for Erin will strike a stroke?
Who'll hurl yon planks where the waters roar?"
Six warriors forth from their comrades broke,
And flung them upon that bridge once more.

Again at the rocking planks they dashed
And four dropped dead, and two remained.
The huge beams groaned, and the arch down-crashed.
Two stalwart swimmers the margin gained.
St. Ruth in his stirrups stood up, and cried,
"I have seen no deed like that in France!"
With a toss of his head, Sarsfield replied,
"They had luck, the dogs! Twas a merry chance!"

O many a year, upon Shannon's side,
They sang upon moor and they sang upon heath,
Of the twain that breasted that raging tide,
And the ten that shook bloody hands with Death!

Uneven Odds

The O' Leary Clan were camped at the head of The Long Avenue while they were carrying out running repairs on pots, pans, milk churns and pongers around Tenelick and Abbeyshrule. Bappy and Nora, both being pregnant were discussing the day's proceedings over a mug of tea when the prevailing winds wafted the mud-thick stench from the school toilets their way. While Babby ran to close the front windows Nora lit the incense Mrs McCormack had brought over from Glasgow.

"What a relief," said Nora as Bappy poured her another cuppa.

They had enough of it though, and were determined to force their men to sort it out with the Master, they worked out a game plan.

"No sex for them for a week," Bappy said tongue in cheek.

"Don't think that'd work though," Nora laughed.

No sooner was Rex home than he was lit upon and had no recourse but to sort it out the following morning.

As soon as she saw Quigley calling Jem O'Leary over the Crossroads Babby was up again. Knowing there would be a deficit of garden implements around the campfire they decided to hide theirs. Word spread like wildfire about the 'school job' and appropriate action was taken to ensure everyone could account for their own accoutrements.

They were delighted when they saw the Tinker lads arriving with butts of spades and coal shovels the following morning.

"Looks like the lads were out late," Nora grinned as she recognised some of the tools from the barges berthed on the canal. Being born beside the canal she was fully familiar with the Bargemen's unusual tools and lifestyle.

"You'd want to warn Jessie so or the Guards will have them gone in jig time," Bappy said as she took another slice of soda bread and spread Nora's newly made Seville orange jam over it.

"Sure they're only borrowing them for the day. They'll have them back before they miss them. It won't be the first time and I'm sure it won't be the last," Nora smiled as she thought of the times she borrowed bargemen's tools for her father 'Big Joe.'

Milling around on the Crossroads while waiting to get a game of rugby or something going, the lads were spoiling for a bit of a row to liven things up a bit.

"Ya played shite last Sunday," nearly did it but it wasn't enough because it was too regular a complaint and could bounce back on you. However, something like "did you give back the money you took from the collection" or, "I heard your sister was at the well again" was sure to cut to the quick. The problem solved itself when Costello's few coppers went missing from under the goalposts, which were often just a jacket or cap, although a big scraw or a stick stuck in the ground would also suffice. Rounding on everyone producing no results, he spotted Jessie's brother Paddy standing by the wall and immediately challenged him to return the washers. Denying it emphatically Paddy turned his back indicating he didn't want to fight. Not knowing better, Costello grabbed him by the collar of his coat and went to thump him.

"Look out, he has a knife!" Mullin warned as Costello jumped back. Jessie and Nora had been standing by the little gate and came running shouting for Paddy to put the knife away and the others to back off if they knew what was good for them.

"Your coppers are here," shouted Seamie as he lifted the goalpost.

"How did it get there?"

"You put it there yourself, I saw you," O'Heeran told him.

"Cheeses, sorry lads," Costello said realising he had nearly started another war.

"No point in saying sorry to us. Say it to Paddy there" Mullin said. Hand extended, Costello went straight to Paddy who reluctantly accepted the apology only because his sister and Nora were on the spot. The Tinker Folk thought the world of Nora and knew they'd be up against it were it not for her and the good people of The Long Avenue. Order restored, the teams were rejigged to allow Paddy to play, taking the sting out of what could have been an arse tightener.

Recently arrived on the fringe of the team, Seamie was waiting for the crumbs that fall from the Master's Table. Hearing a soft voice behind him he turned to see who it might be and nearly fell out of his standing when he saw who had just spoken. It was herself, the heroine of the Clonfide River; the one and only Annabel who had entered his life like Venus just a week earlier. New to the group and a Protestant to boot, she was anxious to impress, and she did that in style. Her long blonde hair, short summer dress and long legs set her apart from the rest, but there was more. Her smile would light a path through the night were the moon and stars to be hidden by the darkest clouds. Having prevailed on her parents to allow her travel with the Hanlons, whose son Pat was one of the outstanding players on the team, she wasn't going to miss anything now. Hanlon was already spoken for, so widening her horizons was imperative if she was to break away from the claustrophobic tentacles of her fellow churchgoers.

How Irish Coffee was Invented

"How did you hurt yourself Granddad?" Seamie asked as he rescued the bottle of Jameson from under the armchair. More or less confined to that chair now because of a weeping varicose vein he kept things that mattered close at hand. Some said it wouldn't heal due to a Tanner's bullet being lodged in the knee but he wouldn't admit to it. The closest he ever came to that was one evening when Tess and Seamie dropped in on him to suss out a problem they knew only he could solve. It was about a cave Tess knew to be beyond in The Glebe but she couldn't pinpoint it. As there was no hurry on them they beat around the bush for a while before broaching the subject. Seamie marvelled at the sheer diplomacy of the two old friends. Both knew where they were coming from and where they were going, but if the subject surfaced a minute before the small talk was concluded all would be lost. There wasn't a danger of it as, the timing was in the tay, as Tess told him later.

"I used it meself the time they were after me and nearly nailed me," he confessed. "I could barely pull the leg after me and knew they were getting close when I saw a badger disappearing between two rocks a bit beyond me. "Better to be savaged by the badger than be beaten to death by the murdering bastards" was my only thought as I flung myself in after it and rolled up in a ball. It must have got a fierce fright because it tore out of there like a mad thing, frightening the shite out of the Brits as well. They knew no man would be stupid enough to hide in a badger's set so shifted their search to the wood beyond the Turlough instead. I lay there for ages until I knew they were well gone and then made it across the fields to Knockagh through Ballintubber Lane. By the grace of God Maggie Connell came on me just in time as I was on me last legs. With a strip off her slip she managed to stem the flow of blood until she got me to her place in Knockagh and onto the settle bed. As soon as the men got home they got me out through the attic to the outhouses just in case the Tanners arrived out of the blue as they had a habit of doing. Maggie said I slept like a log for three days but she might have been adding a bit to it there. Anyway, she had the four corners of Knockagh watched in case the bastards did a "Cromwell" and came back to murder all before them. Those were dangerous days I tell you. You never knew where they were hiding out or who might give the game away. The few that did paid the penalty for being informers. Your man in Lisna got off by the skin of his teeth and only because of his people who were the salt of the earth. He was black and blue for a month and would have been a lot worse but for The Potstick and The Horse. It worked though because it frightened the daylights out of everyone and stopped a fair few from chancing it.

The badger did me no wrong and gave me one of the safest places in Ireland to hide out in during the struggle," he concluded as they marvelled at his story.

"I doubt you'll want to bring the secret with you Paddy," was all Tess said.

"You have a reason girl I suspect?" he grinned as he winked over at Seamie.

"Seamie knows most of the spots Paddy and we'll have to leave the lot to him as there's few others with the interest," she cajoled.

"You're right girl. I'll draw it out for him and if he finds it he'll have found it himself and no one will be a bit the wiser."

"That's more than fair of you Paddy," she said as she got up and put her hand on his shoulder.

"Would to God they were all half as good as you," she said as she wiped a tear away from her eye.

"G'wan now Tess! Few did what Margaret or yourself did and the two of you paid for it. If it wasn't for Cumann Na mBan a lot worse would have happened, but you'll reap your rewards for sure," he managed to say without breaking down in front of the two of them.

"Make the tay Seamie or the water will go up in flames if you don't," he laughed to lighten the situation a little. Not another word was said about it until a long time later when a drop of Paddy and a good story lubricated the memory.

"What was that about Mick Coffey," he remarked to Seamie a few evenings later.

"I was talking about coffee, not Mick Coffey," Seamie laughed.

"And what's that do you mind me asking?"

"The Master was talking about it and said it was all the go above in Dublin."

"And what do you do with it?"

It was like tea but completely different he went on to explain. You had to boil the water as you would with tea and then you put in a couple of spoonful's of the stuff, add sugar and stir it.

"I suppose you dose calves with it then?" he laughed uproariously at the thought of it. Seamie offered to ask the Master to order a little of it so as to try it out for themselves.

A few days later he arrived with a small jar of brown powder and proceeded to set up the experiment. As soon as the kettle was singing he filled two mugs, added a generous teaspoonful of the powder, a level teaspoon of sugar and topped it all up with a drop of milk before handing it to him.

"A cor as ugly as Mrs Esler's cat crossed the old man's face as the liquid slid down his throttle like dishwater."

"Now I've drunk sour doses in me time a mhic but that takes beating. Will you hand me the bottle before I'm poisoned," he grimaced as he drew his hankie from his pocket to wipe the thought of it away.

A decent thimbleful of the uisce beatha seemed to restore his equanimity so he had another go at it while Seamie looked on in wonder as he poured a double-dose into the mug.

"Now that's the Real McCoy!" he said as he licked his lips. A little drop of cream on that and you'd keep the doctor at bay for many's the day. Do you know what we'll call it?" he said, the hint of a smile lighting his eyes.

"No idea Grandad."

"Irish Coffee of course!" he laughed. The thought of offering the recipe to Mulvey for a consideration entered his mind. A couple of evenings later Johnjo and the father pulled up at the gate to take him to Tashinny. He didn't bother much now but the idea of the 'Irish Coffee' was growing on him as he had taken a liking to it.

"With ye in a jiffy," he shouted as he laced up his boots with some difficulty. As Ever, Johnjo was beside him to help and fill him in on the local gossip.

"Better than two women," he joked as he eased himself onto the back of the tractor.

"Take her easy now," he advised as he got a good grip on the bucket seat.

Mad Maggie hung under the hedge until they moved off. As usual she was looking for a few spoonfuls of sugar for the Cuddy though what he did with it was anyone's guess. Some said it was for the poteen but if it was then he knew how to mind it.

Ned was like a two year old behind the counter as they walked in.

"To what do I owe the pleasure?" he smiled as he hurried to make space for the two elderly gentlemen.

"One of the Marys I'd say!"

"Sharp as a tack this evening I note," he replied, the wind gone out of his sails in one sentence.

"Oney coddin', no harm meant me man. Give us a few half wans there when you get a minute."

"A drop of water in it I presume?" he enquired.

"There might be enough in it already," brought the house down as Coffey nearly choked on his Guinness while others slapped the counter and their tables in delight at the repartee.

"You must have met yerself getting up this morning," Ned snapped back setting the tone for the evening, one quip borrowing another in rapid succession until the cards appeared and the serious business began.

On the Brink

Sitting chatting with the Brink on his favourite seat on the cross-roads, Seamie was enjoying his account of the previous night's occurrence in McCawley's. Páidín Murray from Ballintubber was eyeing up María, Ginger and May's well-endowed daughter, and was making fair headway too. Taking after her mother, she was building up an enviable reputation with the women of the parish and knew how to use her best assets, as did her mother. Páidín's people had a bit of land and he could handle himself fairly well in centerfield providing he wasn't given a puck early in the game. Ginger and May had a different view of the matter though as they felt that he was a bit of a boyo and was far from finished sowing his wild oats. A few mature ladies from Carrickboy to Legan were well aware of the fact and hoped they'd never be called in to testify for or against him. Maria's parents weren't going to let him take up with the pick of the parish, then leave her high and dry as he swanned off around the world without 'by your leave.'

A sweet little game of 25 soon started up with Ginger and May stuck in the middle of it. Páidín saw his chance and gave María the beck to join him for a walk in the moonlight. Waiting until her parents were fully intent on the cards, she slipped out and joined him at the corner of the shed where he was bullin' for action. Seeing he was already sweating she dropped the hand to test the waters, and on feeling there was merit in the situation, nodded towards the side door of the hall where the carpentry classes took place every Friday night. Rex and a few of the boys had joined the class at the outset and were making chairs, sofas and dressers by the new time.

The Brink was having a bit of a snooze on a heap of horsehair stuffing for the sofas when in slipped the two of them as if they were cannibals starving with the hunger. Used to sleeping with one eye open and his back to the wall he was wide-awake but couldn't move or he'd give the game away. Divil the likes he ever saw and he'd seen a lot in the same shed, he told Seamie later. Buck naked, the two of them nearly made dinner of each other as they did things he didn't think possible, and certainly had never seen or heard of before. Used to the quick slap, bang and wallop he marvelled at the length Páidín gave her and the way she thanked him without saying a word. The worst of it all was he had to suffer the father and mother of an erection in silence as they tore the arse out of it altogether. Half tempted to tell them it'd be closing time if they didn't quit soon, and all the half empty glasses and drops of whiskey to be dealt with yet, he was trying to figure out something, as well as deal with the full of his hands at the same time. There were more full moons to be seen inside that night than there were outside. As they stood up as naked as the day they were born, in walked Ginger. Picking up her skirt he ordered her into the dark corner to dress while he lay into Páidín giving him the slapping of his life. It was obvious to the Brink that Ginger wasn't out to hurt him because he could have done that if he wished. Nevertheless, the slaps were not something you'd give a wayward child he mused. Over in the corner María was hurriedly pulling up her knickers when she bumped into the extended Brink. Though suffering his own torture, he was able to calm her though he didn't know what way to turn or they'd all be fucked.

By now Páidín had managed to settle Ginger by promising to drain his high field and to sign over a bit of bog land by way of compensation. Standing over him long enough to convince him he meant business, Ginger left no doubts in his mind.

"Grand job girl," he said as he put his arm around María who was fully clothed by now and smiling sweetly.

"A fucking set-up!" the Brink thought as he watched them checking that the coast was clear. Thanking his lucky stars he got away so lightly, Páidín was halfway up the Parson's Hill on the tractor by now. Waving back into the darkness, knowing the Brink would keep his mouth shut if he got the odd bottle of stout, Maria blew a kiss to his erection. If he played his cards right he knew that she, or better still her mother, would look after him when the chips were down. Knowing Seamie was wise enough to know what he was referring to, and that Tess would enjoy the story as well, he spared no blushes. Wasn't that what friends were for anyway?

"Share the day's crack to lighten up a grey world," he remarked as Seamie responded to Hewart's call to deliver a telegram.

He delivered most of the telegrams now. One of the families he loved visiting lived at the far end of the parish. Tim and Allison received loads of telegrams due to her literary work and his interest in model aeroplanes and mining. Their big house on a comfortable farm beyond the Glebe was his favourite place, not only because it afforded him an opportunity to visit Annabel, but also because of the warm welcome they afforded him. He liked going there because, even though they were Protestants, they always asked him in for tea or lemonade. Annabel used often take him out to see the animals, especially the new lambs. He told her he knew a lot about lambs because he often helped Hewart with them at lambing time.

One evening as they strolled around the Glebe he told her about the Lamb that dug the well that was full of gas instead of water.

She thought he was mad until he told her about the Lambs from Finea. She nearly cracked up she thought it was that funny. It was the first time Seamie had mentioned this to anyone since he had uncovered the secret and was paid off handsomely for keeping his mouth shut. Tim was fascinated by this as, being an amateur mineralogist himself, he had been exploring his own farm since first acquiring it from the Land Commission some years earlier. He it was who had led Rio Tinto to search Ardagh Mountain. Their success there led to his promotion and meant he was often away in Spain and South America for weeks on end. Knowing Seamie was good with animals he asked if he'd help Allison for the rest of the summer. He hadn't to ask twice. For Seamie it was a dream come true. He'd be fed and watered in the sanctuary where his true love lived. She was thrilled too and told him so as they wandered around the big house together.

"Tell me the story about Larry the Lamb Seamie," she begged as they sat together on her bed.

"All right so," he said as she snuggled into him with her two arms wrapped around him. Adding legs to everything for effect he reminded her of the morning he had spotted The Lambs in Geoghegan's Field and that the Brink's seat had fallen victim to progress by being levelled by the big machines turning in at the Crossroads.

Reminding her of the first morning he turned up for work he spared nothing in bringing her up to date with the Lambs from Finea who arrived in the middle of the night, and had their machines ticking over nicely when he stopped by to investigate in case he'd miss anything. That wouldn't reflect well on his reputation for being well informed in all that transpired around his little fiefdom. Larry the Lamb took an instant liking to the young whippersnapper who knew his onions and wasn't going to be easily codded by anyone. Reaching a mutually acceptable agreement on what they needed done, and how much he'd be paid for same, they shook hands and went their separate ways.

Not blessed with culinary skills, they'd normally settle for a ploughman's sandwich or a bogman's breakfast. Seami inveigled them into allowing Nora to do the cooking for them. She was happy with the arrangement as it was money for old rope and something to help pay for the Clarinda and turkey meal until they were sold around the Christmas. Meeting Rosey in Tashinny on the way home from Ballymahon he stopped to have a quick chat. Cutting to the chase immediately, she asked him if he might arrange a meeting with herself and Larry the Lamb. Promising he'd sing her praises if she made it worth his while they went their ways. True to his word he had the Lamb set up for her on her way home later. Being a bit backward in coming forward Larry was somewhat shy of women but not unwilling.

"Now Larry, here she's coming. Out with you and chat about the weather and I'll do the rest."

Rosey's smile lit up the crossroads as soon as Larry held her bike. He let Seamie do the talking as his mouth dried up.

"Sure, come up for a mouthful of tea later," was the perfect excuse and they left it at that.

Coming home from the Glebe around teatime he was surprised to see the Lamb sitting on the school wall. The brother was inside the wagon tidying and cleaning and taking down the calendar girls in case it'd throw the tin hat on everything. Cushions were bet beautiful with the handle of the brush and the mugs replaced with a few cups and saucers. As well as that he asked Seamie to get a couple of packets of biscuits and a good lump of a sweet cake from Flynn's bakery. A pot of raspberry jam would put the cherry on the cake Seamie recommended.

It wasn't long until Rosey became a permanent feature at the weekends as she did the tidying and cleaning. Larry wasn't that happy when she told him to throw out the old mattress, but agreed a new one from Sloane's of Athlone would be a better bet altogether. As soon as the mattress was burning she had him level the base and replace the creaking boards saying they would waken the dead. Adding the sheets to the burning pile she replaced them with a set she got from Mrs Mills. The job was oxo after that and everyone slept well if they weren't too busy making ends meet.

Arriving home with the groceries from the town one Saturday evening he was happy to see the boys hard at work. After putting everything away he went into the back room of the wagon to have forty winks as he was feeling tired. A heated discussion between the brothers woke him up sometime later. Not wishing to interfere until they quietened down he was surprised to hear them saying they'd have to cap the well due to the foul fumes coming from it. Likewise, the water was strangely coloured and smelled like dishwater. "Coal" Larry pronounced. "Gas" George insisted. Realising their goose was cooked unless they had an acceptable excuse they agreed to say it was poor quality coal at a hundred feet that made the well unfit for human consumption. With that Seamie coughed and opened the door. To say they were surprised would be putting it mildly. Saying he was tired and hoped they didn't mind him having a nap he was about to leave when George caught his arm asking him how much he had heard.

"Enough," he answered.

"Now Seamie, you'll have to swear to keep this to yourself. Down on your knees there and swear or it won't be good for you," he demanded.

"You'll have to make it worth my while so," he answered knowing that's what Tess would have him say.

Realising he wasn't to be cowed, the bargaining started at a fiver and finished at fifty with the sweat bubbling on the lads foreheads. Pocketing the notes he promised to keep it to himself.

The County engineer arrived early the next day, and on seeing the scene for himself he ordered them to cap it deeply and to move to the other site at the corner of Farrell's field opposite the big stone at the gable wall of Geoghegan's shed where the lads often hid their half crowns after a visit from the uncles from Meath. Seamie had that covered too and now and again replaced the half-crowns with a shilling or a tanner from his treasure throve from the back of the bridge.

Justice being done, they carried on as before saying, 'the divil you know is better than the divil you don't.' That suited Seamie to the ground so he let the hare sit.

A Hard Act to Follow

Dick Skelly NT came to Colehill with a bee in bonnet. He knew that Quigley's act would be difficult if not impossible to follow so he set out his stall from day one. By roll call they knew he was going to be a bastard, and he didn't disappoint them. By ten, when Veronica came in with his tea and biscuits, he had already used the cane half a dozen times 'for sweet feck all' McDaniel said as he tried to ease the stinging from his fingers. Good at maths but better with a tractor he was caught daydreaming and paid the penalty. Doherty was next for whispering under his breath and big Robbie for saying the Romans built the world. Aodh Goo hadn't a clue what was going on but left Skelly in no doubt who was the strongest when told to put out his hand.

"I will in me bollox," left the whole room gasping, even Miss Stakem who had just wandered in cup in hand. Aodh Goo put his fist under his chin defying Skelly to hit him. Dismissing him as not worth the bother he turned away and went to his desk. In truth he had eyes for one only and it wasn't for any of them and it was hard to blame him. Her long, lithe body, stunning good looks and flaming red hair were the epitome of Dev's dream- 'Colleens dancing at the Crossroads was it!' Yes, she could dance her way into anyone's heart. Yet, somehow she settled for Skelly, a mix of chauvinism, Puritanism and savage. There was no doubting his intellectual ability because he had it in buckets. It wasn't enough to save his soul though as far as his pupils were concerned. Seamie whispered to Drim that he doubted the two ends of a bollocks would ever get near heaven unless he changed course quickly.

"A leopard can change his spot but you can't change the spots on a leopard," grandfather chuckled when he recounted the following incident to him.

The 'six wise men' were sitting nonchalantly in the very back row, euphemistically designated sixth class.

Skelly called the roll. The Cúl Fióir Uisce (Kilfirish, a fertile area adjacent to Westmeath just beyond Abbeyshrule Bog) boys were missing, which was no surprise as there was a mountain of work to be done around their respective farms and little time for 'the educmacation.'

Though just as busy in their own right, Seamie's parents rightly concluded that the only way forward was through a sound education. Quigley gave his life's blood for this cause even though he terrorised many in the process. It was his way of keeping absolute control over every youth in his charge and was tolerated by the parents rather than risk their children being bypassed when scholarships came to visit. And visit they did in the form of entrance exams to well-established colleges throughout the land. The Civil Service, agricultural and clerical establishments as well as monasteries and universities the length and breadth of Ireland and England held hope for those clever enough to qualify.

Meanwhile, the scholars had to suffer the indignity of a cold, damp school throughout the long cold winters. Were it not for the unquestioning generosity of the parishioners the fires would have died long before the winter was out. Quigley did his best to keep the big old building warm but it was labour in vain due to the high ceilings, big single-glass windows and porous brick that held the lot together. The high roofs and windy lofts offered little protection either as there was no insulating material to prevent the dampness seeping through the lofty rafters. The children from the outlying areas brought small sacks of turf to school once a week while the locals carried an armful or basketful with them more often. Occasionally, the PP would time his arrival on his white stallion with that of a tractor and trailer load of turf or sticks for the school. This was to give the impression the good deed was done by him. The truth was that he had either talked or bullied the unsuspecting party into donating the load of fuel. He applied the same methods in placing some of his prize bullocks with local farmers. It wasn't worth arguing the toss with him either, as he'd never forget it and would use the altar to belittle those who crossed him. This often took the form of placing particular stress on his enunciation of the amount donated for 'Peter's Pence' or the Harvest Collection.'

"Two and six from Peter O' Donnell I hope that's not leaving you short Peter," he'd say dryly. That was fine until one day Peter stood up in the aisle and told him he was lucky to get it, and if he paid him as much for the grass his bullocks ate he'd get more. The congregation broke into loud guffaws as Fr. Pat threw down the list and continued mass without replying to the charge. Though delighted with Peter's truism they knew he had incurred the wrath of the cleric and there was little doubt as to who would win out eventually.

Though hard to appreciate at the time the youths knew, just like their parents, that education was their only sure way of escape.

Indicating he was not to be disturbed Skelly ordered his charges to get on with their maths exercise while he dallied with the joy of his life. A fascinating creature, they wondered what she saw in such an average guy. They were certain any one of their local sports heroes would be far more appropriate soul mates for her. They had visions of her being serenaded by one of their heroes.

"Any one would do rather than that sharp-nosed cunt" was Lardy Belly's considered opinion after a prolonged discussion about it during lunch hour.

"Stand up, stand up," he roared as he saw Drim's eyes unclothing his beau. Seeing it as an ideal opportunity to display his power over his charges he went into overdrive. Face contorted with rage he was beside them in a bad breath, his stick singing in the air as he whisked it madly about.

Drim stood up. Seamie didn't. Sensing it was back to Quigley's brutality he held firm. He had more than enough of that. Tess had shown him how to cope with Quigley and he wasn't about to let this reincarnation take over.

Leaping sideways, Drim winced as the ashen-faced tyrant came down heavily. The sally rod splintered into several pieces as it struck the side of the desk. Control gone, he grabbed a lump of hazel from the top of the cupboard that would subdue the fiercest in any faction fight around the country. Hand high he was about to come down heavily on Seamie when she spoke through him.

"Touch him with that stick and your arm will shrivel as fast as your budgeen on a frosty morning," a voice thundered inside his head. The stick stopped in mid-air as an agonising pain shot up and down his arm. Flabbergasted and immobile he stood gaping at the two of them.

"No more of that," was all he could say as he backed up to the front of the room. Miss Stakem was gone. She had seen enough. Unable to decipher the voice or where it had come from put the fear of God in him.

"A sensible woman," Seamie said to Drim as they banged fists in celebration.

"She'll search further afield after that display of bullying I dare say."

Truer words were never spoken. Despite his best efforts she rarely ever entered the room after that. Word spread of her sightings at carnivals in Legan and Longford as well as the different Lakelands around the Midlands. Jimmy and JP tried their hand too and didn't go home unhappy either. The lads were delighted for her. However, his influence with the Parish Priest meant she didn't survive long. He pestered her in such a manner that she soon sought a new school well removed from Abbeyshrule. Some said Jimmy was heartbroken because he was known to have fallen for her but he soon got over it because of his ability to field a high ball. Heroes were hard come by and if one could impress on the field of play one would do well with the women, young or old, married or single. All it needed was a quiet spreadbank and not to be followed by a jealous wife or a suspicious husband.

Although reluctant to offer any help or advice to the 'Six Sages' he found he needed their help from time to time so, after a cooling-off period, he had to offer some inducements to placate them.

"Would any of the scholars in sixth class take over while I speak to one of our neighbours?" he'd ask.

They didn't much want to help him except they knew it would take the pressure of the other classes for a while at least. God knows they needed it! They took turns at the task rather than be branded a 'Pet' yet took no prisoners either as they had the inside line on every child in the room and used that to keep order. It was a different kind of psychology. Not that they knew anything about psychology but they did have an intuitive talent for order and control. How often had they seen their parents go about their business in a quiet, inoffensive manner without recourse to threats or physical abuse? That was the reserve of the ignorant they were often reminded.

Rex rarely needed to remind his colleagues of their duties. He set out their day's work for them and they just got on with it out of a grudging respect for his position, but also because work was hard to come by and needed to be well minded. It astonished Seamie that so-called educated people, especially teachers, had to rely on threats to get a job done. It always struck him as a different kind of poverty, that of the mind.

Though far from being teachers yet, they were born leaders. An innate sense of timing and humour took the sting out of learning and brought their charges along with them as they searched the world for the lost pygmy tribes in the Kalahari Desert or in the depths of the Amazon jungle. They'd organise groups around the big map so that they'd pick out all kinds of geographical oddities and then ask them to write them down on the big chalkboard so that other groups would have to find them as quickly as possible. The only difficulty was the decibel level, as it invariably rose with their zealous endeavour. A threat of being dropped from the school team was usually enough to subdue their excitement.

Having talked it over with his parents and Tess he felt much more at ease. They were unanimous in thinking he was more than ready for his move away. That was all the encouragement he needed to give Skelly a withering look and two fingers before he bade goodbye to his colleagues in the middle of one of his rants. With a skip and a hop he was gone as if he hadn't a care in the world. His abiding memory of the sour git was his astonishment at his behaviour and his inability to either comprehend it or to do anything about it. Tess nearly wet herself as he related the story to her on his way home from the counting.

"Serves him right," she laughed as she cleaned their two enamel mugs with the end of her colourful shawl.

"Did I ever tell you Seamie?" meant an evening of pure fantasy. He would sit on the three-legged stool at the side of the hearth with his back to the hob while she would wrap her colourful woollen shawl about her shoulders and bury herself in the rugs and cushions in her easy chair. The kettle was always boiling with the water from her stream or from Bosque, and once he got used to the different flavour, her pancakes were always welcome. A duck egg or two retrieved minutes before leaving home made for a splendid meal. If either he or Tess had been across in Bosque they were sure to have a good bunch of watercress to add a piquant touch beyond the realms of the finest restaurant in the parish. There weren't any of course but if there were Seamie knew they wouldn't hold a candle to her fare. Somehow, she always seemed to know when he was coming to visit. Perhaps it was Billy, or even the fairies on the froth of the river, he thought. His favourite story was the one she told him about the time the pheasant jumped into her arms as she lay in wait in a clump of rushes. But it was her ability to put words together in verse he'd always remember and try to copy. He particularly remembered their agreement to write some rhyming couplets and how they laughed till they cried the evening she recited them.

Waiting until they were finished drinking a big mug of tea she started off.

> *I live beside the river not far from Abbeyshrule,*
> *I often chat the scholars coming home from School.*
> *I pay no mind to money or what the idle say.*
> *I'd sooner share a bite to eat and drink a cup a tay.*

"Now it's your turn Seamie," she said knowing he had something up his sleeve.

"All right so, I'll have a go."

> *I often wander down the way to spend some time with Tess,*
> *We cross the fields to Bosque Well to gather watercress.*
> *Some say she's half crazy and some say she's a bitch*
> *Some even call her 'The Witch behind the Ditch'*

"Good lad Seamie," she cried as she rubbed her hands with glee.

There was a famous story about Oul Maggie which Tess loved and which she proceeded to tell him one evening as he dropped in on his way home from the Glebe. She had heard it directly from the Tinker lassie Jessie and didn't doubt a word of it. She'd have to tell it as Jessie told it or it would be no good. Seamie explained that he was in no hurry as his jobs were done for now.

Ould Madge's entire clan were beyond in Knock for the new Bishop's blessing, Jessie told her. Tinker clans came from all over the country for it. They themselves had only just come back from the hills of Donegal and were encamped by the side of the road not far from the Cathedral. There was a bundle of money to be made from selling rosary beads and miraculous medals to the settled people who were often more superstitious than themselves. The men had a fairly decent coin press they pulled out of an old factory near Derry and in the hands of a good pot mender a bit of tin could resemble a miraculous medal. The settled people were easily pleased. The fact that it only involved a few coppers kept them from losing the run of themselves. Seeing as the medals were blessed in the spot where the Virgin appeared, gave them even greater meaning.

Jessie told her that her granny complained that there was no place for her to sit down and she with the years on her. Some of the helpers brought her up to the front of the altar before the High Mass started and put her sitting down in a spare wheelchair. She was asleep in a minute with the heat of the huge congregation and the tiredness of the long journey from Donegal. Nobody passed the slightest bit of heed on her as they were all watching the new Bishop who could rev up the crowd better than any Missionary. There was great talk about the big church he had built adout on the Island, and how he managed to talk half the world into contributing towards the building of it. Some said he'd soon be a Cardinal if he kept the money coming in from the Americas like that. He was a real showman and every service an act in many parts, just like the plays the McCormack travelling players used to put on nightly on the Long Avenue as the evenings came in and people had a bit of time to themselves.

The faithful flocked from near and far to hear his sermons and songs. He had a lovely voice, Jessie continued. Some said the great tenor, McCormack, was only trotting after him. Anyway, Jessie said that her granny didn't wake up until the bishop was giving the blessing.

"Well, I declare to God Tess!" And these are Jessie's own words, just as the Bishop had his hands up to Heaven, didn't she stand up out of the wheelchair, shake herself, and start walking off down the long aisle to where her own people were sitting.

"A miracle, a miracle!" they cried. "You'd think," said Jessie, "that there was a football match goin' on there was so much noise and excitement. The likes of it wasn't seen before or since. The Bishop downed tools and ran down the aisle after her to bring her back up inside the altar where she, the object of the miracle, could be seen. His two hands were raised to the heavens, one holding his jewel-encrusted crozier, the other the Bible, all the time praising God and crying 'Alleluia, Alleluia, behold the power that the Lord has vested in me!' The poor Bishop hadn't a clue what oul Maggie was saying because according to Jessie she uses the ould can't when it suits her. It was beginning to dawn on her people what was going on, and ideas were flowing from one to the other on how best to milk the situation. They didn't have to do much as the entire congregation were shouting and roaring. Anyway, the Bishop made a huge fuss of her and gave her his own rosary beads from around his waist. He could see himself with the red cap already and he having tay with the Pope himself beyond in St. Peters. It's not everyone who can pull off miracles like that, especially with the age of the old woman. A thousand thoughts must have gone through his mind in that instant wondering if it could have been the holy water that Nelly, his young housekeeper, had given him a few days before! Jessie knew Nelly well. She was an orphan who had run away from one of the laundry houses that the Nuns ran above in Sligo. It was said that they ran a booming business in baby adoption because they also took in the poor unfortunates who became pregnant for one reason or another, and the culprit, whether friend or family, wanted nothing more to do with them. Jessie's family happened on her as she was wandering the road, exhausted and starving, unable to look after herself like them because she had never been shown how. She had somehow fought off a farmer who had given her a lift, fed and watered her, took her to his isolated farmhouse in the back of the wind and tried to take advantage of her when she felt a bit comfortable with him. It was a mistake that nearly finished both of them as she fought him tooth and nail to preserve what her mother told her was an asset that'd stand to her one day. His intentions became abundantly clear once she lay on his bed. Exhausted from days on the run trying to hide from her pursuer she just conked out. She had no idea how long she was in the lap of the gods but woke with a start as she felt his hands on her. Brushing him off only encouraged him as he thought she was his. He was lucky to survive her next move as her knee nearly went through his back. She left him in a heap as she took to her heels and cut across the mountain like a hare. It was falling dark when they came on her wandering aimlessly along the road. Unable to talk from fright, Jessie's mother consoled her, wrapped her up and laid her to sleep in the caravan leaving Nelly to watch over her. It was hours later before she woke with a huge hunger on her. They plied her with titbits rather than sicken her with kindness, knowing that her stomach wouldn't be able for more. Few knew more than them what an empty stomach meant and the danger of filling it too quickly."

"A little goes a long way," was their mantra that stretched back through time immemorial and centuries of deprivation.

It wasn't long until they realised she was different, even more different than them. She could read nature's signs even better than themselves after a short while, and seemed to be able to predict the future in an uncanny way. Certainly she could read palms and had a special way of doing it that only a few like Tess knew how to do. Also she had a gift for winding up people who thought they were cleverer than her and could wrap them around her little finger while you'd be blessing yourself. She stayed with Jessie's family for a good while until Father McCabe found her a grand job with the Bishop when he was beyond on the Islands. The new bishop thought the world of her and who wouldn't? She was simply gorgeous and clever too, as the nuns taught her how to read and write and answer the phone and things. She had a body like a film star, jet-black hair down to her waist and deep-brown eyes that looked straight through you.

She never forgot what the tinkers had done for her and often slipped them a few bob, or anything that might be left over after the big dinners the bishop put on for the important visitors who used call to his Palace in Knock.

Nelly told Jessie in confidence that the Bishop was more than good to her. She had simple tastes and wanted for nothing other than decent clothes and shoes. She told Jessie that the Bishop used to give her money to buy lovely frocks and get her to try them on in front of him at night time when his work was done and he was relaxing with his brandy. She didn't mind because she thought it was normal, and wasn't he normal too when he took off his robes and all. He felt totally at ease with this young, unassuming girl who had such wonderful traits. Her ability to read his mind was uncanny. She seemed to know exactly what he was thinking. He felt safe confiding everything in her though she seemed to know anyway. One thing led to another and in no time they were living together like any other man and woman, except that the Bishop didn't want her to say a word about it because if it got out he would be destroyed, and she too he told her. Nelly told Jessie that she had no problem with that as long as he looked after her and this he did in style. Though she was less than half his age she didn't find him repulsive at all, rather, she enjoyed their intimacy as he was so different from everything she had seen until now. His impeccable manners, education, intelligence and airs left her bemused and delighted. She repaid in kind.

Meanwhile, the poor people in the Cathedral were beside themselves with all the excitement over the new miracle. Some of them tore home for their ailing grannies as fast as their pony and traps could take them, while the rest of them were above crowding around the altar trying to lay hands on the Bishop or oul Maggie. One of the servers told a priest that was helping out with the ceremonies that the cat must have got in and shit behind the altar because there was an awful smell. The priest told him shush and not to be ridiculous. It was the old woman that smelled, and not the cat's shite. He sent the young lad in to ask Nelly to run the bath and have everything ready to get her washed as soon as mass was over and the important people started arriving. This was a great time for Knock he told the server. The likes of it hasn't been seen since the Blessed Virgin was here with the Lads one frosty morning years back. The priests and helpers were shooing the congregation back to their seats because the Bishop was getting over-excited, telling them to move in and make place for all the people who were already coming in from the mountains and valleys nearby because word was spreading like wildfire about the 'new miracle in Knock.'

Tess had Seamie in stitches as she related the whole story that Jessie told her about Oul Maggie and the calculating Bishop.

It was mid-April according to Jessie, one of the kindest to come for years. The birds were singing like thrushes beyond in the trees and the daffodils and daisies were bursting out all along the tree-lined driveway into the Bishop's Palace. He was still trying to get sense out of oul Maggie, but all he could make out was that she wanted money to buy a bit of bread and a grain of salt and some clothes for the childer (children) who were running around in rags and barefoot. Her people were lying in ditches dying of hunger and would he mind giving her a few bob so she could buy a bit of Injen male(Indian meal) for them before that all passed away in front of her very eyes. She could play that tune so well after years of practise. The Bishop, being a little green around the ears, fell for it, hook, line and sinker. He commanded the collectors to go around the aisles again asking the excited congregation to give every penny they had on account of this great miracle. It was their great chance to see the power of prayer at work, and that they would be well rewarded for their generosity. Their offerings would be given to the poor woman who had been blessed by God. More would be raised if she came back the following Sunday when a special mass would be said by all the other Bishops so he could show them the power given to him by the Blessed Virgin. That was grand said Jessie until the Bishop saw the mountain of money the poor people had given in the second offerings. Beckoning the PP of Knock over, he told him to take it all into the Sacristy and count it as quickly as he could.

His experienced eye told him there must have been at least two hundred in the collection. He had rarely seen the likes of it in his short time as a Bishop he told Nelly later. Fifty would be more than enough for the old woman he suggested, the rest could be used wisely in the interests of the Diocese and the Church in general. He confided to Nelly later that night, as they relaxed together, that it was about time he changed his car too because it was common knowledge that the Protestant bishop of Killaloe had recently changed his for a sparkling new Triumph. It wouldn't do for the Church to be outshone by the minority religion. The extra money from the collection would go a long way towards a new car for himself. The other one was nearly five years old now, and with all this excitement he couldn't be driving about in a car that reflected poorly on his office and that of holy mother Church whom he served with all his might. He would go down to Longford as soon as possible and order a red Mercedes from Dick Reilly. He liked red. It would go well with the Cardinal's hat. Dick would give him a good discount for sure due to their monthly poker sessions and he'd get some of the PP's to lose a hand or two now and again to keep the man happy. It was surely God's will he informed Nelly.

He was still trying to humour the old woman to get the best out of her before she left the Cathedral. He could see she was getting fidgety and wanted to hit the road. There was so much excitement that day that it was hard to keep pace with everything. The sick and dying were being brought into the church in droves and he had to supervise everything. Oul Maggie saw her chance, and in the wink of an eye she was gone like a plate of sandwiches in front of a haggard of thrashers. She took a coat from one of her own, threw it over her head and slipped out the door of the short aisle surrounded by the rest of the crew. They were gone like thieves in the night before anyone realised it.

They never laid eyes on her for weeks after that according to Jessie. She cut her stick and was gone the road the same as if she had been swallowed up by the ground itself. The Gardaí went into one Tinker camp after another but they might as well be idle. Those people can smell a guard a mile off Tess told Seamie. Oul Maggie would be spirited away into the hedges and ditches quicker than you could bless yourself if a stranger came anywhere near their camp.

The PP from Drumlish, a decent poor devil if ever there was one, was one of the co-celebrants at the mass in Knock and happened to recognise her because she used to call on him for a few bob on her way back from the hills. He informed the Bishop of his concerns by letter, as he was unwilling to spill the beans on those he considered to be the real poor. She was long gone by then and the rest of her cortège with her. Jessie told Tess that they drank Kiltimagh dry in a couple of days. The Sergeant said it was a sight for sore eyes, Ould Maggie singing "The Road to Abbeyshrule," Jamsey whistling like a blackbird and the son Pat hopping the spoons of his knees and elbows as if he was possessed by a leprechaun. Divil the likes of it was heard in a lifetime according to the Sergeant. Dinny Charlton the box player was sitting adin in the middle of them all playing like a magician and singing like a Christian.

"Now, there's a man that can play," the sergeant remarked. The likes of it hadn't been heard since he cleaned up at the Fleadh Ceóil in Claremorris.

"That same Sergeant is the very one that's adin in Longford now," she told Seamie. He's often seen doing his rounds with the squad in Tashinny and Abbeyshrule and it was he who told the whole story to McGoey one night as they supped pints together while his two Rookies were adout in the could pullin' decent people for havin' no lights on their bikes. She wouldn't doubt a word of it seeing as she knew the creatures herself. Guinness's brewery had to send down a special lorry to cope with the demand. It was all grand the sergeant said until the Bishop's money started to run out and then all hell broke loose. They began fighting with the locals and one another and wrecked half the pubs in that grand little town because the ones who drank porter with them hit the hills when the coppers started appearing instead of the silver. There were men laying around the streets and in doorways the same as if a hurricane hit the town. A few commercial travellers who were dodging the time above in the hotel went down to have a look when they heard the commotion going on. The Sergeant told McGoey that they hadn't a shirt on their back by the time the Tinkers were done with them. One poor lad who was working for a tobacco company near Dublin was sitting in the gutter at the side of the street crying for his mammy. Oul Maggie went over and gave him such a hug that she nearly smothered him with her Eau savage. He got up and started to run, tearing past the hotel where he was staying, leaving his car and all behind him. The sergeant heard tell he joined a group of monks who live on an island above in Donegal who do nothing all day long except pray and the like.

"Now, isn't that a strange one for you Seamie?"

"Well I never heard the beat of it Tess! Only it's coming from yourself I'd find it hard to believe a bit of it. Did the guards sort them out or what happened?"

The Sergeant said that those that were able made it back to their caravans and the rest of them that were lying in quicks and ditches were dragged out by the tinker women and bet along the road 'till they came to their senses. Oul Maggie was above on a stone wall flailing her shillelagh and shouting for them to 'come on to fuck or they'd all be destroyed be the guards.'

They had to lie in their caravans for a week beyant in Creggs before they were able to put a good foot under them.

"God bless the Bishop," oul Maggie would let a roar out of her every now and again and the whole lot of them would split themselves laughing at the good of it all.

"Sure they might as well Seamie! They'd lift your heart if you let them."

The best of it all according to Jessie was that the poor Bishop took early retirement a few weeks later on account of his mental state after the 'miracle.'

Nelly got nearly everything he had according to Jessie, including a grand house out on the Islands that she turned into a fine bed and breakfast. She's always asking Jessie and the sisters over to stay with her as well. They have a mighty time when they do, running around the little cove and swimming in the clear blue waters just a few yards away from the house. They look after her little one, the pure spit out of the bishop they say, when she's busy with guests from the mainland and other parts of the known world. She told Jessie that it was unfortunate that the poor Bishop ended up the way he did because she liked him a lot. He spends the whole day now she said, doing the rounds with a collection box in one hand and a big stick like a crozier in the other.

A Mad Dash to the Midwife

That wasn't the holy all of it either Tess told Seamie. The excitement of the escapade and the dash from Kiltimagh to Creggs, where they were lucky to be let in on a corner of a bog owned by Big Jim Lawless, was too much for Jessie. They were safe there as it was private land and the Guards wouldn't bother them unless someone complained just to get rid of them. Big Jim arrived with a couple of his daughters the following morning and a heap of food that'd keep them going for a week. The little one, AnnMaria was a pure dote and used often come to visit them after that. Well, a few nights after they landed, and just while Paddy and the lads were off after rabbits, didn't Jessie start getting labour pains. It didn't take Oul Maggie long to assess the situation. She let a whistle out of her that'd stop a train and had the whole lot of them around her quicker than you'd sink a pint. Ordering up the best mare immediately she put the hard hand on Paddy, warning him not to draw breath till he wheeled into the Midwife's yard beyant in Lísnacreevagh. This was because they were used to her and she had delivered and saved more of them than any other midwife or nurse.

You never saw a horse harnessed as quickly. While Oul Maggie had Jessie organised in the trap, propped up with all kinds of cushions and rugs, her brothers had the mare and trap turned and everything double-checked and ready for the long road.

"Don't come back near here if ya lose that child," she shouted after Paddy putting the fear of God in him as he heeled the road and sent sparks flying from the mare's shoes as they disappeared into the evening mist.

Children ran into their houses shouting about the headless horseman as Paddy pushed the young mare hard. He knew her form well and all belonging to her too because he bought her of a decent farmer at the Ballinasloe Fair the previous year. He was nearly caught though, because, being his very first purchase he had listened well to what his grandfather told him.

"Count the teeth, study the feet, try her on the street and don't let them cheat you," he warned. That was grand and he nearly had the bargain made when his little sister spotted something strange.

"Why has she two different eyes?" she asked. He nearly shat himself when he checked and saw that the mare had only one eye. Backing off immediately he was about to look elsewhere when he was offered her at half the price. Knowing her pedigree he took a tough decision, handed over the money and led her home. He was the laughing stock of every Tinker from Toome to Tipperary until she began to show her paces at the road races. He'd leave her be until she felt free and lost them before they knew where she was gone. Their tune soon changed as he roamed the range and picked up every rex from Clare to Castlebar, a unique event in every Tinker's itinerary. Ould Madge laughed herself silly when she heard Paddy telling the know-all's it was down to the mare being one-eyed, because she was able to keep an eye out for the cute hoors who tried to take her on the inside. Such thoughts sustained him as he urged her on knowing she was well able for it. Fearless when he was on his own against his peers, his heart was in his mouth now as he drove her on, feeling the full weight of responsibility heavy on his young shoulders. As they hurled across the wooden bridge at Lanesboro fishermen and dawdlers nearly leapt into the Shannon at the sight of the ghostly carriage appearing out of the mist. Cutting through Keenagh to Tashinny on the back road to Barry they met the Redin the middle of the road with a skinful on him. But for the grace of God, good driving and the mare's instinct he wouldn't have been able to tackle the line home to Toome. At least he had a credible excuse for Kitty for a change. Mickeen Keegan wasn't able to sing a note for a week after witnessing the Red's miraculous escape, but it was the damage done to the courting couple's along the bog road that put the head sheaf on it altogether.

It was almost dark as they shot through Tashinny like a furl blast on a fine day, forcing Kieran Gray off his bike and Mary Dolan to bless herself twice with fright. The apparition passed by so quickly they were sure it was a ghost as there was hardly a sound from the mare's hooves she was moving that fast.

Paddy knew Jessie was in bother going up the Parson's Hill because she had gone awful quiet. She had kept the chat going as best she could as long as she was able, but it was the child's turn now and the divil himself wouldn't keep it from making its way into the world any minute now. He thought about stopping at Ned and Nanny's at the butt of the hill, but with the clatter of kids that'd be sitting in to the table for their bowls of porridge, he decided he'd better keep going. As they passed Lisnacrevagh and the Dark Trees she let a scream out of her that'd do justice to the local Banshee. He knew he was done for if he didn't get her to the nurse in minutes. Standing bolt upright in the trap he urged the mare on like never before, the animal responding as if it knew a life, or maybe two, depended on it. Though nearly done, she gave it everything as they passed the fields known locally as the Four Acre just prior to the entrance to Ballynamanagh. The Nugget was standing at the gate chatting to the Potstick when they heard the scream that fairly lifted them out of it. Barely having time to push the girls into the long grass, they shooktheir fists after the phantom horse and carriage. Young Paddy hardly saw them he was so intent on reaching the midwife. As he wheeled at Maguire's boreenhe blessed himself several times thanking the old gods for the horse and for getting them there safely.

Coming in from the milking, Pat nearly dropped the two buckets when he saw the carriage swinging into the yard. On her last legs now, a cloud of steam rising from her as Paddy circled the yard a few times to keep her from dropping, the mare could do no more. Jessie's waters were about to burst as Paddy lifted her gently from the trap, and followed the midwife into the parlour and laid her on the couch. Convulsed with pain she knew she wouldn't be able to hold out a minute longer.

The milk safely in the parlour, Pat was already running with kettles of boiling water from the big pot on the black Rayburn. Well used to the routine, the nurse hadn't to say a word to him except to tell him to get Paddy out and the mare looked after before both fell victims to exhaustion. In truth he had never seen a horse in such a sweat and knew they must have come a long way. Now in full control the midwife knew it'd only be seconds before the child would be with them. The two men had the harness off the mare by now and rubbing her down even though she was wobbly on her feet and ready to drop. All he could get out of Paddy was Lanesboro, but when he mentioned Oul Maggie he knew where he stood. The best thing to do now was to get him and the mare to the hayshed and get them settled and out of the way until he got the good word. The poor lad was in an awful state because the full implication of the mad chase from Creggs had just hit him and nearly floored him with fright. Well used to coping with such situations Pat produced the hip flask and told him to take a good mouthful. That did the trick. He couldn't shut him up after that and got the whole story before he heard the shout that all was well.

Insisting Jessie stayed put for a few days, Pat organised a comfortable shake-down for Paddy while the midwife set Jessie up in a spare room with her little man. She was determined to call Séamus because of her affection for Nora and her blonde beauty. Paddy got stuck in straight away mending pots, pans and cans as only he could. Although worried about the mare initially he relaxed as she came to her oats after a day's rest.

"You've got a good one there lad!" Pat remarked as he saw her rapid improvement.

"I suppose you'll be wanting to hit the road soon," he said casually more to test the waters than everything else.

"They're likely to be here any day now so if it's alright with you we'll hould tough until they arrive. No point in putting Jessie or the child through the mill for the sake of a few days."

"Spot on young man. You'll be grand here until you get word of their arrival. I could do with your help around the yard anyway. There won't be a hole to be found in a hedge never mind a pot or a pan the way you're going."

Knockagh Demesne

Always up to something, or planning some kind of devilment, the lads laid plans for weekend rambles or bartered their books and comics for a tube or tyre or even a jaunt around the fields with the Skelly's in their reincarnated Volkswagen. That was a real buzz and was worth a few Dandys or Beano's as they took the wheel and spun around the high field alongside the Boreen. The brakes were non-existent of course, but it didn't matter much anyway as the car quickly ran out of the home-made juice they had converted into a fuel better and cheaper than anything on the market. Its life was short-lived however on account of Mulvey and Hewart having the franchise on petrol and tvo. They weren't about to lose good money to two young inventors who could change the world, so they copied Henry Ford's motto- 'if you can't beat them buy them out.'

Sundays were roaming days. A group of boys and girls would gather at the cross about midday during the summer to wander through the fields until hunger drove them home late in the evening.

A game plan was quickly arrived at with a show of hands. They were gone in minutes, laughing and playing through the fields to the Giants Grave or over to Knockagh, another of their special haunts. Though a firm favourite, it took some planning as it was a fair march from the crossroads. A vast estate, it offered unlimited excitement and adventure in the dense copses that grew throughout the huge holding. Numerous outhouses, now mostly semi-derelict, had been occupied until relatively recently by Seamie's extended family before moving to the 'mainland.' As with Ballynamanagh and Abbeyshrule, Knockagh was part of the lands owned by The Cistercians from the Middle Ages until the confiscation and plantation in the late 16th and early 17th century. Kenny of Antley acquired the lands much later; some said in a bet between the bishop and the parson at a rough game of poker one Saturday night. Kenny disputed the ownership saying his people were granted the lands for siding with the Farrell Bhuí. But as no one was sure, and it was too difficult to prove, they played for it. It was said he won it by plying the Reverends with whiskey and getting them to sign it over there and then in front of the young housekeeper.

"It wasn't the first time and it wouldn't be the last a bit of skirt brought good luck," he was heard to remark in Hanlons as he ordered fencing for a disputed area the Flowers of the Paddock were trying to get their hands on. They might have gotten it, if Flower himself, who had a questionable role as Bishop of his flock, hadn't been the subject of a lightning visit from his superiors from Dublin. On finding the latest in radio equipment under the 'bishop's' bed he was immediately carpeted, but somehow managed to hold on to power despite his lapse to mammon. Hewart said he couldn't have luck because he was always stuck in some young one from Legan or Rathowen.

A long tree-lined laneway led from Conway's to Knockagh. Both Johnny and Tommy were excellent carpenters who operated from a well-built barn by the side of their house.

If the Sunday came wet and Mass might have to be missed Johnny piled Norah and the boys into the Beetle. It was a wonder how he was able to see out at all with the number of bodies inside, but as he was an ultra-careful driver, there was never any doubt but that he'd get them to the church on time.

Huge oak, ash, beech and chestnut lined the driveway on both sides for about half a mile. These trees, which lent an air of mystery to Knockagh, constantly attracted the young adventurers. However, it was the big oak in front of the semi-derelict mansion which drew most attention. Its huge branches hung low to the ground, wandering around like a lost dinosaur looking for its own. It wasn't unusual for the whole gang of youngsters to be on the tree at the same time, looking more like fairies or elves than humans as they flitted from branch to branch. The older and more adventurous sat on the upper branches acting as lookouts should any foreigners from a neighbouring parish deign to usurp their haven.

From a distance it looked as if it were a tall ship in full sail with the eyrie occupied and the sailors attending to ship duty. One could see for miles from here. The hill of Arva loomed large and boding to the north where Queen Meave led her troops into battle against the men of Ulster led by Cuchulainn. The great Odyssey of the Táin owed its being to such outposts. Uisneach lay South-East between Athlone and Mullingar and had a softer, gentler appearance. Quigley often recounted tales of the three sons of Uisneach and the fabled Catstone that lay to the south of the hill which was reputed to be the exact centre of Ireland and the universe as far as his pupils were concerned. Stories were told of a fabulous city which lay deep in the bowels of Uisneach where the Tuatha de Danann reigned supreme on being condemned to live underground after losing out to the Milesians from the Iberian Peninsula. Croughan Hill away to the west was Queen Meave's headquarters during her long reign and the other entrance to the Underworld thereafter. The lordly Shannon snaked its way through the Midlands, and on a clear day, its sinewy shape could be seen from the upper reaches of the great oak as it wound its way from Lough Allen to Loch Ree and onto Athlone. The Hill of Tara on the plains of Meath could also be seen on a clear day and in itself the whole exercise was an intriguing lesson in the geography of Ireland as enunciated by the Master himself.

A small house and orchard lay at the back of the main building once occupied by Seamie's uncle, also called Séamus, during the early years of his marriage. Later moving to a fine beehive cottage on the hill overlooking the Bosque valley and Tess's river, they were blessed with four fine daughters who became an integral part of the close-knit group of Sunday wanderers.

Most of the apples in their orchard were cookers and as sour as buttermilk but wonderful for an apple tart. There were two trees near the gable end of the house with apples as sweet as any that could be got south of Armagh. The young ramblers knew which were which of course but games were frequently played out with their younger brothers and sisters who had to learn quickly to keep up with the rest. Although their steel was tempered in the hot flames of puberty there was a perceived limit that could be applied to test their resolve. Entrusted with the care of the younger ones it was imperative they came to no ill or they'd never hear the end of it if anything untoward happened. This didn't preclude the normal inquisitiveness between boy and girl or the physical bonds that grew quickly between them. The newcomers were afforded sufficient room to find their own feet, often meaning they had to endure little stratagems to find their way forward. They soon learned the sweet apples from the sour and after a few mishaps here and there they generally settled comfortably into the machinations of the greater group.

Considered the 'Owl', Seamie was given a difficult task to prove his worth. He was obliged to go into what was considered the 'haunted shed' and walk along a plank to retrieve a bottle half way up the hayshed. A huge rambling building of stone, wood and sheeted iron, it was rarely visited by the kids because it had an evil air attached to it. He didn't see that as a problem at first but about halfway across the beam he suddenly began to feel uneasy. A strange feeling came over him as voices resonated around him, none of which he could identify. He felt as if he was been pushed or pulled from the plank. Not daring to look down he tried to blot it out as he inched towards the bottle. Grabbing it quickly, he launched himself far out onto the hay below. Although covered in sweat he felt an eerie chill running through his bones. How was he going to describe it to Smiler and the rest of the crew? He didn't have to. His pale face told it all.

"Sorry Seamie that wasn't fair. My brother John wasn't the better of that for days. Mam thought he had the flu but we couldn't tell her the truth or we'd be killed. Did you hear voices too?"

"I thought they'd pull me off the plank when I was over the machinery and timber. I had an awful job trying to hold on but I heard Annabel encouraging me and that was what kept me going. If it wasn't for that my goose was cooked." They talked it over before re-joining the group agreeing it was best to say nothing about it until Seamie had had a chat with Tess.

Blowing Up a Storm

Tim came in from milking and handed Seamie his flashlight as it was getting quite dark. The wind had risen perceptibly and big raindrops spattered the yard around him as he left the house. The tall trees lining the road looked spooky as he pedalled hard past the fork that led to Keel Mine and the Mountain. Strong gusts hit him head on as he bent low over the handlebars trying to make himself as small a target as possible. Nevertheless, the fury of the blasts forced him to swerve violently from time to time to avoid ending up in the deep drain by the side of the road.

As he rounded the bend there was a sharp blast as the front tube burst almost flinging him from the bike. Somehow, he managed to hold the line before dismounting in the rapidly rising gale. Wondering what might be the best way to proceed, he decided to take shelter in a shanty at the corner of Tim's quarry field feeling it'd be safer there than under the trees where a falling branch could reunite him with his ancestors in the dead centre of Abbeyshrule. Gathering force by now the storm increased in violence, the wind howling through the trees as torrential rain forced him deeper into the shed. He decided to wait it out because even with his limited experience he felt it would soon blow over. He remembered times by the Inny when he and his father had to take shelter from a sudden squall and his father stating it usually got worse before it got better.

His mind wandered as he thought of his new friends. If he wasn't with Annabel he was thinking of her and the times they had together. Thanking God no one knew what they were up to, or more than the priests would be after them for sure. He had never felt such emotion before and the thought of her lying into to him with her firm breasts, created another storm, one far more pleasant than the one raging about him now. All healthy stuff according to Tess but few shared her opinion. Her whole attitude was different to almost everyone bar himself, and now Annabel. Being a Protestant, it was said they had a healthier outlook on such matters according to Tess. He couldn't understand why everyone had such hang-ups about such a natural thing as sex and the country full of children. It'd answer them better to explain things to people and not be making dung heaps out of potato peelings. If Tess and Allison could explain it so easily to Annabel and him why couldn't all the other big heads do the same? He suspected there was a deeper reason and most likely something to do with making money.

Thunder and lightning raged around as he sought a safer corner in the shed. The old iron was being lifted off the roof by the powerful blasts that swirled and furled like demons. A strange crying sound similar to what Tess had told him resembled a Banshee echoed from the graveyard making him more nervous than he already was. With no sign of the storm abating, and the rain pouring through the porous roof, he decided to make a burst for it, at least as far as Gannon's where he knew he'd find refuge. The wind howled through the trees as he raced along trying to avoid the flying debris by sticking as close as possible to the big hedge. A dim light flickering through the wildly swaying branches told him he hadn't far to go. A branch crashing to the ground in front of him forced him to leap sideways. As he did so he felt a vice-like grip tighten on his upper arm flinging him to the ground. Swinging madly he struggled free but was soon held again. Though wild with fear he knew he'd have to turn and face his attacker. Shielding his face he swung around to hit out with all his might but there was nothing.

"You fucking bastard," he roared as he saw the culprit that had left him shaking like a leaf and in more pain than he had ever experienced. A big 'buck' briar trailing from the bushes had ensnared itself around his arm and caught everything as he tried to flee. He could feel blood flowing from a gash inside his jacket where it had gripped tightest, but gingerly easing the thorny embrace free, he cursed it to the fires of hell as he did so.

Holding his arm as tightly as possible he fell against the iron gate as he stumbled into Gannon's yard.

"Who's there?" a familiar voice sounded from the interior.

"Me, Seamie," he spluttered as loud as he could though exhausted from his mad flight through the trees and the pernicious briar attack. Barely able to stand upright he fell into Johnjo's arms.

"Ah me poor gossoon what happened to ya at all, at all? Come in to the fire a mhic. Pull over there father and make room for him. Can't ya see he's drowned or something."

With an alacrity that belied his advancing years the old man cleared a space, put the kettle hanging over the blazing logs and produced some clean rags while Johnjo eased the wet clothes from the exhausted youth.

"Put a drop of the cratur in that or he'll leave us altogether," he snapped as his father put a large spoonful of Hogg's Amulet into the chipped teapot.

"Are ya alright Seamie or what in God's name came over ya at all?"

"No, a bucking briar caught me in the storm and nearly flittered the arm of me, frightened the daylights out of me as well."

"Them's bastards I know. Didn't they nearly do the poor 'Bun' in only for yourself. You couldn't be half careful enough with them. Here, get this into you and you'll be sound as a bog sally," he said as he poured a drop of poteen into the big mug of tea.

"Do you want to blow the head of me as well," Seamie said as the potent brew hit his palate.

"T'won't do you a bit a harm a mhic," old John said as he sent sparks flying from the big log at the back of the fire.

"It'd be a grand night to set the chimney on fire," Johnjo said advising caution.

"If you clayned it when I asked you there'd be no danger of that."

"I'll do it tomorrow so. Haven't you little to give out about and the gossoon here nearly dying on us."

It wasn't long until the traditional mix of home-made Poteen, herbs and an hour's sleep had him up and rearing to go again. Johnjo wouldn't hear tell of him footing it or even borrowing his bike. As soon as a lull came in the storm he had the big tractor out of the shed and ready for the road to Abbeyshrule.

The rapid progress experienced by the airfield developers, led mainly by the Byrne and McGoey families, took a severe setback on the 12th of April, 1958 when a plane being piloted by the vastly experienced Bill Gilday began to experience difficulties, stalled in mid-air and plummeted to the ground killing Joe Hennigan a well-known photographer who was taking aerial photographs at the time. Gilday was seriously injured but lived to fly again after a prolonged convalescence.

It so happened that Rex and Seamie were on their way down the Long Avenue to the Inny for a spot of fishing at that precise moment. As aeroplanes of any description were still a great novelty, they dismounted near the mearn of Esler's field to watch the plane prepare to land. Horror-struck, they watched as the pilot tried in vain to reach the landing strip, only to stall and plunge to earth on the banks of Kielty's River that runs through a narrow ravine dividing Tenalick from Abbeyshrule Barony.

Refusing to allow Seamie to join him, Rex ran as fast as he could to the scene of the catastrophe, arriving too late to do anything except whisper an act of contrition into the ear of the dying pilot and administer whatever aid he could to the injured passenger who was unaware of his colleague's passing. Ray White and Toss Mullin arrived very soon after and helped secure the site removing obstructions impeding the doctor his transfer by ambulance to hospital. There was nothing more they could do except move the deceased pilot and arrange for the regulations to be followed. Rex's experience in the FCA and Civil Defence certainly saved the life of the co-pilot according to Doctor Mc Givney who on being summoned arrived very soon on the scene, as did many other locals on hearing of the tragedy.

Tess told them that Jimmy Byrne was due to fly with them that day but got detained and couldn't make it. Lady Luck was smiling on him then but returned some twenty years later to claim him and two pals when they were killed on crashing into the top of the Galtee Mountains on their way home from an air display in Cork.

Standing alone at the head of the avenue Seamie watched the entire proceedings with sadness. It was some time before Rex joined him but it was obvious he had no wish to discuss anything just then.

"Keep your feet on the ground son," was all he could say as they remounted before heading to Dempsey's Bottoms.

Rex knew nearly every pool in the Inny from Byrne's to Ballymahon and beyond to Shrule where a more famous namesake, the poet, John Keegan Casey, wrote many of his fine verses and is reputed to have written the wonderfully inspirational ballad 'The Rising of the Moon' while sitting beside the old mill and bridge there. Father and son had walked it on several occasions in the past and he had shown Seamie the exact spot at Pallas where Oliver Goldsmith was born in 1730 just a stone's throw from one of their favourite fishing spots. Rex had a wonderfully retentive memory and could recite any verse or even all of The Deserted Village that evoked such wonderful pen pictures of the life and times of Little Ollie. He had even taken Nora to see 'She Stoops to Conquer' in The Abbey Theatre many moons before when she was working with a Jewish family in the city. The Vicar of Wakefield followed some time later leaving both of them infatuated with Goldsmith's prolific output.

There was another swimming pool a short distance below Tenelick Bridge that had a natural flat bedrock-bottom and was a lot safer for young swimmers. It was the Mecca for nearly every youth in the three parishes. It was not unusual to see up to fifty adults and children frolicking together in the clear water on a warm day. One could swim the whole way from just below the eel weir to the waterfall and dive from the high banks into the deep water. A long straight stretch led from the corner after the eel weir to a wonderfully picturesque waterfall about five hundred yards further on. The fall was small, only about three foot high, but powerful even in summer where the water cascading into sandy pools provided a relaxing massage if one could hold one's balance against the volume of water. The bigger children had little difficulty doing so but for the younger ones it was a real challenge. They enjoyed being swept off their feet from the fall but a close watch had to be kept in case of the worst. Mammy Fay and a few like her delegated this role to one of their own and woe beside them should the slightest incident occur. The river was a huge attraction during the summer when all ages homed in on it for a swim, but for most it was their weekly wash if not the annual one. Some of the older folk might not have had a full wash since the previous summer. It wasn't that they were dirty either Nurse McGrath often remarked, it just wasn't done. Most men simply dipped their heads in the barrel by the side of the house or had a hair and face wash when shaving, but that apart, they wouldn't dream of washing their privates in front of their wives or children. If the opportunity presented itself and the house was quiet of a night they'd fill a basin with fairly hot water, and with a clean rag which was always at hand, they would give their privates and armpits a good wash just in case one might have to go to a wedding or funeral in the forseeable future.

'One couldn't be half careful enough' as the Nugget would say.

It was a different routine for the children though. The big enamel bath was taken down from the hook in the corner every Saturday night, placed in front of the open hearth and filled with hot water. The girls went first as it took their hair longer to dry. They screamed as their ears were waxed and their long hair brushed and combed properly.

"If you don't shut up I'll beat the back of you," the exasperated mother would shout as the men folk looked on indolently. Then it was the turn for the boys according to the pecking order. It was an opportunity for the parents to see how fast their kids were growing and to spot any problems like measles or ringworm before it got out of hand. It also prepared the kids for the onset of puberty.

It happened once at the pool that an infamous Peeping Tom was spotted amusing himself in the middle of a cluster of whins by the riverbank. Without giving the game away Mammy Fay sent two of the bigger lads to take care of the boyo. Circling wide, the lads came up behind the unsuspecting pervert and had him in the deep pool before he knew where he was. It was known that he couldn't swim so after being allowed flail about long enough to give him the father and mother of a fright he was pulled clear and sent packing.

A short treatise on the birds and bees and the difference between the sexes was enough to demonstrate to her young charges the whys and wherefores of the differences between one individual and another. Leaving little to the imagination Mammy Fay spared no blushes knowing full well most of the kid's parents wouldn't have the knowledge or conviction to do likewise.

Tess had. She sat Seamie down quietly the following evening when he called on her and told her of the weekend's fun and games. Without the slightest embarrassment to herself or her young confidant she gently explained the facts of life and the many variations he was likely to meet in the society they now lived in.

A Midnight Whirl

Sweeping low along the canal they were just in time to see the 'Whistler' turn towards Tashinny for Derryhawn where he'd spend the night shift trying to draw out the Robin or Dolan on who was doing whom and any other information he could glean for later use.

A faint rustle of leaves showed up clearly on their monitors as they swung by White's. Tess had spotted it too and pointed the craft across the island to hover unseen over the spot where a small group of fishermen were setting up their stands for a night's poaching. The remains of a specially built swimming pool were partially visible beyond the little islands at Tenelick Bridge but the pool had long since silted over. It was possible, on the odd occasion when the water level dropped in mid-summer, to see the beautiful azulejos (bright blue ceramic tiles) that surrounded the pool. These handmade tiles had been imported from Spain during the 1800's, either by Colonel King-Harmon, or Jeffrey White's ancestors. The tiles still had that extraordinary blue lustre which was evocative of the tiny Moorish villages in the Alpujarras Mountains in southern Spain. Swans nested undisturbed there and huge salmon found it to be a refuge on their way back to their spawning grounds at the upper reaches of rivers like Tess's and Kieltys. There were a number of beautiful islands in the wide sweep of the river opposite Whites and Breadens bringing fishermen from far and wide to wade onto the islands and try for the big salmon and trout that fed in the deep pools. A millstream ran fast and furious through the narrow arch beside the long derelict Tenelick Castle and rejoining the Inny near the eel weir. Some of the 'go boys' were known to net salmon, trout and eel there as the fish raced through the rushing waters. However, a close eye was kept on this rich fishing area by Jack Murray, the bailiff of Cloghan, son of Paddy the Hackney Man who provided a much-needed resource in the neighbourhood. Were it not for him the funerals and football matches would have fewer followers. Big Jim Reilly was known to have walked two days just to attend a wake or a funeral. Paddy never passed him because Jim somehow had the inside line on who was dead or about to die. 'It was his gift' Paddy said. More importantly, he got people to buses and trains to attend funerals and weddings beyond in England. His extended family were spread over the world but mostly in the North of England where The Industrial Revolution and good husbandry helped them earn a decent living.

Just below what remained of the once proud castle (later converted to a busy mill), and immediately after the rapids, stood the eel weir. Few living remembered it being in use but it was an indication of the riches this particular stretch of water once held. The Annals told of huge sturgeon being caught here as far back as the middle Ages; certainly the Cistercian Monks in Abbeyshrule wrote of the virtues of sturgeon roe when it was perceived even then as one of nature's great delicacies. The great granite blocks used in the construction of the castle had been quarried near Ballymahon and transported across country lanes by horse and cart during the 16th century. Little remained of what was once a beautiful castle. A few crumbling gable ends were all that remained of what could easily be an equal to Newtownforbes or Kinnity Castles. It was presumed that it was demolished to build neighbouring houses and sheds, but if that was the case it demonstrated an incredible lack of foresight on behalf of the perpetrators as Bill Kilmurray maintained.

The big mill at Tenelick Bridge that was still in fair repair was almost entirely covered by masses of ivy. Seamie and Mikey had often climbed up through the strong ivy in search of pigeon nests while their father was fishing for the elusive salmon that could be seen under the arches of the bridge alongside the castle. Occasionally, artists from the surrounding area and even further afield could be seen capturing the idyllic scene on canvas. The two boys loved to watch them at work and dreamed of being able to replicate such a charming rustic scene in one way or another in years to come.

Breaden's big house by the river was the next port of call. Though now in a dilapidated state through neglect, Tess told them it once hosted sumptuously exotic parties for the rich absentee landlords who came visiting for the fishing and the excitement of chasing the local boys and girls around the big houses. Unable to appease their wanton ways across the water because of changes in the law, they homed in on the isolated areas of Ireland where the laws had yet to be changed to protect the poor and the young from such predators.

Many of the big houses could afford to hire and fire large groups of locals, mostly healthy, attractive youngsters who were prepared to take their chances for a job that invariably led to disaster as soon as the landlord's eye fell on a new victim. Such was the case in days of old she told them. Fortunate in not having suffered a similar fate in her youth she put it down to good luck, the ability to keep her head down and her physical attributes well out of sight of prying eyes. Notwithstanding, she was nearly caught by the short and curlies when a visiting asshole took a shine to her thinking she was a handsome if effeminate young man. She escaped his slippery tentacles by the skin of her teeth simply by conning him into believing she had already picked up a sexual disease which she hoped he wouldn't contract because of its debilitating effect. Fearing he might be caught with his trousers around his ankles and shite up to his eyebrows he beat a hasty retreat to his rooms where he hid out until the coach took him back to his den of iniquity near Bath.

Having escaped by the skin of her teeth she resolved to be on her guard from there on. It didn't stop her surrendering her charms to the odd wandering minstrel or young admirer but the choice was hers and she chose carefully. Anything she could secrete away from her chosen prey was put away for a rainy day. There were so many disaffected unfortunates roaming the countryside in search of a crust that it was unsafe to travel alone day or night. The relatively recent and horrendous genocide perpetrated on an impoverished nation was still etched deeply in the mindset. It would take years to draw a veil across the tragedy that had torn the nation asunder and spread its poor across the globe. Her parents had all too vivid memories of the horror that swept the land but managed, as did most in the area, to keep body and soul together by living of the land and what nature provided. Fortunately, the rivers were flush with fish and all kinds of wild game could be hunted and trapped if one were to take the risk of running into the bailiffs employed by the absentee landlords. Many of those landlords took flight as soon as the Republic was established but those who had managed to integrate in some manner stayed and generally speaking, were tolerated.

Well, well, well

In any other place at any other time Colehill Crossroads would have been a good-sized town due to its location. The views, quality of land and access from the four corners of the wind would have ensured that. However, lacking a good supply of water was its main drawback even though a few wells had been sunk which supplied as much water as was needed for the few farmhouses nearby. That was of little use to the rest of the householders and probably wouldn't have met the overall needs of the community anyway. Bosque well did, but it was difficult to access, and being situated nearly a quarter of a mile away it was never going to be a viable proposition. The area needed a constant water supply, and after the Piper located a powerful spring in Geoghegan's field by the crossroads a committee was formed to decide how best to exploit it. Ned immediately offered it to the school which was totally dependent on his well for drinking water but hadn't a drop for the kids to wash their hands or flush the toilets that stank to the high heavens.

Quigley said the area's commanding position was its downfall. It was too exposed and hard to defend in a sudden ambush. As it lay on a hill on the way to Abbeyshrule, Tashinny, Carrigboy and the Inny it was often party to passing soldiers of fortune in bygone days. Cromwell's murderous mercenaries raped and pillaged their way through South Longford around 1650, as did many others at diverse times. Were it not for the sanctuary of the caves many more would have been killed or forced from the land to work in the sugar plantations in far-flung places such as The Bahamas, Cuba and other islands annexed to the crown by the new navy organised by Cromwell himself.

Everyone knew there was lots of water in the area but there was no running water for the school except what Ned or Hewart supplied. Running water then was harder to get than a packet of rubbers on your birthday according to Ciaran Mullin, and few knew better than him. Fr. Pat in his wisdom delegated the task of finding water for the school to the newly arrived curate, Chris Lynch. Though a great organiser he wouldn't find water unless it was put in front of him in a cruet. His driving ambition was to be a bishop. Abbeyshrule wasn't going to get him there fast so he had to bide his time and learn how to play his cards right. Although he kept in with the big noises and courted the rich he didn't make it as obvious as the PP. Some said it wasn't all he courted but, like a carbuncle, it would come out in its own time Tess said.

Enquiries were made throughout the length and breadth of the seven parishes until it became obvious to the good shepherd that a sacrifice would have to be made. A lamb was decided on and sure enough the two black Lambs from Finea, near Granard were picked. Their reputation for divining a spring was the stuff of legend. Only the Piper could hold a candle to them. He had already proven his

216

worth in more ways than one by locating springs and minerals, even the lost and lonely he could locate and placate. Seamie knew it was he who found his mother's wedding ring when it fell down behind the table of drawers.

He remembered The Piper proving he could do it by inviting Nora to hide her ring in the grass margin anywhere along the side of the road between the house and the crossroads. He found it within minutes. His had to be the precursor of the metal detector that was all the rage in England and the US. The Vietnam War was to attach much more importance to them but the fame fell fairly and squarely on The Piper.

Prior to the arrival of the Lambs he had already located several springs close to the school. The most powerful according to him was the one just inside the hedge in Farrell's field. Dolly was delighted, as it would mean a handsome earner when the kids needed to further their education. She was none too pleased when Ted told her it was a natural resource and should be shared with the school kids. A visionary, he saw much further than his nose and was recognised as one of the sharpest brains in the entire community. Most of his kids took after him though the girls leaned more towards the social tendencies of their kindly mother.

An early riser, Seamie was astonished one morning to see two big wagons, a digger and a strange apparatus which had an enormous screwdriver dangling from it, parked inside Ned's field. Not bothering to eat the breakfast his mother had prepared for him he just grabbed the few sandwiches and put them in his small backpack not sure if he'd get lunch in Annabel's house or not. He felt he would but didn't wish to take anything for granted just yet. Curiosity got the better of him as he turned the corner so he decided to investigate a little further lest he be last to have the inside line. That wouldn't do at all because the whole world knew he was the second-best informed person in the parish after Hewart, and he only because people owned him money and the telephone box was an intrinsic part of the establishment. People who owe money are likely to confess all their sins Tess told him. He wasn't right sure what she meant at first but not wanting to appear a simpleton he chewed on it for a while before solving the equation by beating round the bush. A lengthy discussion with his father while teasing out the line brought the requisite answer.

"By indirections seek directions out," his father advised. He had heard Quigley saying that that was a quotation from Hamlet but wasn't well up on Shakespeare just yet, though he rather fancied Hamlet's other famous saying; "methinks the lady doth protest too much."

There was a lot to learn yet if he was going to be 'as clivir as a jailer' in Pat Carrigy's estimation.

Propping Betsy beside the wall under the big yellow Yew he idled across the road to have a peek at what was going on. They must have arrived in the middle of the night he thought because the Brink's favourite seat was completely flattened to let in the wagons and machinery.

"And who might you be?" brought him swirling round with a start. Introducing himself to a larger-than-life, but affable giant, he was pleasantly surprised when he stuck out an enormous fist in greeting.

"I could do with a well-informed runner," he grinned. "You look after me and I'll look after you," sounded promising.

"It depends on what you want," Seamie threw back at him.

"Be the Holy. We'll get on famously," he laughed through a week's growth. "I won't ask you to do anything I wouldn't do," sealed the bargain. "Now, as a sign of goodwill I'll give you this here half crown and we'll have a chat later this evening or tomorrow if you have time. There's a power a work to be done today so off with you now and 'mum's the word' Seamie."

"That wasn't a bad start to the day at all," he said to himself as he knocked sparks out of the road at the Bull field above Tess's palace.

As early as he was she was already up and about, a wisp of white smoke already sneaking out of the lopsided chimney.

"You'll end up in the middle of it yet a mhic," she wagged her finger as he stalled the bike with his boot hard against the back tyre, whirling it back in the direction he'd come from. Dismounting as if it were an everyday occurrence he stepped over the stile before following her into the dimly lit interior.

"Cutch, ya lazy thing," sent the black cat tearing out the front door. "I'll have to put mangles on that wan. You couldn't blink but she'd have breakfast, dinner and supper gone in the one sweep. Feck the like of it I ever seen!"

"Leave her to me Tess. I'll sort her out soon," he replied as he poured tea for the two of them. Billy landed on the half door with his morning melody as he filled her in on the earlier proceedings.

"I'll not be seeing you at all from this out," she remarked half in jest. "A moneyed man it is we have now. There'll be no standing you at all after this," she smirked as she put her hand on his shoulder. "Delighted for you I am a mhic. No better gossoon ever deserved as much. Off with you now or you'll miss the breakfast with the young miss."

Wheeling into the yard he was just in time to meet Tim who was all set to head off to the mine below in Keel.

"Ah, there you are Seamie," he greeted him with his clipped Oxford English. "Follow me young man. I've something for you" he beckoned as he threw open the garage door. Allison waved as she strode over from the kitchen door.

"I wouldn't like to miss this Seamie," she smiled knowingly.

"Nor me," Annabel cried as she ran from the house with a mere slip of a gown on her despite the chill of the early morning.

"Didn't know you were awake, child," Tim smiled as he hugged her close. It was obvious she was the joy of his life, but they weren't to know as yet, she was fast becoming the joy of Seamie's as well. Throwing off the plastic cover he unveiled a brand new Raleigh and stood aside to let him look at it. Speechless, he could only shake his head in disbelief.

"But, how can I pay for it. This is only my first day with you," he gasped as his mind did the maths.

"You hardly expect us to pull a fast one like that on you Seamie," Allison chided at his lack of trust.

"How was I to know?" was all he could think of saying as Annabel gave him a reassuring hug.

"It's yours Seamie," they almost echoed each other as he began to take in their appreciation of him.

"I'll make it up to you or die in the attempt," he said as he fought to hold back tears that hadn't hit him for ages.

"You can leave your old bike here for emergencies," Tim urged as he took leave of them and headed for the mountain.

Sir Walter Raleigh couldn't have felt half as good as he threw his leg over the bar and did a few circles around the courtyard.

"Hey, let me up," Annabel begged as he circled around her.

"Be careful the two of you or I'll be picking you up of the ground,"

Allison admonished as she let them at it. Sitting comfortably on the bar Annabel laughed as they cycled out to the front gate and did a few rounds of the walled-in orchard before stopping at the ornate fountain in the centre. Despite the excitement of the bike, he couldn't help feeling her warmth seeping through him. Throwing her long blonde hair back she kissed him full on the lips. Instinctively he pulled her closer with one arm. It was enough for now. No point on making anything too obvious they agreed. Putting the bike into the garage he followed her in to breakfast.

There was plenty to do around the farm so he listened attentively as Allison outlined his immediate duties. Pencil and paper at hand as always, he jotted down the main points just in case. They could help him around the yard if they wished and Annabel could help him with the counting, but the mucking out and tractor work he'd do himself as he was well used to such duties with Hewart.

At the back of his mind he knew he had a lot of preparation and planning to do before he set off for college in early September but there was enough time for everything in between. As Tess told him 'Time waits for no man' he had begun to put bits and pieces together for the event. Annabel was leaving too. She was about to head off to a boarding school in the Dublin Mountains and she could hardly wait. Having worked hard to escape the monotony of life in an inward-looking community they weren't about to let it slip through their fingers now. An awful lot had happened in a short time but they were eager to see the world from a different perspective even if they had to go their separate ways for a while. The future beckoned and they planned to be aboard. There was little time to dawdle as he went about his work. As lunch hadn't been mentioned he decided to take a short break and eat the sandwiches his mother had prepared for him.

He rarely went without the backpack Tess had made for him because it held a bite to eat, a small bottle of goat's milk, a few biscuits and a few scones if he timed his mother's baking right. But all kinds of things found their way into the bag. A rabbit, hare or pheasant meant a decent dinner for Tess and himself though he had to be careful he didn't upset his mother by dining out too often.

Three sharp whistles brought him to his senses, as it was the pre-arranged signal that he should return to the house. Annabel was coming over the headland to meet him with an angelic smile on her face. Hand in hand they dallied back to the kitchen where her mother had lunch ready for them. Chatting away together he told them all about the Lamb's delivery earlier that morning and the pact he had reached with 'Larry the Lamb' as he was now known. A shrewd businessman, he was far from being anyone's fool as transpired later.

As they wandered the farm later he told her he was leaving soon just like her. He had to go. There was nothing else for it. He took the little bronze Cross Tess had given him from the inside pocket of his jacket and gave it to her. It had to be from long ago Tess thought because she had found it in the sandy bottom of the river near the well where she used go for a wash, weather permitting. Annabel said it was lovely and she'd keep it forever even if she had to learn the rosary. That started them laughing again and helped them forget the fact they must soon go their separate ways. With that she went to the drawer at the side of her bed and took out the gemstone her father found in the Fairy Fort over by Mornin castle. It resembled an emerald and had a beautiful sheen to it. Her mother told her emeralds brought luck and life and she wanted to give it to Seamie now.

Tim had fashioned a tiny casket for it and attached it to a silver necklace belonging to his grandmother. Undoing the clasp she went to hang it around Seamie's neck.

"You have one already!" she said stepping back with obvious annoyance. "Who gave you that?"

"Tess of course!" he said truthfully. The shadow lifted and she was happy once more. It was a small white stone with a hole in the centre and a star-like indentation at the base. Tess had found it under the fall many moons before he told her and she could have her pick of the two. He told her Tess and himself were talking about relics and the like one evening. She noticed he didn't have a talisman of any kind to ward off the evil eye and told him she'd soon fix that. He often wondered why she collected different stones but it interested him a lot and he began to do the same. More often than not she'd dismiss them but she kept some. Not many visited her except those who wanted a reading. She sometimes read their palms and other times their tealeaves but one day as he was with herMags Murtagh called. Realising they needed privacy he put the kettle over the fire and was about to leave when she asked him to stay.

"I want you to help me pick out the right stones," she said. As before she agreed with some of them and rejected others. Magsbeing entirely fascinated said nothing. When satisfied with the selection she narrowed them down to just six and handed them to her.

"Blow on them and roll them in your fists," she told her

A couple of minutes later she told her to roll them on the big flagstone in front of the fireplace. Ginger thought it was a game and took off across the floor with one of them.

"Leave her be," she told Seamie as he jumped after the young cat. She's gone with the one I was worried about. He listened as she told her neighbour how to cope with her recent crisis and where to look for support when the end came. She also told her who to watch out for, who to avoid and who to bring into her inner circle. She mentioned Nora, which surprised Seamie as he thought they were already friends. She told her of a windfall that was on her way, a journey that lay before her, and of a visit from the authorities and the Church, but she wouldn't elaborate. Mags asked her if she was referring to her confessions recently where she was quietly telling the PP that she was so exhausted after a day at the hay that she had to refuse her man for once in her life. "You did what?" the PP shouted at her. Every head in the short isle turned as if she had just confessed to a murder. "You'll never see me in this church as long as I live," she shot back as she burst from the confessional banging the door so hard it flew off its hinges. Mortified, but delighted she had confronted the tyrant she paraded down the long aisle like the Queen of Sheba.

"No, not at all dear woman," Tess assured her. "You'll find out soon enough," she said as she gathered up the stones and put them back into the recess by the fireplace. Seamie had the tea ready by now and after drinking it, Mags slipped something into Tess's hand, made her excuses and left.

"What did you make of that?" she asked him as their neighbour walked up the road towards the Crossroads.

"Could I do it," he asked her.

"You could if you were interested," she laughed knowing he was fascinated.

Promising to go into it at length another time she reached over the mantelpiece, removed a brick with her penknife, took something out, and realising he took a fancy to it she immediately presented it to him to bring him luck. On his next visit she had a piece of leather thong ready so he could wear it around his neck.

Slipping it around Annabel's neck now, he felt her scent drawing him like a magnet as they eased onto her bed.

Allison meantime had come up the stairs to call Seamie as it was getting dark and he'd need to be on his way home. Hearing the two of them in Annabel's bedroom she thought she'd surprise them. Peeping around the door she was astonished to see them locked in each other's arms. She was ready to roar at them when something stopped her. They were talking quietly to each other, and even though she could barely make out what they were saying she heard her tell him that she'd wait for him to her dying day. Replying that wherever that was he'd wait for her there too they giggled at the good of it. They looked like angels she thought, their golden curls intertwined and falling around their faces like rays of sunshine. They were always laughing. She saw nothing wrong with their youthful intimacy and stepped back quietly to the top of the stairs before calling them.

"Coming mother," Annabel replied. The two of them walked to her hand in hand. It was the nicest thing she had seen in her life. Pure love, there was no other word for it.

Fuel for the Winter

"Well boys, are you all set for the day? Whoa there Blackie! Run in and get me a half-quarter of nugget Mikey. Seamie, will you cut me a small branch from the Willow tree?" he asked as he handed his sharp penknife to the youngster. Not knowing why that was necessary he nevertheless did as asked and was back over the roadside wall in minutes.

"Good lad. That's for the ould headaches. I'd be lost without the Prods and their hanging trees," he laughed heartedly as he saw the understanding flash in Seamie's eyes.

School was out as it was Easter. Many of their neighbours and school pals were already on the bog getting the high bank ready for cutting. The kish(a rustic bridge over bog drains) had to be checked and the rutted tracks made ready for Blackie to draw out the turf on wooden barrows. The Nugget owned a fair-sized plot in Aska bog and that would be prepared before heading to Abbeyshrule bog where his son Rex had acquired a much better one for the princely sum of ten shillings. The Government, led by DeValera, had ordained that a portion of bog land was to be made available to anyone living in the hinterland that could work it. This grant referred only to turbary rights and didn't allow for some greedy farmers who owned the land itself. This in turn led to difficulties in later times as a few farmers from Clonbrin muscled in on the unwary and cut the turf themselves or sought to take it over. There was no such difficulty with the Nugget or the Rex as they guarded their rights by consistently cutting a little each year, enough to do two years normally. The Nugget was not one to take chances.

"Cut enough for two," he advised his son Michael, more commonly known as Rex due to once having a dog called Rex who was never far from his side. Experience told the Nugget that heavy rain could wash them out of the bog or make the channelling of the water highly dangerous. The high bank could slip and bring tons of turf in on top of the sleánsmen. The age-old art of directing the water around the various bog holes was essential for good maintenance. There were many things to bear in mind, pressure, depth, flow, and, of course, the neighbours. Poor work by one neighbour could do a lot of harm and force the water in on one another. The Nugget knew the bog, as did his son. As soon as they reached their patch of bog land they were checking the drains and the Kish that led into the inner bank. This homemade bridge was essential to the success or failure of the entire operation as it was the only crossing of the deep drain that bisected their spread bank.

Joe Mac owned the stretch alongside the Rex. A conscientious neighbour, he treated the demarcation lines between both spreads with respect, which was more than could be said about other neighbours. The Potstick owned the drop bank on the opposite side to the

Rex but in a hollow underneath. In order for the Potstick to work his section it was imperative that those above him treat theirs properly. There was never a dispute between them over how the water was channelled because the neighbours prided themselves on their workmanship, whether it was the safe use of their area, the movement or sluicing of the water into the big drain which would take it safely away from all concerned, or the temporary narrow channels which diverted the water on each day's cutting.

The high bank, as it was known, was ideal for spreading the turf to dry out. This took weeks and was labour intensive. Firstly, the drains had to be secured and deepened sufficiently to take the surplus rainwater but not so much as would dry the surface too much and cause shifting or the collapsing of the drains.

A brief inspection of how the land lay was followed by the slunging (cutting away of the top yard or so) that was useless for burning but ideal for filling in the previous year's bogholes.This topsoil, mainly whins, gorse, heather and clumps of rough grass, required care to cut away properly or the turf underneath which was often kept in place by the upper growth, could slip and take all with it. Years of toil preparing their work had lent a special professionalism to the undertaking. The 'slunging' of the top yard was usually completed in one day. The surplus material being pushed down into the previous year's bog hole forming a platform for the judicious use of the area behind it. Care had to be taken also to allow enough turf to form a wall between the past years cutting and the present. This section of peat land was commonly known as the hill for obvious reasons. It stood above the surrounding spread banks and was therefore much drier. Although the turf on the hill was better quality and dried quicker it was often brittle and difficult to handle. It burned beautifully giving off a pleasant odour and was easy to set alight with some dry tinder such as moss, cipíns (small dry twigs)or paper.

Nothing went to waste in or outside the house. What didn't burn was used in a myriad other ways. Jute, or the more recent plastic bags could be used to insulate roofing in the outhouses or thrust between walls to keep the heat in during the depths of winter. Likewise, the bags could be used to carry heavy loads of turf, turnips, mangles or any kind of fodder for the animals. Cloches made from these bags protected lettuces and frost-endangered vegetables thus ensuring an earlier crop.

"What would we do without them," was Granny's oft-spoken preamble to a neighbourly chat.

Rex invariably deferred to his father in deciding when everything was ready.

"I think we could start soon," was the signal to pull out all the stops. Everything was well organised as usual. He just needed the nod from his father. The three generations would only vacate the bog when the midges became unbearable, certainly not before everything was in place for the following morning.

Blackie, who had been feeding quietly beside the big cherry tree, was harnessed to the cart, which was loaded with the tools for the day.

Out the rutted bog lane, down the long straight road at an easy trot, past the graveyard where Fitzsimons's thatched Shebeen stood, and where most of the dead had drunk their fill at some stage during their lives, and on across the Inny bridge into the charming little village of Abbeyshrule where pints were sunk as fast as the Titanic. Hardworking and hard living they seldom shied from an opportunity if it showed at all. Though rarely partaking of the demon drink the women were compensated with the drug of careful housekeeping with sex as a sideline when their menfolk felt like it. It wasn't the case with all of them because their needs being greater, they sought companionship that gave a buzz no drink could touch. Past masters of Nature's lures they could raise the dead with a tongue or finger. Hadn't their sisters told them all would be forgiven in the confessional, especially if they caught the pastor's attention and drew him into their web?

The Bull Run

'Day-dreamitis' was Seamie's problem according to Tess. It didn't matter what he was doing, snagging turnips, thinning lettuce, milking or counting it was all the same to him. He'd be gone with Tess while you'd be looking around you. Somehow he managed to get the job done but didn't know how at times. He'd spot the old lady soaring over Bosque and would be gone after her in a minute. At times it was a yard brush or graipe but it could just as easily be a fishing rod or the blackthorn stick his grandfather gave him for the 'counting' or to protect him from a frisky heifer or young bull. A good tip on the nose was usually enough to remind them who was in charge.

He was halfway across the Commons one evening when he heard something heavy coming his way. Looking round he was amazed to see White's bull homing in on him. The fact that it shouldn't have been there made precious little difference now. There wasn't a bush or a tree he could turn to and even less chance of escape by trying to outrun the big beast.

"The cave Seamie, the cave," he heard her shout. It shot clean over his head as he dived full length into the depths. His heart in his mouth he lay prone, eyes probing the pitch darkness in search of further danger. This was the realm of the badger, one of the quietest nocturnal animals in the Midlands but also one of the most dangerous if forced to defend its young. Easing towards the light he peeped above ground and spotted her sitting on a stone by the hedge.

"That was a close one a mhic," she smiled as he eased himself out. The bull was by now heading towards Mulvey's heifers in the high field.

"He'll do some harm there I suspect," he said as he imagined White's annoyance and Mulvey's delight at the obvious outcome.

"Shure someone has to do it," she grinned as they crossed back over the style at Bosque and on to her little house beside the road bridge.

"Where in God's name did you spring from?" he enquired as he took her hand while crossing the river by the steppingstones.

"I was after the dinner child when I saw you in a bit of bother."

It was only then he spotted the rabbits ears sticking out of her satchel.

"You didn't do so bad either Tess," he said as he imagined what might have happened were she not close-by.

"Well you can clean it now while I'm getting us a mouthful," she advised.

"No bother Tess. I'll have him cleaned and skinned before the kettle boils," he joked as they went about their chores.

"I don't doubt it child. You're a credit to whoever your father is," she laughed as she saw the look on his face.

"I'm only winding you up child. I know you and all belonging to you and a better father you couldn't have. Any wonder you're able to say your prayers," she said breaking into a fit of laughter at her own good humour.

"You're pushing it Tess," he warned her as he swung the rabbit towards her in mock attack. Picking up the sharp knife from the sideboard he got stuck into preparing dinner for the two of them.

"You just reminded me of a story from long ago a mhic," she said as they worked together.

Asking her what it was about brought a smile to both their faces as it meant more time together and another story to be stored for the future.

She was reminded of it as they stepped across the river.

"Will I tell it to you now or after the bit of grub," she said as they carried on with their preparations.

"Now is as good a time as any. We might have time for something else later," he giggled, as she looked quare at him.

"There was a time," she said when Abbeyshrule was like an island, protected on all sides by the bog, the Inny and more bog. Unless you knew the paths where Eithne reigned, you had no chance of entering the rath that once surrounded the village. Likewise, the big boulders in the river had to be jumped one by one to get across. But the river ran deep and dangerous at this point and it was said that many'sa poor soul fell to an icy grave before some genius cut holes in the stones for grips.

Neighbours by the name of Farrell and Dolan lived beyond near Slíabh An Óir she continued. Their only children Pat and Brigie were inseparable from the moment they laid eyes on each other. As they skipped to and from school in Ballynacarrigy the neighbours knew they'd be together forever and so it was. As soon as it was decent to do so they got married, Pat moving into the bigger house for convenience as the old folk were no longer able for the daily grind. It wasn't long till Bridgie told Pat she was expecting. Needless to say he was as delighted as she was.

"Well, time passed and they had one child after the other until there were seven of them under eight."

"That's impossible Tess," Seamie interrupted.

"Not at all child."

"Weren't there two sets of twins in between as well," she laughed as she saw the look on his face.

"Tell the story Tess and never mind trying to pull the wool over my eyes," he said as he pushed the kettle over the fire.

"Well, it was getting harder and harder to feed his family so Pat found work in the mill by the river. It was often late when he got home and Bridgie worried about him having to cross the stepping stones in the dead of night. Worse still, ice often covered the stones in winter and made it doubly difficult to get across safely. She never slept a wink until he was beside her in the bed and very often not for a good while after either as he'd be like a buck goat after the excitement of leaping from stone to stone with only the moon or the stars to guide him. Indeed, there wasn't even a moon sometimes due to the weather and the like," she chuckled as she saw how her story was winding into Seamie's spirit.

"Go on," he encouraged as he helped her prepare the stuffing with breadcrumbs, herbs and the divil knows what she had concocted earlier.

"Right so," she replied.

"Well, one night around All Soul's Day she lay awake waiting for Pat but he didn't come home. He didn't arrive the next night either, nor the next. In Fact, she never saw him after that. The poor woman was beside herself with grief. The sight of the little kids hungry faces looking up at her nearly broke her heart. She did the best she could under the circumstances. She went down to the river every evening to shout across to see if anyone might hear her but not a sinner passed the way. She trapped a few rabbits that kept them going for a while, but as she couldn't leave the children for long and she couldn't chance the icy stones she gathered them around her and they all fell fast asleep."

Weeks went by until Father Tom missed Pat from Sunday mass and decided to pay a visit. He thought he should check with the Miller first as he was bound to have some information about his daughter and family. The old man, partially senile by now, had no information on them at all so he left to go to the local inn. As luck would have it he happened on Peter the local Garda who took an immediate interest. Asking the priest to wait a few minutes he returned with his double-barrel that didn't do much for his equanimity. All very well until they reached the river again and Peter realised the difficulty of the task ahead of him. He had completely forgotten the stones and nearly shit himself as he looked across the river and saw there wasn't as much to be seen of the stones as he had hoped. Looking at Fr. Tom he confessed that he couldn't possibly do it because of his bad back, an injury he had picked up at football a few years earlier. Tom knew of the injury and left it at that. Cold sweat broke out on his brow as he deliberated the next move. There was no going back now. He recalled his visits to the farm when he was a teenager and how easy Pat and himself could fly from stone to stone, but that was then and a vastly different proposition now.

But being made of stern stuff, and having done it without blinking an eye when he was a kid he decided to take a giant leap of faith by handing Peter his overcoat and missal, stepping back a few paces and then launching himself onto the first stepping stone. Hurling from stone to stone with sweat bubbling through every pore of his corpulent body he landed on the big stone in the middle where he knew he could get his second wind. He could swear he saw something down below but the fear of God being in him now he kept going in case he lost his nerve completely and fell to his death. Blessing himself a half a dozen times, and thanking all the saints he ever heard of, he made one final determined effort before landing in the long grass on the far bank. Peter, who had been deadly quiet during the nail-biting episode, was now cheering him on with abandon. As soon as he'd recovered his poise the good padre shook himself a few times and then cut a beeline for Pat and Brigie's house.

Strange thoughts flew through his head as he opened the Iron Gate that led in the boreen to the homestead. He didn't wait to close it as a sixth sense told him something was radically wrong.

Clutching his rosary he hurried to the ivy covered farmhouse set back against the face of the quarry. Fear followed him like a shadow as he missed the dogs that would normally be barking by now. Not a wisp of smoke rose from the big chimney. Exhausted, he leaned against the doorway. His nerves gave out completely as it crashed inwards leaving him in a shivering heap in the middle of the hallway. It was ages before he could mutter more than a faint whisper. Mouth as dry as tinder he drank a mouthful from his hip flask, a custom that often stood him in good stead. As the wine eased down his bone-dry whistle he gathered himself together for whatever lay ahead.

"Are you there Pat or Bridgie?" he called out as the fear he felt in every fibre of his body enveloped him like a thick fog. There wasn't a sound to be heard as he looked through the window onto the yard once full of life. A few cattle grazed beyond in the 'Ten Acre' as they were wont to call it. Cursing himself for not being more attendant to his priestly duties he vowed he'd spend less time drinking tea with his special lady friends from now on. The sins of the flesh came back to haunt him as he banged on the kitchen door. Convinced a terrible deed had occurred he ran from one room to the other but there wasn't a soul to be seen.

The back door being half open he pushed it out and ran to the sheds. His coattail caught on a bunch of briars bringing him tumbling to the ground as he rounded the corner of the hayshed.

"Curse a fuck on it," he swore as he shook himself free from his entangled jacket. He was covered in blood by now as the thick brambles dug deep into his soft flesh.

"Hail Mary full of grace," he cried out loudly as he circled the house keeping clear of the thick vegetation. The shed door opened inwards with a creaking noise as he lifted the latch and pushed. He was about to step in when a bat flew out missing him by a fraction.

"Holy Mother of God," he stuttered as he jumped backwards. Though nearly out of his wits by now he knew he had to enter the silent house. Not a child or a sign of one. Taking to the stairs he called out as he climbed but not a sound. As he went through the three upstairs rooms a sudden and awful thought struck him. He remembered visiting the house as a young man and helping Brigie take water from the deep well in the back room.

"The well," he screamed as he flew down the stairs to where the deep well stood in the middle of the back room. Falling to his knees in despair he crossed the short distance on all fours.

The cover had been thrown to one side as if in desperation. Pulling himself up he forced himself to look over the rim and into the depths far below.

"And what was it he saw?" she asked as she saw shock in Seamie's eyes.

"Poor Bridgie and her children!" he answered.

"Not at all, not at all a mhic."

"Water, water, that's what he saw. What else would you expect to see in a well?" She exploded into wild laughter as she saw the realisation of her black humour crossing his face.

"Feck you anyway Tess," he said as the full impact of another of her strange stories hit home.

"I'll never forget that one," he whooped as they danced around the kitchen in delight.

Billy was half-asleep on the bush as he went to the river to clean the rabbit. The two cats soon joined him as they smelled dinner and weren't about to miss the main course, or the trimmings at worst. They knew better to give Billy a wide berth though they regularly feasted on one of his less fortunate friends. Pretending to offer a titbit he held it out as Ginger leaned forward to snatch it.

It was in the water in an instant.

"That'll teach you to be greedy," he warned as he nearly fell in himself while trying to contain his amusement.

"I saw that Seamie," she chided as she gazed out through the geraniums.

"It'll put manners on him Tess," he said as he whisked the bedraggled cat onto the bank.

"I bet the kettle isn't boiling yet," he ventured gleefully as he gathered up the skin and entrails for the cats. Despite its recent bath Ginger was in for the kill as it shook itself dry.

Billy's orchestra provided the background music later as they tucked in, chatting all the while about the woes of the world, and how, together, they were going to change them.

Everyone met at the Crossroads for a bit of craic. A game of football or rugby soon got under way if it was mostly lads, or bowls or skittles if it was a mixed bag. Some of the girls were every bit as good as the lads and were sure of a game no matter what. Maura, Dympna, Jo and June could stop a ball as good as the best of them and loved nothing better than a kiss and cuddle as darkness descended. They all had their favourite places, let it be under the bourtree, out in the haggard, or Larkin's shed if there was a half decent shift in the making.

Geoghegan's ditch on the corner of the Crossroads was the Brinks favourite resting place either coming or going to Tashinny. Although well past his best he could still lilt a tune with the best of them. Some said he was as good if not better than Pat Kilduff who used to travel with The Chieftains. His style was half whistle, half lilt but Seamie loved it. He often walked the road to Tess's with him as he tried to imitate his style.

She was sitting on the bridge as they approached.

"I haven't heard you at that for years," she said as she bid them take the weight off their feet.

"Ah, shure nobody listens anymore Tess," he shook his head as he remembered the days they came from far and wide to hear him him lilt.

"I listen," Seamie defended.

"If only there was more like you young man," he remarked as he shook himself and headed to Tashinny.

The following evening seemed ideal, so having finished the few jobs at home he threw his leg over his bike, but not before he had showboated for the Brink and a few of his mates hanging around the Crossroads. He had perfected the way to ride his bike backwards and loved showing off when he had an audience. Sitting on the handlebars he did a few rounds of the crossroads before dismounting beside the Brink.

"It's Duffy's Circus you should be in Seamie and not around Abbeyshrule," he grinned as Seamie mounted backwards again and headed for Tess's.

First things first he thought as he gathered a good bunch of sticks and piled them in the corner for her. Meanwhile, she had the tea made and a few slices of potato cake warming on the pan. Though it wasn't long since he had eaten he couldn't resist the "prata bread" as they called it.

Stories soon started, and as there was no rush now he sat back to enjoy. She had the most vivid imagination possible but her strengths lay in the detail. Whether true or not didn't matter in the least, simply the telling. To his adventurous spirit these stories were better than anything he'd yet read. He could see her clearly as she roamed the bottoms in search of supper.

Her story about catching the cock pheasant took some beating. He could imagine her lying in the long grass in her bundle of rags and the pheasant out for a stroll before roosting for the night. She waited ages for Mr Pheasant she told him but as the evening was kind she didn't mind. Lying low in the long grass she waited patiently until the bird walked straight into her arms. A quick flick of the wrist and its neck was wrung. Throwing it over her shoulder she whistled happily as she hurried home across the stepping stones. He had seen the odd pheasant hanging by the neck at the back of the door alright but thought the Bun or someone might have given it to her. He couldn't imagine her killing anything. She had the easiest way about her of anyone he ever met. Sometimes he drifted into another world when she started on her stories. The tiredness of the day, the warmth of her voice and the heat from the fire ferried him over to fairyland. He'd stroll through the Commons with the giants of the Firbolgs or Tuatha Dé Danann and fight against the one-eyed Fomorians with his blackthorn.

"Are you asleep child?" she'd ask, as she coaxed him gently back to her little hearth.

If the weather was kind the crossroads was the meeting point at the weekends before taking to the fields. If not, there was always Larkins or Hewart's hayshed, though the big beech tree in the playground was equally popular once Coogan had passed on. The neighbouring kids could be relied on for fun and games though there was always something bubbling underneath the surface. It may have been the fact their ages matched like gloves or, more likely, the subconscious need to protect their sisters from either party. As fast as the boys were developing the girls were sprouting even faster and were that bit more aware of their blossoming sexuality.

"You couldn't be up to them," Bappy said to Nora as she related the previous evening's episode where her instincts told her something was amiss when she saw a gang of them seated far too quietly under the shade of the crab apple tree half way to the Piper's. Crossing over behind the hedge she arrived in time to prevent an impromptu inspection of the group by their self-appointed physician and nurse.

"We'll leave that to the doctor and nurse if you don't mind," brought the matter to a sudden close as the boys bolted, Kevin shouting, "Rory Fagin had no bacon- he stole a pig and now he's aching," as he ran up the back of the school field.

Sometimes Dolly would call the two boys to have a bite with her crew but it meant staying for the rosary and the trimmings. Nothing was worth that. It went on and on. She prayed for everyone, even the priest who probably needed it more than anyone. The fact that they had just risen from their own family rosary made the ordeal worse. All kind of ploys were played to try to get out of it but she was a stickler, especially if they had already supped at her table.

Mikey and Seamie were passing the time playing up in the rafters while Bullwire and family were having their tea. Suddenly they heard the back door opening and heard her coming towards them. Beckoning each other to be quiet they lay concealed in the attic darkness. Opening the half door she stepped in, did a quick whirl, dropped the knickers and let fly. Only a miracle kept the boys from falling out of the rafters but they bit deep to prevent bursting themselves as she signed off with a polite fart. That was nearly their undoing. Biting hard on their fists and hoping they wouldn't explode they didn't dare look at each other. They would never be forgiven they knew as they watched her hitching herself up before prising a stone out of the back wall. They watched in awe as she pulled out a ten pack of Sweet Afton and lit up with a packet of matches from her apron. The sweet aroma of the cigarette floated up to where they were lying prone, tickling Seamie's nostrils forcing him to almost choke while repressing a sneeze. Fear of being caught kept them quiet. Hearing the kids calling her she quickly stubbed out the half-finished cigarette, placed it in the packet, put the packet back in the cavity in the wall and closed the half door behind her. They couldn't believe it. They had just been party to a series of secrets and actions that they didn't think possible. Few knew she smoked, not that it mattered as it wasn't a crime and it was obvious that not even her family knew of her one failing. The other matter was that of breaking wind. Mother had told them that it was impolite for men to break wind, but for a woman to do so was unheard of. This led to complications at times, as, when the need arose, the boys would disappear suddenly no matter what was in progress. Rex was in on their little secret and the three of them would have tears in their eyes as they made up the craziest excuses to pardon their sudden departure.

"I thought I heard the fox," was one of their favourite excuses and was invariably followed up by a nonsensical retort by one or other of them.

"A fox always smells his own cocky first."

"What are you two laughing at?" Nora would ask but that only added to the nonsense as more stories were concocted to cover their tracks.

Meanwhile, they had managed to climb down from the rafters without killing themselves. As soon as they heard the back door close they were out and gone, thanking their lucky stars they hadn't been caught.

Aodh Goo's Last Hurrah

"The Summer's landed I see," said Tess as Annabel and Seamie dismounted at the bridge sporting shorts and T-shirts. I'll have to look up me swimsuit" she laughed as they ran to greet her.

"That'd fairly make them blink," said Seamie as Annabel handed her some cakes she'd made during domestic class in the convent.

"Don't be giving them to every Tom, Dick and Harry," she cautioned as Tess gave her a warm hug. Seamie was delighted the two of them had jelled so well as he had had reservations initially.

As they supped their tea they filled her in on all the recent gossip and goings on in their young lives.

Seamie had to tell them about the big fight in the playground during lunchtime.

Danny Murtagh, a likeable lad with a propensity for tree climbing, had to help with the milking before school but as his parents were away on business he had to do it all by himself that morning. As soon as he ate his lunch he lay back against the big oak tree and promptly fell into a coma. Aodh Goo was raging because neither of the day's captains picked him on their teams so he was bulling for a row. Being a notorious bully and seeing Danney's outstretched feet he pretended to trip over them. Getting up like a bastard he accused Danny of doing it deliberately. Protests falling on deaf ears, Danny shrugged his shoulders, brushed himself down and turned away. That was just what Aodh Goo wanted. Planting a ferocious slap on his ear he waited to goad him more. What happened next was to change things forever. Known as one of the quietest kids in the school Danny did his usual, turned away and pretended to walk away. Just as the blow was about to land he ducked and came up under Goo's chin with a header few had seen in their short lives. He fell like a stone, completely blacked out. Big Mary ran with a bucket of washing up water and emptied it over the bully to the delight of all. Strong as an ox he came around quickly enough but the fight was gone forever. He climbed over the fence into Farrell's field and never returned to school again. It was more than his pride could take. He wasn't missed. The hero of the hour was carried shoulder high to shrieks of delight from the girls and wild buck leaps from the boys.

Doc was responsible for kicking a new football, a rare treat in those times, into the long grass in Coogan's garden. This was an unmitigated disaster for the school team as it was hard to prac-tice football without a ball. A sudden hush ensued as the inevita-ble outcome transpired. Coogan was stuck to his shed window as usual during playtime and duly appeared from the inner depths with a pitchfork in his hand, wisps of straw stuck in the black belt that barely supported a pair of greasy trousers. Cursing the children loudly he waddled like a duck to the new ball intend on forking it.

More like a scarecrow than a human, as wisps of hay hung from his belt, waistcoat and flat cap, he was avoided at all costs by the schoolkids. Mikey was the captain of the school team at the time and knew that Coogan had destroyed good chances of winning matches before but this was different. He had led his team all the way to the finals but despair was suddenly staring them straight in the face. Powerless to do anything about it, as old Coogan could and would make life difficult, the Master watched from the window to see if the lads could solve the problem for themselves. Calling Seamie to join him Mikey issued hurried instructions. As Coogan neared the ball he heard glass breaking behind him. He turned in time to see the large pane from his shed window fall in smithereens on the ground. Cursing loudly and about to spear the ball his attention was diverted by hearing more glass breaking. This time Mikey took out the tiny top window from where Coogan used to empty the piss pot onto the dung heap in the yard below. A reddish brown stain formed an unusual mural which the kids referred to as 'the pissed mist' which didn't sit well at all when they took to mocking him. It was a two-way sword as one provoked the other with the kids invariably winning out. Red with rage he moved as fast as his wizened frame could carry him. He couldn't see who the missile thrower was but he was determined to punish the culprit at all cost. Roaring like a stuck pig he shouted out names of potential wrongdoers. So intent was he on revenge he failed to see the dung heap until his nose was buried in it. Clouds of flies and dust rose into the air as he tried to extract himself from the foul-smelling manure. A cheer went up as the children saw poetic justice in action. Seamie had by now squeezed under the rusty barbed wire, and grabbing the ball, he lofted it high over the fence into the playground to the delight of all. Justice was done and the lads held the barbed wire high as he scrambled to safety. Handing him the football Mikey announced that he was the Captain for the day, a great honour indeed. Meanwhile, Coogan had struggled erect covered in all kind of shite. Waddling as best he could into the shed he banged the iron door behind him as he disappeared in a cloud of steam. Doherty, trying to save face shouted feeble curses after the scarecrow.

The whistle blew for the end of the lunch break then and the jubilant footballers headed towards the schoolyard where Quigley called his young warriors into a circle.

"I didn't see all of that, boys!" he pretended, "but what I did see was good team spirit. Show that against Sarsfields on Sunday and you'll beat them home."

His words were prophetic.

Coogan never troubled the kids after that, not even when the odd ball ended up right beside his shed. He never threw it back but neither did he prevent the lads from retrieving it. He took to his bed not long after and didn't leave it until he was "waked." He outlived himself according to Babs.

Bappy had enough to contend with besides putting up with Coogan. She was busy being pregnant like most of the other woman in the Parish. Not only did the Church not allow contraception, it dealt a double indignity as well. Sooner than admit the loss of a foetus and thereby benefit from proper medical care, the poor unfortunate had to hide the evidence. Seamie remembered a neighbour sitting on a bed of blood rather than let him see it. There wasn't a sign of it when he returned to the spot a few days later. The evidence had been disposed of. Talking it over with Tess filled him with dread and hatred for a Church that could treat its people so badly. Worse still, as soon as the mothers were up and about after their delivery they had to be "churched" which meant they had to go to the altar alone to beg pardon for being unclean for having given birth! The women hated this rite but were powerless against it.

The situation was exacerbated if the timing coincided with the Missions, the annual spring-cleaning.

Even the sick and dying somehow managed to turn up for the Missions. Everyone knew they were going to get slated one way or another but it was the women as usual who ended up being blamed for all the sins committed. They ground their teeth at the accusations and the blatant incitement of the Missionaries. Fire and brimstone was easier to handle than becoming pregnant yet again.

"Be faithful to your husband," they thundered. "God's Will is to bring children into the world. Let nothing come between you and the Lord," they roared as the men on one knee at the back of the church grinned at each other.

"Jaysus, I'll have to try that out after the hop next week," said Joey Mullin.

"Who'll you try it on? Some poor idiot of a gossoon who'll take your sweets?"

"I'll get you Egan, you can't talk about me like that. I'll get me father after ya."

"And what'll he do, ride his own ass to Colehill Cross."

"That's shocking talk out of the two of you," Big Joe whispered as he attempted to make the peace.

"Listen to the priests and forget your nonsense, shh, here's Fr. Pat, move over there the two of you or he'll have me above at the altar with the Missioners."

Despite the railing and entreaties from the Redemptorists life went on more or less as normal in the parish. The age-old game of pitch and toss drew young and old into the circle at Byrne's shed before and after the mission just as it did for Sunday mass. The missioners were too clever to get involved in a game as old as time, one in which, if the truth were known, they'd love to be taking part in themselves, McGoey once commented.

It was soon after one of the missions that a strange incident occurred that brought wry smiles to many of the parishioners. Close by the Inny and not far from the mill there lived a peculiar old gent who was often seen roaming aimlessly along the riverbank. As thin as a skeleton he seemed to take a delight in frightening folk by suddenly appearing out of nowhere. Of a different persuasion, he was tolerated due to his strange upbringing and even stranger kinsfolk. A landowner, he was incapable of managing what everyone knew was top quality grazing land thus allowing a brother to farm it for him. Human nature being what it was he was soon nearly penniless but for a small pension from the British Army. The theft of some quality roofing beams from one of his outhouses enraged him so much he withdrew from society completely. The straw that broke the camel's back was the appearance of the same timbers on a local entertainment house. Though rarely seen after that, there were reports of spectral figures being spotted flitting around the front lawns after the witching hour. She wasn't surprised when Seamie told her he had just heard that his skeletal body was found hanging by a bed sheet from the upper window of his rambling ruin.

Most of the neighbours attending the wake were there for one reason only, to find out how he died, how much he had left and to whom. The cognoscenti knew there was only one place it would go but couldn't say that of course. There were suggestions he had been hoodwinked and blackmailed but that'd be said anyway according to Fred Concrief.

Few delayed except the hard chaws who knew they'd get a good drop of whiskey, even though the family were parsimonious in dispensing it. Once the Gawk stood up to leave it was time to get on with the proceedings.

Heavy rain drenched the entire area the following day as the locals gathered about the main gate.

As the hearse attempted to reverse in the narrow gateway the taillight caught the pillar of the gate and shattered.

"Oh shite!" the Sliabhín grimaced, "that's not a good sign."

Pretending not to notice anything, one of the bystanders quietly toe-capped the largest pieces into the long grass while the undertaker went about his business. The poor man never looked better it was generally agreed. He was as clean as a whistle, moustache and wisps of hair trimmed and combed, cadaverous jaws filled out with cotton wool, a fleck of rouge to hide the deathly pallor, and dressed in his best Sunday suit he looked ready for the journey. Candles were lit and placed in the ornate holders on the rosewood table at the top of the bed.

"They'll never get that coffin into the room," Johnjo observed when it was realised the body had been waked in a tiny room off the main hall. It was tried but the pallbearers quickly realised it would have to be brought in sideways through the small door. Little was thought of it until Paddy Murray said it would be bad luck to turn the coffin sideways going out of the room, apart from the fact that the body would fall around inside. A mild panic ensued until Kelly, the postman suggested they take the sashes out of the windows and pass it out that way.

"Now you're talking Kelly. Up there for dancing, down there for thinking," Magee remarked. "You can't beat the man with the pencil."

As soon as the sashes were removed the men lined up under the window to take the coffin from those inside. A sudden gust of wind blew the curtains into the room and over the candles. The tinder-dry lace curtains caught fire instantly. Flames shot out the window forcing those standing nearby to dive for cover. Several of the astonished onlookers took flight not knowing what had happened. Moran cleared the ornate fence into the big field and kept running until he reached the sanctuary of the Clynan road.

"Where are you going, what's up?" Concrief asked as he witnessed the sudden commotion from the Crossroads.

"There's a new crematorium in Tenelick, Fred!"

"Jesus, Mary and Joseph we'll all be cremated with him," Cambell was heard shouting inside the room.

"Get outa me way for Christ's sake, the curtains are gone up in flames. We'll all be cremated if you don't do something."

Mulvey was chatting with Mary Dolan when he saw the flames shooting out the window.

"Jesus Christ Almighty, someone should go for the doctor," he said to Mary who was huddled closely under the umbrella with him.

"The man is dead you eejit, he can't die twice."

"I meant if anyone gets burnt or anything, do you think I'm stupid or something?"

"You can answer that yourself," she laughed.

Meanwhile, Murtagh was organising a chain gang to deal with the fire and get the coffin out before it went up in flames.

The barrel of rainwater at the side of the house had never come in so handy. The flames were soon under control and the coffin out with the minimum of fuss.

"Such is life in a rural community," Miss Mills remarked as order was restored and the small group hurried for their cars before pneumonia set in from the wetting they were getting.

"The divil himself will finish the job," whispered the Sliabhínfollowing the hearse as it moved slowly away from the house.

Murtagh dived into the nearest car to save a drowning. Few followed the hearse as it wound its way to the graveyard due to the incessant rain but McCawley's was packed with parishioners, eager to recount the amazing story to all and sundry.

"I'm a long time livin' and I never heard the beat of it," the Piper's father said as he chewed on the end of his dudeen. "There'll be music, song and dance made out of that for sure," McCawley said, as he filled pints of Guinness as fast as he was able.

"Go up to Mulvey for a few bottles of whiskey a ghrá or we'll have nothing for the rest of them when they come back from the graveyard," he asked his daughter as he directed the women into the snug.

"There's more room in the kitchen Ladies. The Mrs will look after you in there where it's grand and warm. That's a whore of an evening, begging your pardon Ma'am he apologised as the principal of the Protestant school came in out of the heavy rain. I'd hate to be looking in at a coffin in that rain."

It wasn't long until the cards were produced and a lively game of twenty five commenced.

A Child's Funeral

Blackie knew the routine and headed for McGoeys instinctively once Fitsimmons hostelry had been passed.

"A bottle of stout would only give me a thirst," was Clarke's reaction as he peddled past as if he had just gotten out of bed.

"I'll have two pints drunk be the time you get into the village," he laughed as he put down the boot, a smile as big as Lough Ree on his finely chiseled face.

"We'll be in as quick as you," the boys shouted after him as Granddad urged Blackie into a light gallop bringing roars of approval from them. They were off the cart and into the grocery just seconds behind Clarke.

"Well boys, how did it go today?" Ned asked.

"Ah, no bother at all today. It'll be harder tomorrow when we have to catch the wet sods," Mikey replied.

"Here lads, help yourselves," he said holding out the big jar of sweets to them.

They needed little convincing. Reaching into the jar Mikey drew out a couple of Peggy's legs asking if they could bring one or two home to little Ann and Paula. Poor Ann couldn't eat sweets because of her illness. It didn't stop her from smiling though. She would chuckle away in her pram as soon as the boys appeared after being away all day. Paula minded her like a mother hen, and like her two brothers, she was devastated when the angels came for the 'special' one at an early age.

"She's with her own," Fr. McCabe told them when he did the necessary before the child was placed in a white coffin and taken to the graveyard on the carrier of Rex's bike. Word spread like wildfire as the neighbours stood by their doors and gates blessing themselves as the cycling cortege passed slowly by. Poor Peryl, overcome with grief, blessed herself and threw a fistful of holy water on the group who quietly acknowledged her noble gesture. Death was never far from the door when proper medication was hard got. Nevertheless, the strongest survived as always even if food had to be rationed due to the number of children clambering for a share.

Unable to show their deep-felt emotion men ran for their bikes in solidarity and joined in behind the now sizeable group.

Fr. McCabe stood waiting by the graveyard gate as the cyclists dismounted, propping their bikes by the roadside wall. It was only a matter of months since he had left Black Jack standing like a statue by the church gate for a scurrilous reference to the Pope and something else about magic. He was still standing there as people filed out of the church an hour later.

"It'll be a gay while before he thinks of crossing Fr. Francis again," Cella said to Biddy as she blessed herself.

"And that's a fact Cella," Biddy replied. "I heard it said he questioned how the good priest saved Jessie's child and it as blue as the sky above. He has the power no doubt and it'll be a brave man as'll say other."

Seamus and Pat took the tiny coffin and walked silently to the plot prepared earlier by Peter Courtney and Pete Mullin. Laying a hand on Rex's shoulder the saintly priest read the rosary and sprinkled holy water on the coffin before the gravediggers started their work.

"The prayers are for us sinners," Fr. Francis said. "That child went straight to God and will be looking after you all as long as you live." Nora will be fine don't worry. Peamount is the right place for her and she'll be well looked after there. You won't find until she's home with you and the kids. As the lads tapped the top of the tiny grave a tear ran down Rex's cheek. A hard man, he took no prisoners but took nothing else either unless it was by mutual consent. Thanking the good padre who had long been a friend he walked him to his car and tried to offer him a sealed envelope. "I suspect there's money in that Michael so keep it as I've less need of it than yourself. Your needs are greater than mine. You have a woman to look after and kids to rear so hang on to what you've got. Is there something else in it?"

"There's a note from Nora. I didn't read it as she wanted no one else but you to read it."

"Keep the money and give me the note so."

A ripple of conversation flowed as they parked their bikes along the railing before filing into Fitzy's Bar. Although not much more than a Shebeen it was very popular and had just recently had electricity installed. Fitzy turned off the radio out of respect as Rex called for a drink for the closely-knit group.

"Sure you mightn't bother Rex," was the usual reply when asked their preferences. "A bottle of stout so if you please," meant good manners were adhered to even if one was as poor as the next.

"God bless all here!" brought them pivoting on their heels as the priest's soft voice broke over them.

"Jaysus! You too Father," Clarke stuttered at the unusual sight of a priest in a pub, especially this one. "Sorry, sorry Father, I didn't mean to take His name in vain," he gasped at his unfortunate faux pas.

"He'll not be hard on you Jim. Don't worry about a slip of the tongue. We're all human."

"I'll look after that Mr Fitz," he added as his gaze swept the room. "And you might as well add another in the name of God on this sad day," he advised as he stood beside Rex.

"You'll have something yourself Father?" Fitzy queried in a reverential tone.

"I'll have a lemonade to take with me if you have the like."

He knew only too well that his delicate stomach wouldn't be able for the bacteria attaching themselves to the edge of a glass half-washed in a rinsing bucket. Though close by the river the joys of running water had yet to flow in the old-world shebeen.

"Your blessings will come quickly Mike," he promised. "I just popped in to wish you all well and to say the Church is with you on this saddest of days." He was gone before anyone got their breath back leaving a bemused group and a fiver on the counter that would wet several whistles before the day's work was done.

"You put the two of them in it there, Clarke," Rex said as he heard the Morris Minor departing.

"How was I to know it was himself," Clarke blushed at the thought of his taking the Lord's name in vain in front of His disciple on earth.

"Mind that money Fitzy," Rex cautioned when he saw the two shadows slipping in by the back door.

"It's as sound as a bog sally Rex. It'll do the job it was meant for," was his measured reply.

A huge plate of ham and cheese sandwiches soon appeared on the beer-stained counter.

"That's for the mourners," Fitzy said as he fixed the two late entries with a knowing gaze. His right hand man 'Red Biddy' read the scene expertly as soon as she heard there was a crowd gathering. The bush telegraph was primed to perfection and soon had her in the back kitchen preparing a heap of sandwiches.

"Give them a couple of bottles," Rex said as he saw the look on their faces. "It's an ill wind that doesn't blow someone some good," he nodded to the boys.

"Wisha Rex, you're the besht of the bunch and me heart goes out to you so it does," sniggered the Slíabhin as he tested the waters for a worthwhile drink. "Any man as loses a cratur afore it walks is blessed be the Man above."

"And what would you know about childer seeing you never had one? You're too miserable to keep anyone but yourself," Rex blasted back at him. "Look at the cut of you. What happened to you anyway?"

"It's easy for you to laugh Rex. Weren't we on the bog all day?"

"Looks like that all right. Could you not tidy yourselves up a bit before you came in?"

"With what?" he asked. "I hadn't time to go in ta Brady Browns if ya want to know. We don't have people sending us bags of stuff every day and that's the holy all of it," he said as he tightened his torn overcoat across him. The reference to Mrs McCormack didn't sit well with Rex.

"Well, I'll be off so if ya don't mind."

"Didn't the Nuns give you a heap of stuff not long ago? You needn't be putting on a show for me me boyo. I know you only too well. If everyone had their own you'd have less."

"Aye and your crowd would have less too if ye weren't involved with Brady and his gang," he threw back as he turned away.

As he made to move away he felt an iron grip on his wrist.

"Don't start that fucking crack with me Slíabhín or you'll wake up with your ancestors."

"Ah don't be like that Rex. I was only giving as good as I got, but sure I forgot the day that's in it and God's truth me heart goes out to yourself and your little woman. Ye have a pure angel lookin' after you now and maybe she'll be able to help the likes of me too. Shure wasn't I oney going to tell you sumthing about 'the Crutch' but you mightn't be interested at all."

"Out with it and stop beating around the bush like the rest of them."

"I'll tell you all about it so if you give me a drink. I have a fierce thirst on me after the bog."

Fitzy caught the nod and put a pint bottle of Guinness in front of him.

"Blessings a God on you Rex," he said after taking a huge mouthful. "I needed that better than me dinner. Wasn't I passing the way the other day when I saw the Crutch' hopping over the wall behind the Abbey and I said tomeself 'now what would a man like him be doin' adin there? As soon as I turned the corner I hid me bike and hightailed it back so as I could see him without him seein' me. I hid down behind the ould wall and as sure as I'm here, didn't he disappear before me eyes with a bag of something. I had to hide adin in the boultree bush in case he'd come out of nowhere. You won't believe this but as quick as you'd bless yourself didn't he pop up beyand the other side of the road with the bag still on his back. Now there's only wan way he could have done that and that was to go underground. Now there's sumthing for you Rex- a man keeping all that to himself and he having more than enough as well," he shook his head at the thought of anyone doing the like.

"It was a good while after he was gone because I was afeared he'd return, when I slipped into the abbey and spotted where he had been working and where he had covered over his tracks. It didn't take me long to clear away the stones and there in front of me own eyes was the secret tunnel that we all heard about long ago but could never find. Well, I covered it back up as quickly as I could but didn't I spot this which I think might be worth a bob or two."

With that he fished out what appeared to be a copper brooch that seemed to be fairly well preserved.

"He dropped that somehow I imagine," he said, all the while keeping a weather eye on Rex. "Would it be valuable?" he asked knowing Rex had more than a passing interest in the like.

"It might, mind you, but I'd like to see where the tunnel goes first. Not a word to a sinner until we have a good look around or I'll be dug out of you. I'll be doing a few weeks work fixing the windows soon and I'll have a look around if you're interested in dropping in by chance," he winked. Meanwhile Fitzy read the situation perfectly popping another bottle in front of the Sliabhín.

"Sound as a sally Rex!"

"Not another word to the world."

Content that he had looked after his business he beckoned to Fitzy to settle his bill.

"All done Rex, taken care of by the good priest himself. 'Better to have a friend in court than two in hell' as they say. Safe home now, I won't be long after you meself. As soon as I put the run on the stragglers I'll hit the hay for tomorrow is another day and with a bit of luck better than this one for both of us."

"G'night all," he waved as he lowered his head going out the back door for fear of a late night visit from the squad from Longford. T'wouldn't do to have to let the Sergeant win his hard-earned collection now he thought. For win he'd have to let him or he'd be the worst in the world after robbing him at the cards in Tashinny only a few months earlier.

"Give to God what's God's and the divil sweep the rest of them," he thought to himself as he threw his leg over the Raleigh and headed for home.

No sooner had he gone than Clarke excused himself saying he had to go home or there'd be no milking done in Cloghan.

"God help the poor cows so!" said the Monkey as he nearly fell off the high stool laughing.

"Fuck the lot of you so. You'd think they'd milk themselves."

Little did they know the Monkey had been listening into the earlier conversation between Rex and the Slíabhín. Clever as a jailor, he slipped out without being spotted and headed across the graveyard to investigate the story. If he could only get his hands on the monk's long-lost treasure he'd be set up for life. Though he never had much he always had enough. His wizardry with the women and at the pitch and toss kept him in more than beer money. The luxury of a late night visit to a parlour of pleasure was his one motivation. Proud of his prowess in this field of fancy he rarely paid and never went hungry. Nevertheless, he made ends meet in his own inimitable fashion.

Never a mean man, he knew his strength and depth was much appreciated by those who valued such attributes Nor was he lost for female followers. Oft quoted, some said he lent length to passion where mere mortals failed to follow. Though never verified, or so they say, he was said to have plunged deep into the face bank in the interest of science when times were hard or colours were flying. "Devoid of bacteria" was his proclamation on being quizzed on the merits or demerits of the situation. "God gives for good reason," he was wont to say when asked if he'd approve or disapprove.

As Clarke had left earlier in order to be home for the milking it didn't occur to the Monkey that he might have been on a similar mission. Forgetting that a new grave had just been dug for Maggie Coutey, Clarke had fallen headlong into it. Try as he might he couldn't get out of it as it was over six foot deep. "Bad cest to P Coutey and his big spade" he swore as he prepared himself for a final leap. Despair gripped his heart as his fingers clung at straws before giving way as he fell back with a thump into the darkness. Half Christian, half pagan, he resigned himself to Mother Nature and promptly fell asleep dreaming of tunnels and dungeons that led to the strangest places. He found himself wandering from one labyrinth to another until he came to the junction that led under the Inny to Byrne's on the right and O'Connell's on the left. He decided on the left fork because of his fear of water. Then all hell broke loose.

As with most bars and dens of iniquity the secret became the profit of all. Fitzy was up to speed by now as the walls shared their secrets and the shadows spoke volumes. Years of babysitting the blind told him more than any oracle could. If he couldn't gain from it he'd be part of it and so it was. The stragglers gathered around the front door felt the full force of Lucifer as shouting and roaring rose from deep within the graveyard. Such wailing as would raise the dead sprung from the depths.

"Ah suffering Jesus it's the end of us all!" cried the Slíabhín as he ran for his bike only to fall headlong into the quick with fright. Grabbing the pitchfork and the yard brush Fitzy handed them to Seaneen and Mattie and leapt to the fore like a revolutionary of old.

"Follow me lads," he urged as he stepped over the low wall and into the cemetery. Fuelled with false courage the stragglers followed him at a respectful distance, each stepping back out of politeness to let one another follow Fitzy in an orderly fashion. Their false courage soon deserted them when they heard weeping and wailing that hadn't been heard since the Vikings put the monks to the sword. Suddenly, a vision of two savages appeared shouting and roaring before them. Fitzy stood his ground but the others took flight and would still be running were it not for a burst of laughter from the Monkey and Clarke. Realizing how comical the situation must have looked their sense of the absurd rose to the surface and took the fear out of the situation. Clarke told them he was taking a short cut home when he fell into the open grave. Unable to get out he lit a fag while considering his situation. There was nothing for it he thought only wait for the morning which wasn't far away now either. Sitting back he promptly fell asleep and would still be there were it not for the fact that the Monkey fell in on top of him a short while later. Certain he had died and gone to hell Clarke made one final effort to elude Old Nick thinking it was he who had come for him. With one last desperate effort he leapt onto the Monkey and clear out of the grave. Scrambling to his feet he was astonished to hear the Monkey's voice coming up from below. Cold sober now, he realized the Monkey had fallen into the same trap as himself and it was he who was whimpering for Old Nick not to take him this time.

Promising to share the spoils if his soul was saved for longer he cried like a Banshee. Looking down at his terrified face Clarke burst into uncontrollable laughter before reaching down to pull his bewildered companion from the jaws of hell.

As they stood together beside the ogham stone the hilarity of the situation gave rise to a thicker plot. In a few seconds they hatched a plan to give the lie to the truth.

Deciding to play the Banshee rather than admit their stupidity they agreed on a more devious plan which would further their cause and keep the nosy from venturing near the tunnel until they had time to do so themselves.

"We were beyant in the ould Abbey when we saw strange lights coming from where the tunnel is supposed to be and decided to dally over behind the wall where we wouldn't be seen," said Clarke. "And declare to John the Papist didn't the two hooded figures walk clean through the wall with sacks on their backs."

"Well, we took to our heels and like two proper eejits didn't we miss our footing and fall back into Couty's new grave. What they had to go and dig it there for is beyant me. Thinking it might be the safest place to be for a while we hid in the shadow until we heard ye coming and nothing would do Clarke only act-the-fool as usual. Well, I agreed too I have to admit. No good pointing the finger when your own is stuck up your arse," he guffawed as the open-mouthed crew threatened to throw the two of them back in again for frightening the bejasus out of them.

Getting Ready

Pints of porter were being pulled by the new time as gangs of thirsty workers kept filtering in.

"You'd think there was going to be a drought or a strike above in James's Street laughed young McGoey as he carted out a tray of porter for each table."

"Damn thirsty work," the Master quipped as he watched aloof while pretending to be reading his newspaper.

The boys were amused knowing there'd be no hurry on the men that evening. Tomorrow was another day and it could look after itself.

"Well Clarke, are you ready for it?" Rex asked as he pointed to the empty glass and nodded at Teddy to fill another. Recognised as the finest sleánsman in the county when he was sober there were few who could keep in to him even after a hard night of it. He was as natural with a sleán as a drover with a blackthorn on the way to the Mart in Ballymahon.

"If he was born in Tipp or Kilkenny he'd have been some hurler,"

Tom Fitz said as he helped Teddy with the pints. Pete Ledwith was losing the rag playing patience in the corner while Quigley was sitting over by the front window reading the Irish Press and keeping one eye on everything as well. Few knew he had a glass eye because it married so well with the good one but he gave the game away in a fit one day and frightened the daylights out of all his charges.

"It was amazing how he managed to see so much," Peter Courtney remarked when he saw him picking up the change from the counter.

Toss Mullin strolled in laconically just then, his waders around his knees, fly rod over his shoulder and a brace of salmon sticking out from his satchel.

"Any luck," asked Pete pretending not to notice.

"Divil the much apart from these two," he replied as if it was an everyday occurrence. "I hooked a big one but it went in under a tree at the aqueduct and snapped my line. I'll get him again though."

"Not if he sees you first," Seamie piped up to roars of approval from the others.

"Ah young Seamie is cutting his teeth! We'll see how lively you'll be tomorrow after a few wet sods in the kisser," he smirked as he pretended to enjoy his own joke knowing full well he had been beaten to the punch.

"Out of the mouth of babes," Quigley quipped good-humouredly. It was lost on Toss though. "Feckin' little know-all," he said as he went out to the lounge where some of the visitors might be more amenable.

"Which of you is going to get the water?" Grandfather asked.

"I'll get it," Seamie volunteered as he jumped off his bike and got the big bucket. He could hear the others chatting as he crossed the stile into the field. Though he thought he knew exactly where the well was he was unable to locate it. There was no well to be seen. He remembered his father and brother going across that stile and knew it had to be here somewhere. But where? Thinking they must have got it from the stream he filled the bucket, wrapped the plastic bag over the top and tied it securely before taking off after the others. It wasn't fool proof but it would help to keep most of the water from spilling as he rode gingerly along the deeply rutted lane. Small groups were busy unloading bog barrows and tools while others were tending fires or checking water channels, one of the most important aspects of safety according to his Grandfather. Everywhere he looked he could see movement, people arriving on bikes, sitting high on iron-shod carts drawn by mules, horses and donkeys with the odd Massey Ferguson chugging away here and there. The dry morning got them all out early, he thought to himself as he passed Jimmy Connell's gardens. The little shopkeeper who went around the houses with his van full of groceries, was feeding a few calves in the haggard alongside Askey Boreen. Good husbandry by generations of his family had reclaimed soggy bog land into a fertile island where crops of potatoes, carrots and onions grew faster than on many a farm. His ability to cross seeds in the fertile bog land was already legendary and brought a steady stream of buyers for the lettuce and cabbage plants as well.

"How's the young footballer?" he shouted as Seamie passed by. To which salutation the youngster responded warmly with "Never better Jimmy, I'll be pulling them out of the clouds shortly."

"No doubt you will gossoon, do doubt you will, but don't take your eye off Clarke for a minute or he'll leave scraws in your ear," he advised knowing full well the tricks that particular gent got up to.

"Don't worry Jimmy. Tess warned me about his tricks. She also told me how to cod him too so we might have a draw before the day is out," he laughed as he remounted carefully not wishing to spill the precious bucket of water.

The forest of ferns by the roadside were as tall as himselftherebyhiding many of the groups scattered across Askey bog and beyond to Cíol Fíor Uisce, the fort of clear water. Knowing Grandfather would be curious as to who was early and who was late he stood up on the pedals to get a better view. The Dolans, Courtneys, Cahills, Mulveys, Mitchells and Butlers were well ensconced by now, some even having camp fires going in preparation for the first break and breakfast. Teatime at ten meant everything to everybody on the bog. It meant a respite from the hard work, a chance to warm the hands from the sopping sodsas well as providing fuel for flagging energy in the early morning chill. For the young it was a chance to walk and talk and they were gone as soon as they had eaten a few hard-boiled eggs and a couple of heels of McNamee's bread, their favourite.

Meanwhile, back at the bog, the boys were keeping a close eye out for grandfather's next move. The moment he stood up they were away, clearing drains like prize jumpers at a gymkhana.

"Good lads. Did you get all the news?" was his first question on their return.

A long and difficult day's work to be done, the boys were back in harness in seconds. The work was too important, too essential, for one of the neighbours to hold another up. That could be done differently and in more cunning ways another time, but this work would lead to good storytelling on cold, wintry nights by the warm glow of the self-same sods.

"Tom Mulvey said his shovel was stolen last night," Mikey gushed.

"It was hardly his own," Rex laughed as he winked at Clarke.

Clarke took up the cudgel then with another rare one about the previous night when he was coming up the road from Maggie Teague's after a feed of rasp and a wink from Molly.

"A nod is as good as a wink to a blind horse," Molly told Nora the following day as she shook her head at another missed opportunity.

"Ah maybe you're better off. Sure he'd only be slobbering on you after a feed of pints," she joked as she took a piping hot soda cake from the oven.

"He wastes all his goodness on the fecking Guinness," she moaned as her sister laughed at her.

"Did he ever shift a woman?" she asked knowing the answer full well.

"He was a boyo in his teens but something happened that turned him off," replied Molly.

"I wonder would it have anything to do with any of the Egans. It's said he got a fierce beating after one of them left the country in an awful hurry. She got married to an older man beyond in England soon after and little has been heard of her since," Nora half asked, half wondered.

"Ah sure wouldn't half the parish be gone if every woman had to go," said Molly as she thought of her own situation.

"There's more ways of killing a cat than drowning it in milk," she laughed heartedly as she changed the subject.

Clarke warmed to his subject when he saw Nugget pretending not to hear him.

"I could have sworn it was Dolan I saw sneaking past Fitzsimons's with a shovel strapped to the bar of his bike. It wasn't his either because I heard him asking Sam Farrar earlier if he'd loan him one."

"Did he not give him one?" Rex asked.

"He told him he hadn't one for himself as he had already loaned out the ones he had."

"The poor man is far too generous for his own good," Nugget pronounced as he spat on his hands and eased himself down the ladder into the bog hole.

"Aye, and wasn't I heading to Colehill after that when I spotted the same bike adin under the widow's window," he said as he tossed a tempter up to Mikey.

"He bet you to it," laughed the Nugget as he slid a haymaker in Seamie's direction. Blessed with peripheral vision, he ducked, but spinning like a top he side-smacked it onto the barrow, raising a triumphal fist as Grandad acknowledged his dexterity.

"Keep some of that for Sunday a mhic," he winked as he tossed a regular one.

"There's work to be done lads if we're to bottom this out before the midges come for their dinner."

Cnocanoir (the hill of gold) stood away across the heather near Williamstown. The De Danann had mined for gold there before they were banished to the Underworld according to the Nugget who knew more than his prayers as Kate Kearney once said of him when he enquired if she still had a longing for the 'Buck.'

"That's for me to know and you to find out," she laughed as she put a plate of rasp in front of him. He was on the run then and knew the last place they'd look for him would be under their own noses. They'd have a hard time finding him anyway as a secret trapdoor led from the cellar to the fairy fort in Lisnacreevagh where even the bravest Brit wouldn't go.

The whole area had a mystic sense and seemed lost in time as the crew eased into full throttle and sods came flying up from the two cutters below. It was a lovely place to be on a warm summer's day Seamie thought, but this was still spring and the cold sods would soon alter his optimistic outlook. Rex was in charge of the wheeling of the turf and had Blackie strapped to the barrow when he arrived with the water. Mikey was laying on the first few sods and turned to greet him. Grandfather saw his opportunity, winked at Clarke and they let fly two sods in rapid succession. One sailed high over Mikey's head but the other caught him flush on the side of the jaw. If looks could kill the two sleánesmen were already dead in the bog hole. Dancing with rage as he brushed the slimy substance from his hair and face with the sleeve of his jacket he glowered at his Grandfather who was roaring laughing at the good of it all.

"Keep your eye on the ball a mhic," he advised the hapless youth.

"What are you laughing at?" he growled at Seamie.

"Nothing, I was laughing at the ass," he answered doing his best to try and keep from bursting out laughing. This infuriated Mikey even more forcing Rex to step in to keep the peace.

"Fill the kettle there a mhic," he advised as they walked out the bank to where a nice fire was glowing in a circle of stones. Blackie grazed contentedly as they filled the kettle and settled it neatly in the centre. As soon as that was sorted he was off out the high bank leaving Seamie attending to the fire and the making of the tea.

"She's ready boys," brought proceedings to a timely halt as the sleánsmen climbed out of the deepening bog hole. Though pushing sixty the Nugget was still able to keep in with Clarke. Clever as a fox he knew when he had enough and needed little persuasion when the shifts were changed. Two hours constant was enough for any man he advised.

"Change like the weather and you'll get the best out of any man," he told Clarke as he took a mug of tea from Seamie and a heel of bread that'd feed half the parish.

"The eggs are done too," the young chef informed them as he transferred them into a ponger of cold water to cool them off.

"Have ye no eggcups," Clarke remarked dryly as he was given a handful of duck eggs.

"You wouldn't know what to do with them," Seamie replied with glee as his grandfather slapped his knee with delight.

There was no hanging around after the impromptu breakfast. The laden skies were heavy with rain and it would only be a matter of time before they were routed from the bog. Leaving Seamie to tidy up they got back to business and soon had sods flying as they got their second breath, keeping Rex tipping it tidily back and forth across the kish to keep into them.

Clarke and Nugget were used to working together and soon had a good rhythm going. The two youngsters stood each side of the wooden barrow and took the sods as they flew off the sleánes before layering them on as deftly as a stonemason. No sooner was the barrow full than Rex was gone out the spread bank having left the empty one for the boys to fill. As usual, Blackie stepped sure-footedly out the soft bank and across the Kish to the high bank where the barrow was flipped over as the animalturned quickly on the rains.

Hour passed hour as the crew kept up a steady pace. A shout went up as the boys spotted their mother swinging in the road on her bike, a basket of goodies on the carrier, and more in the font basket also for the midday lunch.

"Couldn't be a minute sooner Rex smiled as he relieved her of the bike and basket."

"I suppose it's the usual Nora," he remarked as they walked in the high bank.

"I'm not a magician," she answered sharply with a hint of a smile.

"Only coddin' girl," he joked as she made a half-hearted swipe at him.

A quick wipe of the hands with a clump of wet moss took most of the bog dirt away and eased the Nugget's aching fingers. It was well known that turf held little if any bacteria and was often used with bog moss to cover a wound when nothing else was available. However, they all knew Nora wouldn't be happy with them handling food with dirty paws so a quick visit to an adjoining bog hole sufficed to satisfy her strict hygiene rules.

"I heard the Curlew calling as I came over the road," she said to no one in particular. It wasn't lost on them however.

"We'll have rain so!" Rex answered as he shot a glance at the sky. It wasn't long until they were knocking back mugs of tea with hunks of soda bread and a mixture of duck and hen eggs. Nora knew only too well how hard the work was and did her best to provide the food that would keep the energy levels up and the tempers down. That was no easy task either because the nature of the work, the oft-times wet and dangerous conditions, the early morning cold and the sheer drudgery of the hours of monotonous toil was enough to test the patience of Job.

However, on a fine day with a full belly and the crew revelling in the constant repartee, it was as close to a pleasure as one could expect under the circumstances.

"I mind the time my sister Agnes was crossing the fields to Knockagh with the bit of grub for myself and the brother," the old man began.

It was a heavenly day with nature full of itself as she came to the point where she used to cross Tess's river. As bad luck would have it the two planks had been washed away by the recent flood and there was nothing for it only wade through the stream or jump it. It wouldn't have been her first time either but being well on the way she had to think twice before risking the unborn. Hanging the basket on the end of a fallen branch she stretched it safely across. Then standing well back before taking a good run at it she took flight. Despairingly, her fingers clutched at straws as her feet found soft ground and with an anguished cry she fell backwards into the waist-deep water. She didn't say if she lit candles or not, but she hadn't much time for that either because the child had enough of the waiting and decided now was as good a time as any to make an appearance. As fortune favours the brave she coped with the situation as nature ordained, and holding the new-born high, she waded through the stream to find a safe place to exit.

Well, no better place than Tess's river for that either, because just then that little woman, being closer to nature than anyone, was making her way back from Knockagh, and hearing the anguished cry and spotting her friend's dilemma she hurried to pull mother and child from the fast-flowing river. Nothing would do her then but to accompany them and see them safely to where Mrs Connell or Farrell would be only too delighted to look after the new arrival. Meanwhile there was mother and child to attend to so, needing no advice, they both stripped to the pelt. Being a soft day they weren't unduly worried. Tess handed over her slip to wrap the child in and as much as she could spare of her other clothes so that both would have enough to preserve their modesty. As soon as they reached Knockagh they were hurried indoors to a blazing fire where they were mollycoddled like chicks with a clocker.

"Now there's a story for you!" Granddad said as he kept one eye on the heavens.

"I wouldn't be at all surprised," he grimaced as he thought of the work to be done before the leaden clouds burst and left them running for shelter. "We'd better tear into it so," he advised as he eased himself up and strolled into the little copse of Sallys and Elders that afforded shelter and privacy for one's necessities.

"Get out you fucker you," brought the crew to their feet as Smullin burst from the shelter and out the bank as fast as his two legs could carry him.

"And you ya cunt you if you know what's good for you," he shouted at the Briar who took off through the undergrowth like a young bull.

"That put the wind up on them," he remarked as he joined the gang around the fire. Not knowing what had just taken place they were agog with interest and began firing questions like Vincent Gill himself.

"It's a strange oul world childer," he said shaking his head. "Them two cunts should be locked up as they're a danger to humanity. I caught them lying beyant in the clump of ferns. At it good o they were. It's a pity I didn't have the spade with me or I'd have hopped it on the hoors, begging your pardon for the rough language Nora."

Saying he'd explain later, he finished another mug of tea before lowering himself down the makeshift steps and tearing into it like a man possessed. Clarke had no option but to do likewise knowing the Nugget was not to be tangled with in this state. Up above, the boys were fielding sods by the new time wondering what had gotten into everyone. Rex signalled that it would soon blow over because his father couldn't keep up that kind of pace for long. He was right.

"Put on the kittle one of you or I'll be dug out of this bog hole," he exclaimed as he wiped the sweat from his brow with the back of his hand.

"Done," said Rex as he flicked the rains and steered Blackie out to the high bank.

He growled for an hour afterwards as he was visibly shook by his encounter in the bushes. "There's no place sacred any more with the likes of those two fuckers watching gossoons like women," he confided later as they were supping pints at the bar in McGoeys.

The rumble of thunder in the distance brought a sudden end to the day's endeavours. Loading up as fast as they could there was no time wasted getting out of the bog.

Forked lightning flashed around them as they darted into McGoeys just as the heavens opened. With Blackie safely tethered in Rooney's shed Rex came in after them as a fierce clap of thunder lifted the boys out of it.

"It's nothing lads," McGoey laughed as he handed them a couple of Peggy's Legs and a Macaroon bar as well.

"Don't pay a blind bit of heed to it lads. It'll be over in an hour and you'll get home dry," he predicted.

The bar filled up rapidly as the storm forced everyone to shelter where they could. Most made it to one or other of the bars depending on their usual custom. It wasn't long until the banter started and the big story of the day brought a good card school around them.

"I'll catch up on the hoors later," Rex promised as he knew a couple of thumps would keep them well removed from the young lads.

"It might and it mightn't," Clarke cautioned as he told them in confidence about the time they had accosted him and seemed to relish the beating he gave them. "Two fucking perverts is what they are," he added. "And not the only ones around the parish either I suppose you know?" brought quizzical looks from those seated around.

"Aye, there's a few more of their type around but harmless enough compared to those two beauts", the Buckalero added.

The hare being well risen now, a few onlookers began to offer their tuppence worth in the hope of being let into the game of stud.

It was just what Nugget and Rex were angling for. The Buckalero read the signs like a psychologist and stirred the pot like a well-trained apothecary.

"Grab their interest, suck them in and clean them out," they laughed later as the counted their winnings at the Crossroads before parting for the evening. Although it was well past teatime Nora had everything ready as soon as she heard the iron shod wheels coming up by the school. Blackie sensed home now and his feed of carrots. He wouldn't tolerate much of a delay they knew, so leaving the old man dozing, they clicked the animal onwards. As good as any well-trained dog, Blackie broke into a light trot keeping close to the hedge as he tipped along.

"A sight for sore eyes," Peter Cassells told the Brink later. As he was about to mount his High Nelly from the spudstone by the bull field gate he heard the crew coming. Mounting quickly he followed them home to Ballynamanagh marvelling at what a well-trained animal could do. Margaret was waiting at the gate with the bunch of carrots when they arrived.

"You need have no fear of that animal Ma'am."

"We wouldn't want to be waiting for the men to make it home on their own," she laughed as she helped the Nugget from the cart.

Bosque Well

St. Sinneachs well bubbled out under the oak tree on the road opposite Taghsionad Graveyard and supplied the water for the baptismal
and water fonts in the surrounding churches. Bosque well, which was
down at the bottom of Harrys Field in an place known as the Giant's
leap, supplied most of the drinking water in that area. Both were crystal clear but Bosque, though shallow and near the surface, rarely ran
dry even in the hottest summers. The big flat stone that almost covered the circumference served as a seat when the kids were on their
travels through the fields. It was alongside a huge flattened Rath few
people in the parish knew anything about until it showed up clearly
when spotted and photographed from the air during a fly-over by a
slow-moving East German Stasi spotter plane in the 80's. Looking
more like lazy beds than a Rath it may have been used as such during the famine of 1845 to 1850 but it hadn't attracted attention as yet.
Tess's river flowed past this point and a good trout could be caught in
the sandy depths if one had the right equipment or knowledge.

Sitting back in her comfortable sugán chair she listened intently as Seamie filled her in on the latest news.

She knew he often brought home pinkeens from the river. These little fish were perfect for big game fish like pike, bream and tench, as well as salmon and trout. They would be kept alive in one of the water barrels beside the turf-shed and scooped out for the weekend fishing as well as making a delicious sandwich if combined with the bitter sweet taste of watercress. The watercress and pinkeens could be used with a salad during summer being perfectly complimented with a mug of buttermilk and a slice of his mother's or Tess's soda bread. Nora's rasp was special but it was time consuming and disappeared all too quickly especially if the boys were hungry. Most of the country folk made rasp and potato cake as they were easy to make and the ingredients were almost always available, potatoes, milk and flour, and, of course, the ubiquitous pinch of salt. The traditional breakfast of bacon, egg and sausage became a feast when rasp or potato cake was added. This invariably occurred on Sundays and special occasions such as birthdays and feast days. Boxty was slightly different in so far as other ingredients such as vegetables and meat could be added too. When finished, it resembled a pancake and was often described as such.

Tess had her own recipe. Her rasp was made from goat's milk in which she added water from the stream lending it a slightly piquant taste and a disconcerting colour. The end result was green rasp that made his stomach churn the first time she offered it to him. He had to rush out the door and add it to the rockery by the side of the house where it proved super-effective as a fertiliser for her roses and multi-coloured geraniums. He soon developed a liking for it though as it was an acquired taste, just like buttermilk, which had taken him ages to get used to. The fact that there was precious little else to eat if he wanted to stay a while longer to hear her stories also helped his taste buds develop along unconventional lines. This meant spending quality time with the old lady. As dusk fell he would light the candle for her, and on the odd occasion the oil lamp if she had any oil. The area around the waterfall and the going-in of the bridge was a trap for all kinds of flotsam which, when dried out in the garden or in the corner, kept a good fire going. He took it on himself to be the great provider, often leaving big bundles of sticks and cipíns to keep her warm during the long cold winter nights. She often slept in her armchair by the fire if the weather was cold and the nights brought on severe frosts. It was strange he thought, that he never detected an unpleasant odour from her despite the fact that she never seemed to wash other than her fairy face. He did his utmost to make her little habitation as comfortable as possible but it was almost 'saothar in aisce' (labour-in-vain), as the rain did it's damnest to get through the poorly thatched roof and into every nook and cranny. He stuffed handfuls of dry straw and rushes into every spot he saw light coming through.

"You'll smother me altogether a mhic," she'd often say as he endeavoured to keep the chill of the winter from her old bones. Remembering there was loads of used plastic fertilizer bags in Hewart's shed, which also housed the engine oil for tractors, he packed them tightly with rushes that he cut with a scythe he had found in a disused outhouse in the haggard. Baling twine bound tightly around a bag of rushes also kept the icy blasts from whistling under her front door. Though persistent heavy rain still managed to pour down the inside of the walls at times they were fairly happy with the patchwork. A small channel he had excavated between the flagstones led under the front door and down the garden to the stream where it joined the winter water surging to the Inny. There was no other door but she always referred to it as her front door.

"It's like a new house," she remarked as he inspected the recent improvements.

"You won't know yourself Tess. You'll have to have the Missions," he laughed as she made a face at him. The Church, other than the saintly Father McCabe, showed precious little interest as they were too busy calling on the big houses or anywhere else they could get money. Fr. McCabe helped occasionally but he had many demands on his charity especially from the Tinker folk. Passing by in his little Morris Oxford one day he saw Seamie crossing the style into her yard.

"Is Tess within Seamie?"

"Say I'm not here Seamie," she whispered from the back of the door.

"She's gone over the field I think. Will I call her?"

"No don't bother. Give her these few things for me. I'll call another time when she's more disposed towards me," he winked.

"Thanks Father, she'll be glad of them."

"Call in to me one of the days if you have time because I have a few things for you and your brother."

"Thanks Father, I will."

As soon as the coast was clear she was out like a shot to see what he had left.

"Sorry Seamie, I wasn't ready for him and I didn't want him to see me with my hair down," she smiled as they inspected the big paper bag.

"There's enough here to do you a week Tess."

"I'll make a cup of tay and we'll have a bit of Flynn's bread and this lovely blackcurrant jam. Are you in a hurry a mhic?"

"Divil the bit Tess, I have something to ask you though."

"Draw up your stool child and tell me what's bothering you."

Her obvious interest in all that happened in his young life made it doubly easy for him to confide in her. He had no secrets with her nor did he feel the need to have any. The recent events in Knockagh had puzzled him greatly. Although he was used to hair-raising stories from both Tess and his grandfather he felt that what had happened the previous Sunday was very different. There were few things that bothered him but the strange feeling that came over him as he walked the plank in the hayshed in Knockagh was high on the list. He felt sure he wasn't hearing things when those unearthly voices tried to force him off the perch onto almost certain death on the rusty machinery far below him. She listened intently as he recounted his strange story.

"Don't be worrying a bit about it a mhic. It minds me of a time long ago when Jack and meself were crossing Knockagh on the way to Edgeworthstown. The wind was rising and the rain forced us into that self-same shed, and you won't believe this, the exact same thing happened to us. We were only a few minutes there when the wind started howling and roaring as if it was the end of the world. Damn the likes of it I ever heard. Well, we got a bit frightened in case the whole shed came in on top of us. Jack said it'd be better to move in under the main roof girders because they were likely to hold even if the rest gave. No sooner had we moved than the most awful screeching and crying surrounded us. If there is a hell then it can't be any worse nor that a mhic. I held up me Miraculous Medal and begged the Blessed Virgin to save us as we were mortally afraid. Suddenly the wind died down and the howling and crying died away too as strange figures flew away out of the shed to the big hollow in the field by the river. It took me a long time to find out why the spirits were haunting the hayshed but I did. An uncle of Simon Keegan who was working for Colonel King Harmon came across some leather-bound documents in the lea of an attic he was repairing in one of the outhouses beyant in the big house in Forgney. Realising they might be worth something he spirited them home and a while later gave them to a brother of Father Pat who promised to check them out. The papers referred to Cromwell's invasion of Ireland and the Midlands especially. Though he spent little time around Westmeath or Longford his special forces did. His two right hand men, Ireton and Ludlow, were responsible for guerrilla activities in areas where Cromwell had no interest, or where he thought there was little to fear. It happened that several groups of the old Irish families such as O'Rahiligh, MacEochegan, MacAogáin, O'Farrell and a few others met up near Lough Sheedon before marching to Knockagh. Word reached them that Ireton's group was passing through Granard on its way to Galway, and that it was likely they'd hold up in Knockagh where there was plenty of wild boar and deer to add to what they plundered from the villages along their march. The Irish posted sentries in Ardagh, Legan and Abbeyshrule to keep watch on their march. As luck had it Ireton's advanced guard headed for Knockagh where they intended to rest up for a few days before passing on to Lanesboro where they could ford the Shannon. Waiting until they were bedded down for the night in the hollow, the locals descended on them with a vengeance seldom seen in the Midlands. Putting most of them to the sword they spared a few to tell the tale. Their success brought a terrible revenge from Ireton and his Scottish mercenaries. Rounding up every woman and child they could find they savaged them before putting them to the sword in the same hollow. It's said that their cries and screams could be heard for miles. It's a savage spot Seamie where nature itself laments the loss of its innocent ones. I'd give it a wide berth if I were you. All we can do is offer up our prayers for the poor souls." Tears flowed down her cheeks as old memories flooded back.

She had a thousand stories and loved telling them. It was a pity she often said, that nobody wanted to listen to such stories any more. They were all so busy running here and there they had no time to stop and have a chat. The odd one that did only stayed a few minutes before getting fidgety when she started to tell them a story about the fairies frolicking under the bridge, or dancing on the foam when the stream was in spate.

"Well I like them Tess. I heard Mother telling Mrs Murtagh that you made one of the tinker kids very sick one time. How did you do that? Was it the power of prayer or what?"

"Not at bit of it a mhic! I saw the gossoon eating the berries of that little tree beyond and I knew he'd be sick in a minute. Sure enough he was. The timing couldn't be better thank God as Oul Maggie thought it was down to me. God has strange ways of working child and if you keep your wits about you you'll be able to best the best of them. Look at Mr Fox and Mr Hare for example. They're forever up to their tricks. The hare spends most of his time giving a wide berth to the fox except in March when the fox wouldn't look the side of the fence the hare was. I've even seen the fox laughing to himself while the two hares were boxing. Fun and games is what it's all about child. Learn from them and you'll have nothing to worry about."

"I thought as much but I didn't want to say anything."

"Just as well child as what they don't know won't bother them."

"Have you another one Tess?" he asked knowing full well it was grist to the mill for her.

"I was thinking of a few lines of a poem coming back from Abbeyshrule the other day and I began thinking you might be better at it than me."

"Gosh, I doubt that Tess but I wouldn't mind having a go at it if you were to give me a hand."

Setting a target of a week to produce something worthwhile they parted company for the evening.

Lying in Wait

Just passing the time until college was ready he wasn't about to waste valuable time either. His new bike got well broken in as he sped the road to Annabel's open arms. Besotted with each other they used every trick in the book to be together. Knowing they were being closely monitored they bided their time.

It wasn't easy for them either. Normally comfortable together the thought of being away from each other for so long made her nervous and him awkward.

Her door was kept open as her mother requested but that hadn't been a problem before. It was now. Somehow, he felt her mother would arrive out of the blue and catch them smooching. Neither of them wanted that to happen because they knew it would put an end to everything. Up to now they were considered just school pals but nature being the way it was they felt sure her mother would fear their imminent departure would push them closer together. Sure enough, steps on the stairway signalled Allison's approach. Adjusting their clothing they stood talking by the window while gazing over the fields to the valley of the Mass Rock.

"How are my two young lovers," she laughed as she entered the room. It was a throwaway phrase but enough to bring colour to Annabel's cheeks. Squeezing her hand he diverted her gaze, pointing to a fox that was strolling along the perimeter of the Rath in search of lunch.

"Even Mr Fox is afraid to enter the Rath," he remarked to Allison as Annabel relaxed and hugged her.

"It doesn't stop you though Seamie," she laughed as she remembered the stories he had recounted of his hideout in the cave deep inside the Rath.

Tess had taken him to different Raths where not even animals wandered when hungry. He soon learned to shake off his fears as the old lady showed him why the animals usually avoided the overgrown interiors. It was a place where badgers hung out. Their huge burrows and rank cesspits were best avoided for fear of broken limbs and possible attack. Everyone knew the badger was deadly when cornered. Stories were told of their ability to lock their jaws onto a leg or arm until the bone snapped. The only way to make them release their grip she said was to snap a branch. He prayed he'd never have to resort to that.

"Animals are not stupid Seamie," she'd caution as they gingerly stepped around the clearly marked areas. Little grew there except noxious weeds and blackthorns whose barbs were capable of inflicting deep puncture wounds and debilitating tetanus too.

"Always best to give them a wide berth," she warned.

She didn't need to elaborate as it was only recently they had learned that Bilsheen had been so affected while hunting rabbits in a similar fort. Laid low, he couldn't play football for weeks and lost a power of fitness in the process. The story of his misadventure spread rapidly and reinforced the fear in people's minds. Nevertheless, with patience and care, Seamie forged a secret path to the cave where he spent hours daydreaming of far-flung places like Timbuktu and Too-womba courtesy of Quigley's passion for geography.

It took him a while to convince Annabel it was safe to follow him to his hideout, but when she did and saw the manner in which he had kitted it out with all kinds of unwanted articles he had sequestered from various outhouses and sheds around the area, she clapped her hands with glee and threw herself down on bags of wool inviting him to join her. He didn't need to be asked twice. Rolling and tumbling like puppies they let it all go as they roamed across the fields, up mountains, down valleys, across wide rivers and into deep canyons where waterfalls washed over them as they dived in and out of gem-filled caves hung with myriads of stalactites and stalactites. Knowing that only weeks were left to them before they went their separate ways brought them ever closer. Promising to wait for each other no matter how long it took or how far removed they were from each other helped console them as they made their way back to the river's edge.

Tess thrived on superstition. Her knowledge of nature allowed her passage to places few would dream of. Her cures lay in her knowledge of shrubs and plants that grew in the dense undergrowth of the Forts and Raths around the area.

Her collection of naive poems captured every vestige of how she used Nature to her best advantage. He laughed to himself when he thought of the encounter between herself and Oul Maggie, the Queen of the Tinkers. Tess beat the old witch at her own game by being more observant and tactful but it was much more than that. She knew nature and knew how to use it to her advantage.

"As plain as the nose on your face," she'd laugh as she explained how best to harness it's powers. She had lived a long life on what was within her reach. Not for her the so-called luxuries lining the shelves in the bigger shops. A half pound of butter and a pot of jam was enough to add to her griddle cakes and potato bread. His mouth began to water as he thought of the bread fresh off the griddle. He could see the butter melting on top and almost reached for the slice she was handing him. He had to check himself in case anyone was passing by just then. He got many a strange look as he went about his business and knew that he was perceived as being a 'bit touched.' But what did they know? They were not party to his other life where Tess toured with him and he with her as they sailed across the evening sky in search of anything wild or wonderful.

Well used to her encyclopaedia of stories he had little difficulty remembering them. Her poems were a different story entirely. Though blessed with a good memory he still had difficulty remembering her home-grown poems.

She wasn't over-happy with his notebook and pencil at first but gave in when he explained that his grandfather had advised him to start writing little stories for himself as ultimately it might lead to some good.

"Wasn't it how our own Padraic Colum started out," he added.

Her poems were earthy and of everyday events and held him spellbound. As soon as she started, he whipped out his pencil and jotted down as much as he was able to while she waxed lyrical about her fantastic encounters.

"Going up be the quick I chanced on a hare
Dancing around in the fresh morning air."
"Good morning dear lady, its early you're out
And what might I ask is your business about?"

"Now, I didn't reply as I waited my chance
To see if I'd rise him to give me a dance
But divil the bit, I'd be waiting there still
If I hadn't to hurry on up to Colehill."

"You've heard of the child so?" he said with a grin.
"And the length we're all waiting for it to begin.
It's a quare day indeed when the fairies in mirth
Dance with the Heavens at a wee laddie's birth."

"True for you sir" I answered right back,
If you had nature adin you you'd jump in me sack
And make a good soup for the poor souls beyant
Or would you rather I hit you a belt of me plant?"

"Now less of that Tess! I'll tell you what I'll do.
Carry on as you are and I'll make you a stew.
But if you don't mind I'll stray from the plot
And get you a game bird instead for your pot.

Drop in on your way from seeing the boy
On account of the colours you saw in the sky.
Tread soft as you step near the cluster of trees
I'll be there with a pheasant, or more if you please."

"That's kind of you sir, I'll bear that in mind
But I've often heard such from those of your kind.
I'll hide in the grass as I've oft done before
And hang him to season behind me front door."

"Whether front door or back I'll hazard a guess
Not many will pull a fast one on Tess.
Let me know how the child is on your way back
For I'd rather be mad than jump in your sack."

"As sure as you're there he was as good as his word.
He had everything ready, even the bird
As I came a strolling down by the road."

Although he tried to jot down her poems as she recited them it was almost impossible because both of them would get carried away with the madness of the moment. He could see himself lying beside her as they waited for the pheasant to walk straight into her arms.

"I think he's coming Tess," he'd whisper in her ear as they lay side by side in the long grass.

"You'd hear the grass growing child," she'd reply with a nudge as they readied themselves for the fray.

At her signal he threw himself on top of the feathered feast.

"Hould him, hould him child," she'd giggle with glee as she danced a jig around them.

"He's a fine bird Seamie. He'll fill the pot for a few days I'll bet. Hould his legs there now 'till I put him out of his misery. You did well there a mhic. He never saw you 'till you were on top of him. I couldn't do better meself and me at it all me life."

The journey home was always hilarious as they talked of the many ways of putting food on the table. It wasn't the first time he realised that Tess was a power unto herself. She'd survive where many a stronger person would fall by the wayside.

He soon figured out that most animals of the fur and feathered kind were as much creatures of habit as humans. It just needed patience and practice to observe their movements. The best time to do that was at cockcrow or as the sun sank away in the west. An early bird too, he was in his element as he rose with the dawn chorus and was off rambling the hedgerows in search of anything unusual, let it be animal or vegetable. Long used to the snare, it became an essential and indispensable tool as he wandered the fields. Experience and Tess's wisdom taught him where to place his secret weapon. It seldom failed and often provided sufficient fare for two houses, Tess's and his. His mother soon left him to his own devices and let him come and go as he pleased. There was little else she could do about it as he had built up an armour-plated aura to shield himself from unnecessary hassle. He could thank the old lady for that. Not only had she built up his confidence but placed an impenetrable shield of her wisdom and magic around him. Although he was grateful for it then it was years later before he realised its full worth.

As summer sped past he used all his available free time to test himself against the wiles of nature. She was a willing accomplice. He began to think she was reading his mind as she was always out and about before him. He'd switch his intended ramble from one area to another but it was saothar in aisce as she only laughed at the good of it. He'd hear her animal impersonations long before he'd see her. His brother Mikey often wondered how he could possibly hear it when it didn't register with him for another five hundred yards.

"You get used to her," was his only explanation.

Though prone to error initially he soon conquered the ins and outs of how she was able to read his mind.

"A game of chess a mhic," she'd say as they ambled along by the bushes lost in conversation. She had such an innocent way of prising out information that you'd never suspect she'd use it to her advantage later.

He smiled when it dawned on him how she was able to 'read his mind.' He began to use her little mannerisms to ferret information from family and friends. It wasn't long 'till they were wary of him and how he seemed able to know what they were thinking or even what they were planning.

He was in charge of his little kingdom and felt in control. It'd be hard to best him now he felt as he went his way as if inspired by the gods.

Although grateful for her many nuggets of wisdom he was at a loss to understand how or why she had picked him to be her protégé.

"A shut mouth catches no flies," often sprang to mind as he remembered her wise counsel.

The Bean Sídhe

It was a wild stormy night when even Billy came in from the raging gale that lashed the house like a cat-o'-nine-tails. On hearing the forecast for high winds and torrential rain Rex and Seamie cycled down to Tess with bundles of baling twine to tie down the thatch. They had already planned to do some patchwork thatching but were waiting on bundles of dried reeds from the Inny estuary. It would be a while yet before everything was ready so it was imperative the existing roof be held in place until the work commenced. It was ages since it was properly thatched but a number of her neighbours had carried out some temporary work during the summer leaving it fairly secure. Nevertheless, a storm would wreak havoc unless it was properly tied down. There weren't many she'd let around the place but Rex, Seamie's father, just like his son, had spent many hours with the woman many considered a witch. Neither father nor son entertained such thoughts, the exact opposite being the case.

They often chatted about her as they fished the Inny and the Forgney River that often threw up surprisingly fine specimens of native brown trout. Rex told Seamie about the salmon and trout he used catch at the waterfall above Tess's and of how she had her own way of capturing them. She had shown him how to take trout from the pools by gently tickling their belly. It was a rare art form which, try as he might, he couldn't master. However, he was adept at nightlines both in the stream and at the point where Tess's river entered the Inny. The only problem was the other lads who were up to the same tricks and thought nothing of poaching from one another. 'Honour among thieves,' Seamie had heard Tomás O'Duinn saying while referring to poaching salmon from the river or a fine cock pheasant from its roost in a neighbour's field.

That started Rex on another story about the time he got married and the difficulty he and Nora had finding accommodation. The world and his mother would willingly have put them up for an apple and an egg but as they were on the short list for a new house they accepted the brother's kind offer of a room in his beehive bungalow at the back of Tashinny. They were very happy there as the two men worked together in Bord Na Mona and Rex had already been promoted to chargehand. There were several spin-offs for those in the know, and being able to organise your own team for footing the turf was one of them. They quickly organised a heap of hardy youngsters to help them in this backbreaking work. It wasn't hard going but the constant bending and lifting was a killer. It wasn't uncommon to see a line of youngsters lying flat on their backs at the tea breaks. Being young however, they quickly recovered and got on with the job knowing the rewards were well worth the effort and pain. Of late, his cousins from Ballynamanagh had begun to join them thereby making the resultant profits even more rewarding as a whole. Uncle Seamus was profitably employed by the 'King', a relation of the 'Potstick's', and was making good money from the government by draining poor land throughout the Midlands. The whole gang worked well together as Seamus's daughters often helped with the turf footing as well as the potato picking in Ballintubber and Knockagh. Needless to say the girls would prefer to be doing anything else, but money in the pocket and half decent clothes were huge motivators at a time when few of their pals could afford anything better than homemade knickers. Only their own would have the privilege of seeing them anyway, Big Mary giggled as she reminded Nualsheen of the previous summer when they were all swimming nude in Lisnacreevagh and were sent packing by the midwife who accused the girls of being 'wanton' in front of the boys. She'd have been better of minding her own business they agreed because she only drew attention to what was normal prior to that.

Leaving Seamie to keep their mutual friend company for the evening Rex continued on to Ballynamanagh to tie down the covers on the new turf reek. He knew his parents would be concerned about the turf getting wet after all the care they had taken to get it home dry. Bill Newman was always sure to oblige once his own turf was safely home. Nothing was done for nothing of course but Bill could be relied on to do a good job at a fair price. There was nothing Bill liked better than an evening's storytelling by the fire in Ballynamanagh.

The cats hung close to the fireplace as the wind wailed like a Banshee outside. Billy's odd chirp from the comfort of the window ledge was answered by Methuselah's occasional hoot from the attic as he thought twice about venturing out on his nocturnal hunt. The lines of baling twine had anchored the thatch well, otherwise Tess and company might have to find alternative accommodation for the immediate future. The swirling wind blew the smoke back down the chimney every now and then forcing them to open the little window despite the heavy rain. Keeping the fire low and the coals burning brightly minimised the risk of a repeat performance.

She was in the middle of telling Seamie about the big blizzard that brought the whole place to a halt a few years before he was born when a loud thumping sound seemed to come from somewhere outside.

"What's that Tess?" Seamie asked as they looked at each other.

"I'm as wise as yerself a mhic," she answered putting her enamel mug on the hob before peering out the window to see what the strange sound might be. The wind was whistling through the big poplar like a Banshee crying.

"There's devilment afoot I'm afeared," she said as she shook her head with annoyance.

"It's hardly the little folk because they're not mad about this type of weather when the souls are stirring and getting restless agin. I'll bet me soul it's your pals who are up to their tricks."

"You could be right Tess because Smiler and the lads said they'd get me back for the fright I gave them last year."

"You could hardly blame them a ghrá. I'd have been thinking the same thing meself if I were in their boots. Quench the candle there and we'll see what they're up to."

You're right Tess. There's Bullwire and Dowler at the corner of the bridge beating two tin basins together. That's what the sound was I bet."

"The fire is low Seamie. Run the bamboo up the chimney with this white sheet and I'll scream like a Banshee and we'll see who the brave soldiers are."

"Done," said Seamie as he quickly tied the sheet to the bamboo and ran it up the chimney. Meanwhile, Tess had opened the little window a couple of inches and as soon as he gave her the signal she let out a blood-curling scream that nearly wedged him half way up the chimney.

"Cheeses Tess you frightened the shite out of me there. Are you sure you're not a real Banshee?" he asked as he gathered his wits about him.

"No point in having it if you can't use it," she cackled as she beckoned him over to the window to see a half dozen lads running for their lives. Snoozer nearly fell into the river as he tried to jump up onto the bridge and had to be helped by Poperty, who, despite being as frightened as the rest, ran back to help the unfortunate. As they got him safely on dry land she let another ear-piercing scream out of her that had them running like mad things up by the Bull field towards the crossroads.

"That fairly put the wind up them," she laughed as Seamie got the fire going again and set the black kettle singing over the flames.

"Say nothing now until wan of them brings it up and you can have another laugh at the good of it. They're hardy boys to be out on a night like this but shure your every bit as hardy yerself."

It was a wild wintry night like this that a sorry story happened above by the Blue Doors she told him. Snow was falling from early evening as it was close to Christmas and the evenings fell faster than apples in the autumn.

She never missed an opportunity to teach him how to look after himself, how to look after the ones he loved and how to learn from the mistakes of others. She used parables like Jesus to light the way.

Talking about a tragic set of circumstances that blighted the lives of those near to him, she told him about a neighbour who took advantage of an innocent abroad, abused her thrust, and destroyed many in the process.

It was nigh on Christmas with snow falling from early afternoon. The children hurried home from school before the cold got into their bones and laid them low for days. Few stirred out except the hardiest of men or those on a mission. The few that did hurried about their business or sat huddled around roaring fires in village bars engaged in idle conversation for want of decent discourse. Perhaps he should have stayed at home tonight he thought? The years were catching up on him and the thought of facing home into the driving snow didn't appeal at all. Hadn't he lots of drink in the house from last Christmas, enough to do him for the rest of his life if the truth were known? There was poteen for a sick calf, the odd cold, sore muscles after breasting hedges or chopping timber for the fire, and several other uses as well. There was sherry there too from the church raffle and a bottle of Crested Ten that'd be kept for the parson's annual visit. That was more than enough for most emergencies he felt sure.

The cards not falling well for him he decided to call it a night and hit the road. Losing didn't bother him much though he'd prefer to win where possible. Known as a cagey player he rarely lost much, but it was the company and the excitement of winning that appealed to him.

Wishing his playing partners a happy Christmas he readied himself for the road and put on his big topcoat.

"If you hold on a while I'll throw your bike up and you'll be home warm and dry," Tommy offered as he was turning up the collar of his overcoat.

Thrusting the pot of jam deep in the pockethe bade goodnight- and left. It was letting it down heavy as he opened the front door and stepped out into the night. Waving to the girl sitting alone in the car with the engine running, he wheeled his bike to the spudstone and started for home. His thoughts turned to the young lassie waiting patiently in the car and how strange it was the way life threw people together. His topboots left deep prints in the snow as he struggled to mount his old bike. Finally, wobbling between the ditches he managed to get his leg over the bar and set course for home. Candles and oil lamps outlined the few houses as he laboured onwards.

It wasn't long till his pals did the same and went their separate ways. Snow covered the country as the old man struggled with the strong gusts that threatened to blow him off course or into the ditch if he wasn't careful. He wished he hadn't stirred out this night and cursed his bad judgement. Passing the preaching house he felt a little more at ease. Near home now, the thought of the warm fire urged him on. He had raked it and covered the embers with ashes to hold the heat and keep it burning slowly so the house would be tolerably warm on his return. Like many another throughout the parish he lived a simple life, one uncluttered by extravagancies or anything more than the pure basics. Unlike Tess he had the few acres passed down through the ages from generation to generation depending on who ruled the country at the time. The British forced many to change or lose what they had. What was religion anyway, a dream, an idea, a marketing tool, a big business? Who knew or cared? He thought little of it. He needed little, the basics, a loaf of bread, a half-pound of sausages, a half-pound of streaky bacon, a pot of jam, a half-pound of Hogg's Amulet, and a pint of Guinness of a night. What more would a quiet man need?

"Look out," she screamed as the old man wobbled and fell in front of them as they turned the road. A sickening thud said he was dead or badly injured and all hell would break lose in a small community unused to such tragedy. Desperate to avoid disclosure they dragged the corpse into the garden and beat a hasty retreat before anyone coming from the village identified them or hit on the horrible truth. Vowing her to secrecy he begged her not to say a word to anyone. She was good at keeping secrets and it paid her to do so. He treated her well, gave her money for sweets and stuff and took her everywhere with him. As soon as she heard the old lady snoring she'd slip into his warm bed backing onto the fireplace. Her own bed was freezing. There were things she's have to do of course but it was better than being stuck in the corner listening to the granny giving out the pay.

It was late next day before a neighbour, who occasionally popped in to check everything was in order, tripped over his body and raised the alarm. Simple science and basic logic soon ferreted out the truth and after severe questioning the hapless girl told all. It took time to sort things out but by then another life replaced the old. The authorities decided nature had meted out its own justice and turned a blind eye as they took the boat to another life, away from the pointed finger and the wagging tongue. The eternal cycle had repeated itself once more.

"That's shocking sad Tess," Seamie said as she finished her story.

"Truth is stranger than fiction child. You can hide but you can't escape from nature," she said as she wiped a tear from her eye.

"That's how life is and we must respect it and be wary of it if we're to lead half-decent lives," she counselled knowing he would do his best.

"Will you be alright going up by the dark trees?" she grinned as he looked wryly at her.

The Midnight Raid

The squad arrived from the town one Saturday night just as a 'heated discussion' had been sorted by Ned. The Sergeant entered by the front door forcing the locals to run for the back door. The two young Guards waiting each side of the back door marched them all back into the lounge. Some of the women protested they were only there because they had no way of getting home as they were waiting on their men. As arranged, the Rookies let them go or stay as they pleased saying no action would be taken on this occasion. It wasn't worth the trouble. Nor did the Sergeant want to get a name for harassing innocent women. Vincent Gill, the eccentric owner/editor of 'The Longford News' would destroy him with a few well-chosen words as he had done with many before. Hell, he could even be shifted to Valentia Island or worse still back to Kiltimagh, where he had recently been promoted. He didn't want either.

"Well, well. What have we here now lads?" asked the Sergeant as he pulled his notebook from his top pocket. "I'm surprised to see a law-abiding man such as yourself entertaining so late, Mr Mulvey!"

"I was trying to get them out Sergeant. You can see for yourself they're all drinking up. I was waiting for the musicians to finish The National Antrim and then they'd be gone."

"I don't doubt you at all, at all, Mr Mulvey. Had you any idea when they might start it though? I thought I heard Mr McLoughlin reciting 'The King of Colehill' as I was at the front door."

"They were just about to start Sergeant. We were waiting for him to finish his monologue, and you can't rush a monologue Sergeant."

"You're absolutely right Mr Mulvey and thanks for correcting me, a monologue it was."

Mulvey paled. It was bad enough being caught but you hadn't a chance in hell if you insulted the Sergeant's intelligence. His survival instincts shot to the surface. He had nothing to lose now anyway.

"You'll have a cup of tea while you're waiting' Sergeant, the Mrs will have it ready in a minute. It's a hardy night out."

"I'll have a bottle of stout so Mr Mulvey. You're right it is a hardy night out."

"Sit down there Sergeant and I'll have them gone in a few minutes."

"Ah no great rush Mr Mulvey," he smiled as he unbuttoned his big coat, hung it on the peg and sat down on a high stool.

"You were playing cards men, I see. Who got the winners?"

"Divil the much was in it Sergeant, It was fairly evenly divided," Rex replied.

"Deal us a hand there so," he said as he pulled up a stool. Chairs that had been quickly abandoned were pulled back around the card table. Ledwith innocently put his hand on Rex's chair and nearly lost it without anyone noticing a thing. Rex's vice-like grip was nearly enough to discourage him from ever playing cards again. He came from good stock though and settled for another chair, even if it was the one he had lost on earlier. McCawley circled round his chair seven times to settle the divil that was under it and then sat down with a contented sigh.

"After you Sergeant," Rex smiled as he pulled his chair up opposite him, careful to keep the mirror on the wall facing him. The 'Buckelero' Dolan sat beside the Sergeant and opposite Rex, but at an angle so he could keep an eye on all the proceedings. Flashing a full pack of Sweet Afton the sergeant endeared himself to the players. Accepting gratefully as they were long out and dying for a smoke they thanked him profusely. McCawley and Ledwith took one as well even though they never smoked in their lives. The lads might want one later when the pressure came on and it wouldn't do to have them at a disadvantage against the Sergeant they reported later.

"Sit down men," Ned said to the two young guards, as he gratefully accepted the reprieve.

"You'll have a mineral or something men," he enquired as if it was an everyday occurrence. They looked over at the Sergeant. He pretended not to notice and went on sizing up his opposition. The two guards nodded in unison. Mulvey gave them the nod to slip into the music lounge. They didn't need to be asked twice. They had been surveying the talent as the chief was settling himself in and knew their chances were good with the uniform and all. You'd never know your luck in a hay barn with the wind rising under the skirting one said to the other as they slipped into the music lounge.

Meanwhile, the Sergeant was feeding out the small talk to test the waters around him. They looked like simple country folk but he knew better than that. Many's the smart aleck had been left sitting on their arse by the same simple people. Wasn't he one of them himself he boasted to his betters. Using his natural intelligence and native cunning he quickly rose to the rank of Sergeant.

His knowledge of the ways of mankind earned him early promotion, and not in the arsehole of nowhere either. Longford was as near to the Big City as he wanted to be for the present. He'd use the promotion and the proximity of the Big Smoke to enhance his experience before applying for one of the plum jobs near Croke Park where he'd get to see most of the big matches by organising his forces there. Yes, he knew the type alright, simple people who'd pull the rug from under your feet before you had time to draw a breath and not a hair out of place.

Mulvey signalled for Packy and The Pirates to start playing once again but quieter this time. A few dancers hit the floor and in minutes the place was as lively as before. The two Rookies soon forgot the Sergeant as they hung their greatcoats on the peg and sat at the bar to watch the talent. The girls from the town gave them the come-on look but it was the quieter, innocent-looking country girls with their averted gaze that tore at their heartstrings. Young bucks sent sparks flying from the maple floorboards as they swung their partners around the big dance hall. It wasn't long before the guards were off their stools asking for a dance. Packy was eying up the talent too as he played a selection of foxtrots and waltzes to keep them swirling. The two Rookies were allowed lots of legroom by those who had arrived by motor just in case they'd ever be unfortunate enough to be observed with no lights or worse still, no tax on their car. The odd good-natured bump was no harm and was all part of the showmanship but they weren't about to step out of line on a night like this.

The Sergeant was enjoying himself as he took another hand and upped the betting a little each time. The good card players bided their time. There was no hurry now that the Sergeant was in full stride and it was safer here than anywhere else. Hadn't they the police to protect them if anything went wrong McCawley laughed as he and Rex relieved themselves in the culvert outside. There was no time for stratagems now either as they heard the Sergeant coming in behind them.

"Grand night men!"

"Bedad it is," Rex replied as he held the metal door open for him. Fresh pints stood in front of the players as they sat down to recommence play. A half power stood beside the sergeant's almost empty glass. He raised it in salutation wishing everyone in the room a good Christmas. Voices joined in unison as those about him wished all belonging to him well. The serious business got under way once more as they settled back into the play.

Though busy as a bee Mulvey kept a sharp look out on all the proceedings in case of the slightest trouble. There was none. Johnjo, a much-respected customer since he and his father had come by a small fortune from the Argentine, kept an eagle eye on everything in the bar while Packy Cambell smoothed ruffled feathers whenever there were any in the Lounge. It was one of those rare nights he confessed to Father Pat soon after when all seemed lost but everything was gained.

Mulvey gave the nod when he saw the Sergeant slipping a look at his watch. There wasn't any point in prolonging matters unduly.

"You'll have to finish up soon lads, it's getting on. Some of us have to work tomorrow, isn't that right Sergeant?"

"Whatever you say Mr Mulvey, you're the boss," the Sergeant said as he pulled in another hand.

"We'll have a game of poker to wind it up so lads, is that all right Mr Mulvey?"

"Whatever you say Sergeant, a round of the house won't take long."

"Deal them yourself so for the last one," Rex urged.

"No, no, go on, I'm only the visitor. I don't want to clean you out altogether."

Rex stripped the cover of the new pack that Mulvey gave him, asked the Sergeant to cut them and then dealt a hand to those around him. Mulvey closed the door to the lounge to lessen the noise. The few customers who had been chatting at the bar and taking a half-interest in the game lowered their voices and turned round to the players. The betting started at a shilling, was raised and went around the table to the Sergeant. He saw McCawley's half crown and upped it another. A few hands were thrown in, four stayed on. People were drifting away from the dancing and heading out the back door. The young guards were having the time of their lives. They were in and out to the hay barn like cocks after oats. The country girls timed their minerals to perfection. As soon as the two guards sat down after a set they were up beside them pretending to get their orders in.

"Here, let me get that," they would say and that did it. A few mouthfuls were gulped down before they hit the floor.

"Will you come out for a breath of fresh air girl? I'm sweating!"

"I don't mind if I do sir, I'm fairly hot myself."

"Tommy's the name, what's yours?"

"Oh, mine, its, its, Mary, no, Bridget, I'm all confused with the heat, sir."

"Come on so Mary Bridget, never mind calling me sir, we'll get a breath of fresh air out at the hayshed."

Mulvey kept the stragglers moving as he sensed a grand finale. It had been a great night and he'd have some story for the PP and the Bishop on Saturday night. Meantime, the cards had to be completed and the house cleared before it got too late.

Rex took the bet and upped it again. Johnny Dolan stayed. Pete couldn't see any merit in a little forest and dropped out. McCawley sensing that Rex was on to something decided to milk it and doubled up again. The Sergeant checked his cards once more, put them face down and took aten bob note from his top pocket.

"Ah shure, I'll bet the note so lads."

He was on a roll and it would be foolish to bet against him. Mc-Cawley threw his in. "Just yourself and myself so Rex!" he said as he sensed victory.

"I only have ten bob left Sergeant so I can't rise it unless you let me borrow a pound or two."

The Sergeant looked up quickly, too quickly!Rex knew he had him.

"That's fine with me," he replied but he knew his goose was cooked. He was about to lose and loose heavily.

"Give me a fiver there Mr Mulvey and I'll give it back to you in a few minutes," Rex asked as he turned around to the bar giving Mulvey a hint of a wink. He felt sure he had the sergeant.

"Is that alright with you Sergeant?" Ned asked.

"No bother at all Mr Mulvey, only I don't want to rob the house," he laughed as he tried one last bluff. Rex threw down the fiver. There wasn't a sound to be heard. The dancers and musicians were long gone and the two young Guards were propping up the jam of the door waiting on the Sergeant. He paled visibly. He had been allowed to bluff all night and thought he'd try it again but was caught. He threw his cards in face down. Dolan gathered them up before anyone tried to find out who was bluffing, but not before he stole the merest of glances himself. The Sergeant knew he had been set up but put a good face on it as he stood up and shook hands with Rex.

"You had them me good man, no hard feelings, we'll have another go at it some other night, I'll let Mr Mulvey know the next time I'm around the place."

As he reached for his overcoat he saw himself and Rex in the mirror.

"Caught by the bollocks again!" he cursed inwardly.

There was nothing left to do but make a gracious exit. He knew he couldn't charge anyone for after hours as it would be seen to be bad form.

"I'll see you another night lads please God," he promised as he headed for the squad car closely followed by the young guards.

Johnjo was watching from the parlour window until he saw the lights disappearing beyond the Parson's hill. There was silence as he closed the door behind him, finger to his lips as if to warn of imminent disaster, his pallor that of a convicted prisoner on the way to the gallows. A sudden intake of breath and a cheer that reverberated off the high rafters signalled emancipation.

"They're gone lads, they're gone."

The place went wild. Chairs and stools were thrown back, caps flung to the rafters, half ones demanded as they celebrated their escape and Rex's win.

"What did you have anyway Rex?" Billy Ganly asked.

"A pair of ducks," said the Buckalero, who wasn't going to make anyone the wiser and knew better not to.

"You did it again Mikeen," Mulvey laughed as he clapped the victor on the back. "We'll have to give you the freedom of the house after that. You can run your slate as high as you like now Mikeen."

"There'll be no more slate Ned. I'll settle it now and leave it at that."

A Game of Cards

"I thought you'd never heave it," Seamie's father said to him one night as they were coming home from Tashinny.

"How did you know I had it?"

"Well, it was as plain as the nose on your face. If no one else had it then you must have it. If they had it they'd have heaved it when I went into them with the knave. I had the Ace and all you had to do was take their king."

"Well, you always told me to hold on to it as long as I could or creel them when I couldn't."

"Dead right you are a mhic! That reminds me about the time a few of Hewart's relations came down from the North- grand fellas they were too with lots of money and not a bit afraid to show it off either. They usually arrived around Orangeman's Day because it was a lot safer here than there; what with bullets flying, women crying, people dying and all for nothing except to keep power where it was and the poor in their place. But that was changing too after years of banging their big drums in people's faces. But that's another story as the fella said. You were adout in Hewart's yard pegging up empty cans for them and they trying to shoot themselves, I mean they were trying to shoot at the cans. Ah you know what I mean. Anyway, I was passing the haggard gate when Hewart called me over."

"Are you going as far as the village tonight Rex?" he asked.

"I might, you'd never know," said I. "Well, he told me the lads, George and Roger were going over the road for a game if I wanted to come along. I got the feeling it wasn't out of the good of his heart he asked me because he knew I'd give them a run for their money and make it interesting for them at least and, sure, he might even get a crack at it himself too. I was after cleaning the slate above in Mulvey's the week before and I had a fair bit over as well. Don't say a word to your mother now for she'd have my life if she thought I was running up a slate again after her putting a stop to it before. Needless to say the word got out and Hewart heard all about it. McCawley must have told him and sure he probably asked him to ask me as well, to make a night of it. I left it a kinda late to cycle over the road so as to give them a bit of an appetite for the game. They were in ripping form so they were with McCawley lorrying whiskey into them."

"Just in time Rex," said he, as he put a half one in front of me. "The lads put up a bottle for the players."

"Thanks but no thanks," I said.

"I gave up the whiskey ages ago. It doesn't agree with me. I'll have a pint instead if you don't mind."

McCawley nearly fell over himself as he caught the half-wink.

"You're an awful bastard," said he to me later. "I nearly believed you myself. You fairly pulled the wool over their eyes there."

Frank told his Mrs to look after the bar as he pulled out the table and produced a brand new set of cards.

"Will I deal you in boys?" he asked the Prods.

There'd be blue murder if he hadn't after them coming the whole way down from the North. They were well aware of the stakes in Mc-Cawley's and they'd have been in with Murray and the Bishop as well if Father Pat knew they were carrying that heavy. They talk about the Papists and the Prods a mhic but sure they'd have them all joined together long ago if they'd only let them play together never mind pray together.

"It's them feckers above in the Dail and beyant in England that I blame. We could have the best of football and cards if they'd only let them at it. It suits those fancy pants to keep people divided so that they can train the soldiers to keep the workers in place while they're at it. The only thing that's keeping the Brits above in the North is power and money. They couldn't give a shite whether it was a Catholic or Protestant that was killed as long as they're in control and their big submarines are able to come and go. It's the same beyant in Spain where they can keep an eye on the Mediterranean and Atlantic as well."

The Prods sat down, Hewart included, with Frank and myself making up the school. Frank cut for deal. Divil the much happened as we played up and down for an hour or more; nothing much won or lost until Frank asked them if they wanted to up the stakes a bit as the night was getting on. You'd think they were after getting a blessing or something. It was entirely up to us but they wouldn't mind a bit if the betting was open they said. It got a bit saucy after that. McCawley couldn't catch a cold. I was doing fine myself, up about a ton at that stage, enough to feel fairly safe. The boys were cleaning McCawley. He must have been down five hundred and likely to lose more. Hewart and the boys couldn't believe their luck. Frank knew he couldn't hold out much longer as he was almost out of cash and had already cleaned the till. The Mrs nearly killed him with a look as he came out of the bedroom with a small wad of cash.

"How much is the pub worth lads?" he asked the boys. The poor woman went weak at the knees and had to be given a drop of brandy to revive her. The lads were flummoxed. They didn't know what to say. Frank was serious though. That settled it. We lay into it then and the likes of the cards that fell after that was something wonderful to behold. It's the old story again. When you have nothing to lose or couldn't care less, things turn. Lady Luck saw two lads at the pin of their collar and sided with us. Or maybe we saw we had them. She was with us and we could have won with a pair of ducks just like the night with the Sergeant. The two lads had to ask Hewart for a loan before long. He was doing all right himself until then but the lads were losing their shirts.

"We'll soon have to quit lads," Frank said. "It's long past closing and you'd never know when the Gardaí might drop in," said he full of the joys of life again. "We decided to have a round of the house and leave it at that. I think the lads were cowed at that stage. If they weren't, then they were by the time it came to the last hand.

It was my deal, the last one of the night. I dealt the queen of Spades to George beside me. Frank drew the jack of hearts because I knew by the way he looked at it and asked the Missus to get a drink for the road for the lads. They weren't even finished the other one yet but I knew he was giving me the nod. Roger got a king of hearts later in the deal. Hewart got the ace of hearts on his last card and Glory be to God! I had the five of hearts in my hand. You can't beat a good deal a mhic! It keeps the interest in it. The lads were a bit to the Kildare side by this time. Frank's whiskey was working well. I wouldn't mind but he told me after that he had to send the Brink up to Mulvey for it. Well I needn't tell you how that hand went. The boys hadn't a bean between them in the end and they owed Hewart a packet as well. They were awful quiet going out to the car with Hewart, but fair play to them they wished us well and said they'd be back another time. As soon as Frank heard the car at the Parson's he let a cheer out of him you'd hear here. I was a bit late home that night because Gannon was keeping an eye on proceedings as usual. As soon as he saw Hewart heaving the Ace he hightailed it up to Mulvey's to get them all down, knowing that I must have the five. Oul Ned was gone to bed but Martin came down along with White and the Bull and a couple of the Kenny kittens from Legan. Paddy Fallon came in with a quare one from up the country. Mary D came tipping in on the high heels with them as well. She was after making sandwiches above for the lot of them and brought a box of them down with her. She's a great girl is Mary. An awful pity someone wouldn't make a woman out of her and all that's going for her," he said in full earnest.

"Nothing would do them only play a few hands more but sure it wasn't worth their while. None of them could hold a candle to Frank or meself. Sometimes you just know you can't be bet and you can bluff like a second-hand car salesman. Don't say a word now to your mother a mhic or she'll kill me.

According to Frank he'd have bet the pub if things had got much worse. It's a long road that has no turning and he kinda knew his luck would change sooner rather than later. It'd never have worked if I was losing as well. I was just about able to keep into them until the whiskey began to work. Frank knew it too and went for the big one with the Boys from the Wee North. The bigger they are the harder they fall. Frank stuffed a wad a notes in my pocket and there it'll stay for another day."

Remembering Her Passing

That was then. His best friend had passed away in front of his eyes leaving him alone and desolate. True, his family was there for him but it wasn't the same. Family is one thing but a special friend is another. It took him more time than he thought possible to get over her passing. He might never have gotten over it were it not for the fact that he knew she was close by and would always be.

The memory of her passing would live with him forever and cause him sleepless nights as he fought with himself for leaving her alone when she needed him most. He thought of the evening he arrived at her front door and pushed it in when there was no reply.

To have found her in such a weakened state was almost too much to bear. He couldn't fathom how he could have left her alone for so long just because he was otherwise engaged?

Football had invaded his life and taken over. Everything else was secondary, or so he thought. His selfishness hung over him like a dark cloud as he mentally beat himself up for such thoughtlessness.

Her last words haunted him for ages until she herself came to the rescue. No one else could have done so. Typical of her wise ways she re-entered his psyche through the form of another woman- Annabel. Their friendship had mushroomed under her careful guidance and left them proud of their intimacy and all that came with it. For Tess it was a simple case of young people in love and she would allow nothing or no one to spoil that. Steadfast in her ideals she offered them the sanctuary of her home far from prying eyes, social mores, or the undue influence of Mother Church.

He never knew if she was aware of their intimacy, nor did it bother them as they shared precious moments under her hospitable roof. They did their best to recompense her for such joyous times by adding what they could to her few home comforts. Gathering sticks, running errands, collecting herbs or watercress was a chore they relished not only because it was for her but for themselves too as they roamed hither and thither like elfins. In truth, they were almost that due to her knowledge of the ways of the world and that of nature itself.

She thought them the rhythm method before even the doctor could expound on it. There was no way she was going to let an unwanted pregnancy destroy their young lives as it did so many others of the parish and the country. Wandering along the river with them as they fetched water from Bosque for her she'd share her life's experiences and use it to guide them. Although she often roamed around Bosque and the Commons she never bothered bringing anything bar watercress, herbs and mushrooms home. It rarely occurred to her to bring a bucket with her and if she did she used it for everything bar water as she considered the water from her stream to be safe enough. Even when Seamie told her of coming across the decaying carcass of a sheep in the water further up towards Knockagh she didn't wince, telling him the river, its rocks, sand and gravel would be enough to treat what was a normal occurrence. She doted on Annabel as much as him and longed for their company as much as they desired hers. They felt there wasn't another place on the planet that came anywhere close to that sacred sanctuary. And that it was.

Though she had passed on to her eternal reward he felt sure she was always there when he needed her. He knew instinctively she'd do that. Though sceptical already of the Church's hold on Heaven, he knew Tess's version was bound to be nearer the truth; that the physical being is replaced by the soul in search of peace and tranquillity. She was closer to nature than any theologian or pseudo-religious could ever be as far as he was concerned. Yes, there were many holy men and women she readily agreed, but they had little to do with organised religion. They were the mystics, druids and witches, the Morrigans, Cuchulainns, Brigids and Patricks who had a special power from nature and over nature. Their fervour came from nature itself and had been gleefully accepted into the folds of Mother Church and local folklore.

Just days before her passing, she had entrusted him to her favourites, Brigid and Ann. She saw Christ more as a mystic endowed with special gifts than a god sent to change the world. Her argument that some are endowed with celestial gifts found favour with him. That McCormack, Caruso, Gigli or Picasso could be blessed with such talents had little to do with them, and more to do with their gift, was easy to follow. Likewise, that a seventh son of a seventh son could carry a cure from one generation to another was also a gift, but, again, more to do with maths than man. The mere fact that he should be so lucky to have the advantage of her wisdom was proof enough of another world for him. Not for him to question why, more to accept that nature has its peculiar path to follow and mankind bit parts in a huge machine. It didn't take him long to realise the wisdom of her ways and the depths of her understanding of where everyone fitted in such a simple but majestic organisation.

Despite his trust in her beliefs, which fitted so well with his own, he was devastated by her departure. The thoughts of her lying there alone brought out a cold sweat on him. His family did what they could to soften the blow but it did little to alleviate the pain of her loss.

He could still see Larkin's face as the enamel bucket bounced off the bonnet of his car. Telling her he'd be back as soon as possible he prayed someone would come along but there wasn't a soul or a sound until he heard the Volkswagen starting above at the hayshed. Hearing her cry out he rushed back in to her. Death was close and she knew it. Now he did too. He had to get help immediately. Rushing out he grabbed the empty bucket and lofted it knowing it was the only way he'd stop Larkin who was about to pass the house.

Screeching to a halt, he was ready to kill until he saw Seamie frantically beckoning to him.

Jumping from the Volkswagen he made a run at him with stick raised but was astonished to see him stand his ground.

"Have you gone fucking crazy or what ya little…" but the words faded to a whisper as he saw his ashen face. He realised something was seriously wrong as he tried to speak. Words failed him. He could only point to her open door. Instinct told Larkin that something serious had occurred as he stepped quickly inside. It took awhile for his eyes to adjust to the darkened interior. Seeing her prone form on the little bed in the corner he rushed to her side with a groan. She was fading fast. Asking Seamie if he'd stay with her, he hurried for the doctor.

Though back in minutes with the doctor and curate close behind, she was almost gone. Anointing her, Fr. McCabe whispered an act of contrition in her ear as she began to slip away.

He continued praying over her as the doctor did his best to revive her. It was too late. She was already passing through the portal she often spoke about. Her last words were to Seamie and though inaudible to the others he heard her perfectly because he wanted to. "Mind yourself a mhic, take care of the ones you love and I'll take care of you no matter where you are." Tears burst from his eyes as he tried to speak, to ask her to stay, but she was gone. He knew instinctively that her hour had come because as he caressed her tiny hands she made a last effort to entrust him with a medallion of some sort. Kissing her forehead he gave her a little hug and let her go where she wanted to go. A short intake of breath and she was gone. Fr. McCabe put his arm around his shoulder and hugged him close commending him for his alertness and how he had managed to grab Larkin's attention in the nick of time. Saying he'd return later he asked Larkin if he'd stay awhile until he left Seamie home and got Rex and Nora down to organise things.

"I'm staying here!" Seamie said in a voice that left them in no doubt as to his intentions.

"Very well so! I'll drop in on your mother and father and they'll be along shortly." Already the news was spreading like wildfire because the priest and doctor were spotted rounding the crossroads together. It didn't take the neighbours long to figure out what had happened. No sooner had the priest left than they started arriving to pay their respects.

First to arrive was Rex and Nora, closely followed by Mrs Weed who happened to be visiting at the time. The postmaster put in a few quick phone calls before hurrying along to get the inside line. Despite his alacrity he was beaten to it by the Bun who was coming over the Parson's hill when he spotted the cars outside Tess's. Knowing this to be most unusual he decided to investigate. Rex asked him to keep everyone at bay until Nora and Mrs Weed had laid out the old lady and kitted her out for the long journey ahead of her. Satisfied that she was looking her best despite the circumstances, the ladies started making sandwiches with the bread and ham Hewart kindly provided. A few minutes later saw Mulvey and McCawley arrive with a few bottles of whiskey and enough porter to set the parish drunk. All they needed now was Carrigy to arrive and a decent farewell could be afforded old Tess. No sooner said than done. Just as they were about to send for him he arrived with the accordion and sat himself in the corner where he'd have a bit of comfort. Knowing his place, he waited until Rex gave him the nod after the older women had finished their keening and weeping. Starting slowly with a few quiet airs it wasn't long until he gave it the holly and had everyone tapping their feet and humming along. Johnjoe joined in with his harmonica barely taking time to draw breath as Carrigy played every tune they knew. Seamie asked the Brink if he'd lilt a few, and true to his calling he lilted as good as Pat Kilduff, maybe even better! Seamie was delighted knowing Tess wouldn't have wanted it any other way. She must have read his mind because just as a few of the neighbours began to drift away the sound of Tim's jeep entered his consciousness, and to his great joy Annabel stuck her head reverently in the half door. Not wishing to be too obvious he waited until she and Tim had paid their respects before offering them a seat.

"It's time we were heading home too," the Nugget said as he helped Margaret to her feet.

Although he knew she must be as old as her stream he never thought that she'd leave like that. In truth, he never thought of her dying at all. He could see her throwing her leg over her broom and waving goodbye as she went off to join her ancestors, nothing more. Now he was confronted by the realisation of her passing and he couldn't take it. As he examined the medallion closely he was surprised to see that it was the silver medal that was struck for the Eucharistic Congress in 1932 when her favourite, Count John Mc-Cormack sang so brilliantly in the Phoenix Park. Like many another she had travelled by barge; it being the cheapest form of travel at the time. She often spoke of how McCormack, on hearing how far she'd come, and how she did the cooking on the barge for the boys, invited her to join him for refreshments at the side of the enormous stand in the park. Thanking her for her support and complimenting her on her fortitude, he presented her with a specially struck medal in honour of the occasion. Now it was his and he felt doubly honoured.

A Thorny Problem

He felt trapped. Since Tess had passed on he had been a bit lost, uncomfortable even, without her. No one had ever got that close to him or could take him to such far-flung parts of the planet. He didn't even want to go near the place. Though he often passed on the way to Ballynamanagh he never stopped. It could have been so lovely. The little stone-bridge with the waterfall and the stepping stones that he often used seemed a distant memory now. Thistles and nettles grew tall where geraniums once reigned supreme. A couple of times he thought he saw a flicker of light through the window. Probably the reflection of the moon he thought to himself. Aware of her presence in the past he didn't know if she was still keeping an eye on him or not. He'd prefer if she didn't for the moment, or at least until he found his feet again. He had her beads, the pebble from the pool and his memories of her and felt there was no need for more.

Although he tried hard to blot them out her stories came flooding back whenever he was alone.

The caves around Carrick were now his sole possession and he wasn't prepared to share them with anyone. Certain no one knew of their whereabouts except himself he had drawn maps of each one and hid them safely in the dry interior of the cave he loved the most; the Giant's Grave in Lisnacreevagh. Some of the others were equally dry but lacked the dimensions of his favourite.

It was just as he crossed the high field that he remembered Tess's story about how the Lisna Giant got his name.

It was long ago she told him. Long before even Cromwell darkened our shores. It was even longer back than the time that the pagan goddess Etna drowned in the Inny in Tenelick and gave the river its name. It was certainly before Queen Medhb was slain by Furbaide while bathing off Inchleraun on Loch Rí. However long ago it was, the Fir Bolg, a race of giants who couldn't be beaten in battle by normal means were outwitted by the Tuatha de Danaan with magic and forced into the Underworld.

As always some escaped and hid in the caves throughout the Midlands. Time moved on. Poor nutrition, the constant fight to protect their families from the ravages of the Vikings, Norse and English as well as internecine strife rapidly reduced their numbers and physique. This combined with the mini Ice Age of the early 18th century, and the subsequent horrors of the famine of 1845-50, left few giants in the area. One group remained however; the Giant McCormack whom Tess herself was directly related to. The Clan had survived plague and pestilence by hiding out in the caves around the area and had gradually integrated themselves into the changing community. Though Christianity found favour with the Irish, due to its proximity to their older beliefs, it still couldn't permeate thousands of years of belief in Mother Nature.

The 'Giant' McCormacks were exactly that. Their family blood-line often threw up huge men who were fierce and fearless in battle. They defended the vast Cistercian lands of Teffia and Annally dur-ing the Middle Ages as if it were their own and roamed the wilds of Knockagh, Ballynamanagh and Tenelick to keep the foe at bay. Over time, a quirk in nature threw up an exact opposite to a giant. This individual was also invariably called the 'Giant' as it seemed somehow to reinforce the belief rather than give the lie to it.

Moving on

There was a change going on and he felt it. He knew in his heart that this would be their last time together as kids. The girls who roamed with him were growing fast too and would soon be moving on just like him. He thought for a while that it was a pity they were all growing up so fast but it couldn't stay like this much longer. His brother Mikey had been home and told him about the college and all the sports and different things that went on there. He proceeded to tell him about the films he had seen on the big pull down screen in the recreation hall and the table tennis and snooker tables where any of the boys could play. He had seen some films in McCawley's hall and thought they were great gas; all those guns blazing and the cowboys and Indians and all. He had an idea he'd like to go there but it was early yet and he still had to get the results of his Primary Certificate. Mikey told him he'd have to have a good certificate if he stood any chance of being let in to the college at all. Having read everything he could since his 'awakening' he had no worries about the entrance exam. He had long decided he was not going to be stuck in the outback just because he didn't know his sums or where America or Australia was. He delighted in the books and comics sent from Glasgow by Mrs McCormack, a family friend and distant relative. He almost devoured them in his quest for knowledge before trading them with his friends for some minor treasure or other. Most of his pals had no idea who Roy of the Rovers was but he did, and Superman and Spiderman as well.

Lost in reverie he failed to hear the jeep pulling up. A polite cough brought him quickly back to earth. Jumping up in surprise he was amazed to see Tim and Annabel side by side a short distance away.

"Annabel saw your bike so we thought we'd look in on you. Are you alright Seamie?" he asked concern showing in his voice.

"Just saying goodbye to an old friend," he answered self-consciously.

"Sorry I didn't hear you arriving."

"There's nothing to be sorry about young man. We know you're hurting but you have a new life in front of you now. She'll be with you for sure so don't be worrying your head about a thing," he advised as he stepped back to let Annabel advance. A shy embrace and a kiss on both cheeks spoke volumes.

"I'll leave the two of you at it so," he said as he waved while stepping over the style. A toot of the horn and he was off.

"I missed you so much Seamie. Did you not want to see me or what?" she asked as she held him tightly.

"Nothing could be further from the truth," he assured her as they knelt to say a little prayer for their old friend. Job done, they walked hand in hand to the style.

Insisting on walking her home he hid his bike behind the oak tree at the back of the holy well.

"The divil swipe anyone that touches it," he laughed as they headed towards their hideout near the Mass Rock.

One of the many gifts she gave him prior to her passing was the ability to ferret out places that few had any knowledge of.

The sound of Ted's jeep coming over the road spurred them into action. Gathering up their bits and pieces they double-checked for any give-away signs.

"Am I alright?" she asked as he helped her over the stone style that led to the Boreen.

"You'll never be alright," he joked as she made a pretend-swipe that ended up in a big hug. Hand in hand they ran down the bowery lane just in time to flag Tim down and grab a lift home.

It had been another amazing adventure on the road of life. There was precious little more to ask for they agreed as Tim turned the old land Rover. Bidding goodbye for the moment they went their respective ways, he high as a kite as he waved after them. Looking over the wall into the graveyard he gave Tess an enormous conspiratorial wink before recovering Betsy from behind the old oak tree.

The Beginning of the End

They were circling round the Turlough when it dawned on him exactly what Tess meant when she spoke of 'the watery cave that brought the brave to an early grave.' He had often queried her on that particular one, but apart from her penchant for riddles he wasn't able to draw her out on its whereabouts. It was Annabel who solved the riddle by explaining why the lake disappeared almost every summer. Her father had told her to steer well clear of the lake, which, although crystal clear, could be deadly dangerous because it was prone to disappear overnight, and sometimes in minutes. The reason was simple enough. The mining company had come on an underwater river that fed from the lough.

It was said that a man called Lane had miraculously escaped drowning by calling on St. Sinneach to save him. He was on his last gasp when a hand seemed to pluck him from the depths and place him on the tiny island where he lay until the water drained away exposing the centuries-old pilgrim path that led to the Mass Rock.

Like many other so-called 'pilgrim paths' it existed from the dawn of time providing safe passage through difficult terrain to a place of sanctuary; a ceremonial stomping ground or a market place where everything was bartered, women, children, horses, mules, donkeys, goats and food of all kind. Matchmaking was endemic at these seasonal gatherings and could make or break a Clan depending on the nature of the barter.

They weren't thinking of this as they prepared for a swim in the warm sun; the fear of being dragged into a subterranean world overcome by their youthful desire and the magical draw of the shimmering, clear water. Stripping off in the tall reeds they vied for first-in. Surfacing some distance out in the deeper waters he looked around for her. There wasn't a sign. Panic surged through him as he thought of the dreaded consequences of their rashness. Suddenly, she rose from the lake like a mermaid and struck out towards him. He felt the gods smiling on him as they joined together in a spiritual and physical bonding devoid of fear or consequence. Joyfully splashing about, they ducked and dived as they sought each other in a sensual game of hide and seek. Closing their eyes for a moment they dived in separate directions before rising to the surface and joining together again. Soon instinct drove them to the lakeshore where a bed of ferns and reeds lay waiting for them. Safe in the knowledge that their privacy was absolute, in a micro-system of melodious harmony, they lay back and listened to the medley of sounds. Bullfrogs croaked their territorial warning as larks soared far above sending their sweet sonnets down to the young lovers below. A blackbird sang his heart out in the leafy beech behind them. It could have been Billy and they wouldn't have been a bit surprised if it were. Tess had spies everywhere. He knew she'd be keeping a look out for them and wouldn't allow anyone or anything to spoil their joy.

It was at this precise time that he began to imagine things for the first time. It started innocently enough and may have been triggered by fear of being found out 'in flagrante delicto.' Either way, as they lay in joyous union he thought he heard voices nearby. Putting his hand over Annabel's mouth to signal somebody was close by he pointed in the direction of the Mass Rock. Her eyes said it all as she nodded her understanding of the situation.

"Someone's coming," he whispered as they edged deeper into the reeds.

"I didn't hear a thing," she whispered.

"I'm certain I heard voices," he said. "The strange thing is though, it seemed as if they were talking in Gaelic," doubts assailing him as he saw puzzlement and fear in her pretty face.

"Look! There," he pointed. "They're going over towards the Mass Rock."

"You're losing it Seamie, I see nothing."

"Over there, Look," he pointed. She followed his line but shook her head as she looked into his eyes.

"There's a group of people walking after a priest or bishop," he indicated, wondering why she couldn't see them.

"Look!" he pointed, "there's soldiers waiting to attack them. They're walking into a terrible trap. We'll have to warn them." With that he leaped to his feet pointing frantically towards the quarry where the spectral procession had gone.

"Ah Seamie there's no one there," she cried as she threw her arms around him as he half dragged, half lifted her with him. How she held him from falling to certain death over the quarry wall he'd never know but she did. Her strong arms enveloped him as he struggled in vain to free himself. Her love and fear were stronger though, as driven by a passion greater than his she won the day and soothed the savage beast within him. It wasn't the first time either.

He realised then that he was hearing and seeing things- very similar to his earlier experience in the haunted shed in Knockagh.

He hadn't mentioned it to her before, but if ever he needed to do so it was right then or he'd lose her forever.

Explaining what had happened in Knockagh he begged her understanding. As always, she accepted his explanation and hugged him tightly. Swearing to keep it to themselves they decided to call it a day. He already knew that he'd have to see Tess to exorcise the demon or demons. She was ahead of him as usual.

As they rose to collect their clothes he felt a sharp pain across his shoulders.

"Bucking briars," he cursed as he eased round lest they do more damage. Another pain cut into him forcing him to cry out. Annabel had gone deathly pale. Standing behind them and ready to lash out again was her father. Throwing herself against Seamie she took the brunt of the blow. Seeing the blood he whirled around and dived headlong at Tim's legs forcing him into the water. Dropping the whip he pummelled with both fists as they went under. As they rose for air they saw Annabel dive away from them and realised something strange was happening. They could feel a strong current pulling towards the centre and knew the lough was about to disappear, and within minutes at that. Leaping, running, crying, he plunged in as far as possible before striking out after her. He could feel the pull of the swirling waters and could see her being dragged into the vortex. With desperate strokes he reached her and grabbed her outstretched arm. The will to live kicked in and she kicked out with all her might, but it was too late. Even their combined kicking power wasn't enough to combat the power of the whirlpool. A last knowing glance that they'd go together was enough to reconcile them to their fate. Realising it was pointless they just held each other and left it to the gods.

"The Cross Seamie, the Cross," he heard a familiar voice through the swirling mass of water taking them through time to wherever it was to be. Reaching out despairingly, his arm closed on something solid. Annabel was slipping from his grasp but grabbing her long hair he somehow drew her back to him. Wrapping herself around him she grabbed the stone too. With a hollow sound the whirlpool disappeared leaving an enormous bed of flattened vegetation. Fish flapped in the muddy shallows as they stood against the cross that saved them. Now they were standing tall on what was obviously bedrock or some kind of road. The Lough was no more. It had gone to its underground haven. They had witnessed at first hand another of nature's marvels. Though choked with emotion at the enormity of their predicament they knew Tess had done it again. Tim stood forlorn in the mud not knowing what to do. It was over. His rashness had almost cost their lives and he knew it. As he spluttered his excuses and tried to express his sorrow they walked away from him hand in hand. Picking up their flimsy clothes they strode into the duck pond close by and washed the mud away. Both knew there was no going back now. A new era had already started and nothing would ever be the same again. They watched in sadness as Tim, shoulders slumped, limped away from them. Realising they were close by the Mass Rock they climbed over the wall and knelt to thank God and Tess for saving them.

They didn't need to debate their next move. It was as clear as Bosque Well. Pledging their troth forever they joined hands in the cupstone and touched foreheads. It was the ritual Tess told them that

Diarmuid and Grainne used in this very spot while escaping from their pursuers. If it was good enough for those two way back then it was good enough for them now. Though fast approaching twilight the heat hung in the air as they climbed up towards the mound of the Limekiln. Sitting near the top they gazed back over the scene of their misadventure. It was hard to imagine that a day that promised so much could end like this. Tim would be at home by now and Allison would have heard it all from him. The fact that he had followed them told them he was suspicious of them. Logically, he must have discussed it with her and by failing to discuss it with them meant both of them had decided on a certain course of action. Either way it spelled trouble, more embarrassment and the likelihood of being sent to Coventry at least. Reluctant to leave their present state they lay back on the warm ground. It must have hit them simultaneously because they turned to each other knowing what their next and final move was. The Limekiln had been used recently, explaining why the ground was still warm. Both knew that the silent effect of the suffocating carbon dioxide gas had contributed to many deaths in the past, especially among the travelling community. Tim told them that the heat attracted vagrants during cold snaps because the ground was warm and the gas emitted was colourless and odourless. He had heard of a tramp that was found dead by a LimeKiln in a neighbouring parish. The poor unfortunate fell asleep and woke up dead. Such was the effect of burning lime he said. Now, as they lay together, their thoughts turned to Tess's paradise where souls freed from this planet found their way to a sanctuary in a far-flung part of the galaxy commonly referred to as 'Heaven', as it existed in Man's consciousness long before Christianity. If Tess thought it existed it was good enough for them. She had guided them this far and they felt sure her philosophy would bring them further. The rigours of their fight against the force of nature and the attendant troubles with Tim had exhausted them both. They fell asleep in seconds wrapped in each other's arms.

Allison was doing her level best to bring them back. Having lifted Annabel clear and sat her with her mother Tim was urging Seamie to his feet; his arm around his waist as he led him slowly to where Annabel was coming round, but it was obvious he was still away with the Fairies. Through a purple haze sweeping down the valley he saw Tess waving from afar. Her face lit up the entire area as she seemed to wave him away from her. Shaking her head to tell him it wasn't his time she turned slowly and floated away. It was his cue. His one concern now was for Annabel who wasn't with Tess either. If not there with her then she must be here with him. Then he spotted her beside her mother. Fanning air into their lungs they soon had them in recovery mode. It had been dangerously close to exit time. Though devastated, Allison was coping with the implications involved. That her dear daughter had decided to quit this life rather than lose the one she loved was clear, but what might happen later wasn't.

'Greater love than this no man hath' flooded back through the years to her. Together the four of them walked slowly to the jeep that was parked by the graveyard wall. Still suffering from the side effects, Annabel was yapping away, though mostly random, and unrelated to her recent experience. Seamie, mute, kept his counsel and his gaze averted as they sat in the jeep. As soon as she had them home Allison plied them with water and lemonade. Being a doctor herself she knew there would be no lasting ill-effects but as for the psychological effects she wasn't sure about that at all.

She never took her eyes off them as they slept soundly for a considerable period. It would help the recovery process she knew. As soon as they were rested they had a chat over a cuppa, and rather than create an unnecessary scene it was decided that a shut mouth catches no flies, and that there was no point in alarming people further. Seamie agreed that that was a good idea because his parents wouldn't understand it anyway and it might also affect his college situation. Although Tim wanted to drive him home he said the fresh air and the cycle would be better for him.

The Last Hurrah

Standing chatting with the Brink a few days later he saw Tim's jeep coming up by the Bull Field. Excusing himself, he drifted over towards the school wall that might offer a modicum of support should an argument develop. Not that he was anticipating one but better to be sure than sorry. The few days in between might have hardened Tim's attitude. Pulling up alongside him with the window rolled down he enquired in a quiet voice if he was fully recovered and if he needed anything. Replying that he was fine he thanked him for his solicitude.

Taking a letter from his inside pocket he handed it to Seamie saying it was from his daughter and that he'd wait for a reply if he cared to read it now. Thanking him, he said he'd prefer to read it later in his own time if he didn't mind. Assuring him he had no problem with that, he turned the key, swung the old jeep round and headed back home.

Deciding to cross the fields to Bosque there and then he knew he'd be better able to absorb the news whatever it was but he feared it wasn't good. The heaviness of the world sat on his shoulders as he hurried through the fields. He didn't even hear his mother's shout to take the buckets with him. A fox sat up from his slumber as he hurried along, but recognising that the youth had no interest in him, he lay back down again.

He thought about entering the cave but felt it would be better to carry on as he intended.

Sitting on the Giant's Grave he pulled the letter from his pocket and began to read.

Dear Seamie

It is with great sadness that I write this last letter to you. Rather than lose the love of my dear parents, and most of all you, I've decided to go away now. I've been accepted into an enclosed order on the Continent where I can spend my life in the service of God praying for all of you. I've bound my parents to silence so please don't ask them where I'm going because they can't tell you. They also know they will not see me again and reluctantly accept my decision. I could never live a normal life with my father again.

I have no regrets Seamie and will never forget our time together. I hope and pray you won't regret it either.

Tess taught you well. Me too. I know she'll always be with you and I promise I will too. Go with God. Walk tall as you've always done and remember that all you have to do is ask if you are in trouble and I'll be right with you in spirit though Tess could well be with you in another form.

I know this is a terrible blow for you and I beg your forgiveness. I want you to live the life set out for you and I know you'll have many friends and that for sure you'll meet someone special who will love you as much if not more than me. You deserve it. Somehow, I know we'll meet again, if not in this life then in that other planet Tess often talked about called 'Abbeyopia.'

Your soul mate,

Annabel

Tears burst from his bleeding heart as he fell to his knees in dismay. Madness enveloped him as he thought how close they had been to being together forever. Better to go now than live a life without her. Although he half understood her dilemma he couldn't identify with it. Deep in the darkest recesses of his mind he sought the only answer possible. He'd head for Abbeyopia where Tess was sure to be. She'd understand for sure. There was nothing here for him now. He was about to leave home anyhow, and the thoughts of starting a new life without the love of his life, was not worth considering. Casting around in his mind he considered how best he'd achieve his plan. He felt the baling twine in his pocket and knew exactly what he'd do. There was a heavy stone with a hole in the centre on the bank of the river where they used to swim. They often sat on it to dry off in the sun. It was perfect. As he hurried to the stone he heard a sound he hadn't heard for ages. Looking up, he saw Helena alighting on the very stone. Shaking his head in disbelief he walked slowly towards her. With wings spread wide she waddled towards him. He went down on one knee as he used to do before she flew off to join her flock. Plopping down beside him she nestled her long neck in his outstretched arms. It was all he needed. He knew now that life had to go on and this was the sign Tess sent him. He poured out his heart to his feathered friend and suddenly felt at peace. With a pat on her head he bade her fly away as all was well. She understood perfectly. With a few steps she took off and wheeled away towards Tess's house. The significance wasn't lost on him. Consigning every word to memory he tore the letter in a thousand pieces and let it flow past the well and over the sand bank they lay on in another life.

It was one of the toughest challenges of his young life. He had weathered setbacks, suffered the pain of being alienated, walked the plank of adolescence and ploughed his very own furrow, but this was different. He had experienced the loss of a soul mate once and it nearly killed him.

She didn't need to be with him at all times, nor did he need her to be. She had taught him all she could in the few years they had been together. It was time for him to stand on his own two feet. He knew that. Slipping quietly into the turf shed he untied Shep, took down his rod and headed for the river closely followed by the collie.

Coining it

There was one more duty to be done prior to making his departure. Necessity and tradition obliged him to make the rounds of friends and neighbours to solicit much-needed funds and to announce his intentions. Neither was necessary as their generous nature provided for the favoured few.

First port of call was to Maria McCrone and her long-suffering husband Joe. Long-suffering and tolerant because of her idiosyncrasies, meaning he'd never have to say an act of contrition prior to exiting this life according to his neighbours. It took him a long time to do so as he saw half the parish out before him. Maria, in her many moods, was a joy to listen to as she went her wild and wonderful way. If money was even scarcer than usual she had a plan that almost always worked. She'd trade a song for a spoonful of sugar as quick as a beautifully knitted baneen for a week's groceries in Codys by the crossroads. Fiddling with her purse in the shop one evening Cody asked her for the money for her few groceries. It was obvious she hadn't two coins to rub together but she continued with the pretence.

"You're all out today Maria," Cody remarked as he saw the new bonnet and knew she'd try to barter it for the groceries.

"Win gold and wear it," she replied instantly.

"Sow cabbage and eat it," was his immediate, if slightly pointed reply.

"Come along now Maria, there's customers waiting," he prompted.

"There'll be time after us Mr Cody," she replied as she put the few items into her wicker basket.

"No time like the present for paying your bills Maria," he almost pleaded as she made for the door.

"Me hat's worth ten times that me man," said she as she saw him pick up her latest creation.

Although he had a collection of her brightly coloured hats and scarves he was not averse to accepting them in exchange. He didn't have much of an alternative he knew but was wise enough to know he'd make a pretty penny for them later when he'd take them up North to the Orange parades on the Glorious twelfth. The ladies loved them and paid a handsome price for the unique designs, even if the colours were definitely those of the Tricolour. Green was green, orange was orange and white was white. It mattered little as fashion was all and pretence everything.

Her husband Joe had a lovely pony and trap that was their pride and joy. As brightly painted as Jem O'Leary's wanderly wagon, it represented Maria's gaudy sense of humour which, even though handmade with great care, stood out much more than a tinker's caravan. Nevertheless, it bothered them as little as it bothered the tinkers. Though their children were grown men and women now they accompanied their parents to Mass every Sunday morning, hail, rain or snow. Bluey, their sweet-stepping pinto seemed just as proud to clip along, as Joe and Maria were to have their brood around them. There was no room for anyone else but they always offered a lift anyway.

"Ah, shure the walk'll do us good," was the usual polite reply.

"So you're off away from us a mhic," Joe said as he searched his waistcoat pocket for his contribution.

"I'll be back for all the big games," he assured him as he spotted the half-crown.

"I suppose you have no change on you gossoon," he laughed heartedly as he pressed the coin into his half-opened hand. It wouldn't do to be seen to be greedy he knew so the pretence of unwillingness only heightened the value of the contribution.

Politely retreating, and thanking him profusely for his generosity, he explained that he had half the parish to visit yet and little time left to do so. "Shure don't we know that only too well a mhic. Off with ya now and if ya fall don't wait ta git up," he laughed heartedly with Maria.

The Door to the Underworld

"The divil himself wouldn't keep in with you," his father said as he arrived puffing at Carrickboy. Used to homemade boneshakers he was amazed at the freedom of his new bike. He thought of the times he cycled the length and breadth (width) of the parish on bikes that didn't deserve to be called such. They weren't as bad as the Bun's though. In truth his was the last straw literally!

Though it was hard to believe it could be done, he hadn't bought an inner tube for his High Nelly for a lifetime. Stuffed with hay, straw, or best of all reeds from the lough at St.Sinneach's lake, he sallied forth to the mart at Ballymahon or even further afield as if it were the ride of a lifetime, the dying embers of a Woodbine clutched between his thin lips. Not given to verbosity as Grandfather often remarked he nevertheless managed to be quite entertaining and a fair hand to tell a story as well. High winds, rain, sleet or snow prevented him from going about his daily chores. His daily meal consisted of bread and jam, nothing more.

Seamie watched his movements like a hawk as he passed the way while delivering telegrams to the four corners of the wind. Though Tess's thatch was porous enough the Bun's was another story entirely. The age-old rafters stood out like the bones on a skeleton through the wafer-thin thatch hadn't been touched since his brother passed away some years earlier. It was hard to know if it was laziness or lack of interest. When the woodworm infested rafters finally gave up the ghost he simply cleaned out the cowshed and moved in. It served him well for a few years more until it finally succumbed to neglect and fell in like the rest.

"It was lucky I was out counting," he related later while chatting to a farmer from Tonlagee. He didn't tell him that he never had more that two or three animals but that was an unnecessary detail and not crucial to the overall effect of the story.

When asked how he coped with the loss he replied that he put the chickens out of their house and moved in there.

"And what happened to the chickens?" he was then asked.

"Sure they went up in the rafters. What else would they do?" he replied as nonchalantly as if it were an everyday occurrence.

It was well rumoured that a tea chest of cash was found buried under the collapsed roof after the brother passed away. No one knew what became of the money other than the fact that a few calves appeared around the place and a field dividing their two tiny farms was bought. Although an obvious and logical development it was said to be the dearest field in the parish because the owner, another neighbour of the same name who was renowned for his tightness, held out for the last shilling. The Bun didn't care. Money meant nothing to him. Some said he was easily relieved of it by one crook or another. Despite his apparent miserable existence he seemed as happy as Larry as he hopped off his bike to chat with his neighbours and the few friends he trusted. He didn't have many because he had been bitten too often.

Bill Newman, a true friend if ever there was one, owned a nice farm of land directly across the road from the Bun's. It boasted a series of good springs that were said to come from St. Sinneach's lake over by the Mass Rock. Tradition told of an underground lake or, more likely, an underground river that was said to follow a course from 'The Mountain' between Moydow and Ardagh to Abbeyshrule bog and on to Cnoc-an-Ór on the Westmeath border. Bill often called to see the Bun but they were more likely to meet in the Nugget's in Ballynamanagh than anywhere. There they would join up with the Cuddy, the Potstick, the Horse and the Fiddler to while the evening away with all kinds of tall tales and storytelling The Cuddy's ghost stories grew wilder and wilder and his captive audience bigger and bigger until it was suggested an extension be built to accommodate them. The fact that a cracking little Shebeen grew up around them may have pre-empted its construction. The narrow forums gave way to sugans and three-legged stools while the all-too-powerful poteen, was replaced by Jameson's Redbreast and Crested Ten.

The Horse nearly brought the house down when he launched into an extravagant story about the double-breasted prostitutes beyond in Athlone.

"How do you make that out," was all grandfather could say as tears rolled down his ruddy cheeks.

"Sure, it was the clothes they wore. What else do you think?" the Horse continued as his gob-smacked listeners doubled up with the laughter.

"I suppose you mean they were wearing double-breasted waist-coats," the Potstick ventured unable to control his mirth.

"Not a bit of it boys, they were walking two a breast that's all," was his parting sally as he dived for the door to escape the good-humoured banter that flew after him.

It was a pet day- the sun was cracking the stones as Seamie ped-dled past Lisnacreevagh Boreen towards Cummin's Cross. Word was out that the Banshee was heard near the lane a few nights beforehand but they weren't sure if it was the Cashel one that had gone astray or the one that normally hung around Belton's Crossroads. Peddling past Maguire's lane he spotted the Bun sneaking along the far hedge. Curious, he alighted immediately, parked Betsy safely out of sight and ducked back to the Boreen making sure to keep him in sight as he moved quickly along the thick hedge that divided them. Sens-ing he was either after something or up to something he wasn't about to miss anything. Either way, he wanted to be party to the proceedings. It soon became clear that he wasn't hunting. His deport-ment demonstrated a certain furtiveness and fear of being watched or followed. Despite his youthful years Seamie was well used to be-ing able to conceal himself when the need arose. After all, he had managed to keep secret his hiding place under the big Bourtree/elder beside the school up to the present. No mean feat when you consider hundreds of kids passed the way daily.

Unaware of his presence, the Bun eased through the thick hedge and continued towards the Fairy Lís at the mearn(border) of his land and Munis's. Given a wide berth by even the most experi-enced hunters due to its deep and dangerous marshy surrounds, it had a little island in the centre in which a fine Lís stood in splen-did isolation. Even Munis kept clear of it on his odd visit to that outreach of his empire. There was nothing to entice him inside either because access was almost impossible due to the marshy ground that surrounded it. The Bun obviously had no such fears as Seamie watched him pick his steps in a zigzag manner that kept his feet dry and brought him safely to the outer perimeter of the Lís.

Taking careful note of his steps, he crept ever-closer keeping cover between the two of them. He was certain now he had something to hide or was about to do so. His curiosity rightly aroused he had no problem following as the imprints of his wellies showed clearly in the soft lichen. Advancing step by step he placed each foot carefully in that of his quarry noting that, although the top layer was spongy, it was obvious there was a sound base underneath.

He had just reached the safety of the raised bank when a litany of muffled curses forced him to lie low. Scrambling up through the dense undergrowth he managed to keep himself concealed while keeping the Bun in full view. He was attempting to clear thick thorny briars from a cluster of rocks in front of him but it was obvious he wasn't having much success. That particular type of briar was notorious for extracting blood and as far as Seamie was concerned the blasted thing seemed possessed. His terrorising encounter with its first cousin in the Glebe came quickly to mind as he thought of the dark night it frightened two souls out of him as it attached itself to his coat sleeve leaving him thinking it was an evil spirit trying to take him to hell with it. The memory held fresh with him as he held his position and saw the Bun break a thick stick to help him with his labour.

"Mistake number two," he thought as he remembered Tess's advice.

"Don't ever break a bough or branch adin a Lís."

Deeply conscious of that as he went about his tours of the ten townlands, he knew spirits still stalked their old hunting grounds and would resent intrusions from any but the little folk.

Wielding the broken branch as if it were a sword or axe, the Bun lay into the dense clump of briars with gusto. Suddenly, he was crying out in pain as a thick bramble recoiled and dug deep into his unprotected wrist. He let out a sharp cry as he jumped back, blood flowing freely from an open wound.

"The curse a Jaysus on ya," he swore as he dropped the branch and tried to stem the flow. Stumbling back, he fell heavily banging his head on a stumpy bush as he did so. Though his situation was delicate Seamie knew he couldn't leave him like that. He'd explain his presence later but for the moment he'd have to risk that rather leave him in mortal danger.

"I was after rabbits Brian when I heard a voice and came in to investigate," he lied.

It was obvious he was more than surprised to see the youth but as he was losing blood quickly he accepted the youth's help. Putting his jacket under his head while tearing the sleeve off his shirt he searched around frantically for a good bunch of lichen. Using the top part only, and making sure to keep the soil from it, he covered the wounded area and tied the torn shirtsleeve around the lot. According to Tess the lichen would work fast and protect the affected area.

He had gone very quiet and was as white as a ghost as Seamie squeezed a little water from a handful of lichen he had dipped in a pool beside them. A gentle shaking soon saw the blood returning to his ashen face. He was over the worst now Seamie felt but he'd have to get him out of there as quickly as possible. 'A hardy hoor' as the locals used say, he was soon struggling to his feet. Handing him the stick to steady himself Seamie offered his shoulder but it was clear he was coming round when he declined.

Tightening the baling twine around his waist he shook his head as he steadied himself.

"Them cursed briars are possessed," he said as they stepped gingerly back along the tracks.

"Don't bother talking now Brian," Seamie urged as they walked back slowly towards his shanty.

Pointing to where he kept the key hidden behind a loose stone in the gable end, Seamie withdrew it gingerly and opened the door. Anyone with a mind to do so would have walked through the same door as if it were paper, but that was neither here nor there he thought as he eased him into the only chair in the little room. Heaps of dry tinder and cipíns(small sticks)lay in bundles in the corner near the open hearth. Being well used to lighting Tess's fire Seamie had a good one going in jig time. The kettle was soon singing as he prepared a jar of tea for him.

"You're a quare hawk lad," the Bun smiled as he blew on the tea. Needless to say, there was neither milk nor sugar nor did it make a bit of differ to either as they supped from the two jam jars.

"Who'd want mugs," Seamie joked as he thought of the value of the jars. Although he had never been in the shanty before he correctly deduced how he coped with the nocturnal visitors in search of something to eat. Lines of jam jars stood shoulder to shoulder on the makeshift mantelpiece over the fireplace. "Rodents and the like would have to venture further afield in search of supper," he suggested as he showed him how he kept the batch loaf safe as well. Concealed in thick brown paper it was safe inside a biscuit tin that was the usual present given by Hewart every Christmas.

"Indeed, I saw the hoors nibbling at it but it's got the better of them so far a mhic. You couldn't be up to them though. They'd mind mice on a crossroads they would."

Seamie laughed with him as he felt he was well on the road to recovery by now and was at ease with his presence. Time had told him that if he kept his counsel people would trust him. It always worked. Everyone knew he could be trusted to keep his mouth shut if it wasn't going to harm anyone by doing so. There were secrets and there were secrets. Some didn't deserve to be called such but others…

"I'd better tell you what I was up to Seamie," he began.

"That's your business Brian," he said as he pretended not to be unduly interested.

"There's not much you don't know gossoon and I know for sure you'll keep it to yourself. Tess told me the divil wouldn't get news out of you if you didn't want to tell him," he continued.

"Well, it lets people trust me and gets me to places where few other youngsters get to go," he ventured as he saw him preparing to tell his story.

"Them Lís's and forts have more to tell than most," he said as he lit one woodbine from the ashes of another.

"The Maguires are here as long, if not longer than most of the people in the Parish. It's said that we came out of the caves beyond in the Commons and maybe it's true, but a lot seem to have come out of there as well. It's said that my great, great grandfather was hiding out with a group of rebels after Sarsfield and St. Ruth had nearly freed the country from that bastard Willy the Orangeman. St. Ruth, the bollocks, lost his head in Athlone through not trusting Sarsfield and it was all downhill after that. Those that were able had to fight and run and keep at it until they made it to the safety of the marshes and bogs around Abbeyshrule. They were helped by their own of course, lying low until the Dutch murderers gave up and went after richer spoils further south. The low lands of Longford offered little to them, although many's a settler from Cromwell to King Billy, found nice ground around here. Indeed, they're still here though they're as Irish as ourselves by now," he nodded as he warmed to his story.

"That same fort over there has hidden many's the secret down the years a mhic. Priests and parishioners hid there during the worst of times. There was a fair sized cave there all the time but what they didn't know was that the 'Mad' Maguire had found another cave leading off the small front one and kept it to himself until he was on his death bed. He passed on the secret to his son who was my grandfather. The secret was passed from father to son until now. Now that there's only meself left I was thinking of telling Tess, but sure, as you know her better than meself, I might as well tell you or the secret will die with me. They say you should never bring a secret to the grave with you or your soul will be tortured with it forever. Now I don't know if that's true or not but I don't want to take a chance on it either Seamie. I'm sure as sixpence you'll mind the secret well until you know what to do with it. I mind the time my father brought me there the first time.

You'd never think there was a cave there at all at all it was that well hidden. It's hard to say how they stumbled on it but it was a long time ago. I think it might have been in my grandfather's time when one of the other Maguires- no relation- was caught stalking the place. He disappeared overnight and was never seen again. That wasn't unusual around here then or now. You know full well about the Mulveys beyant in Toome. I'm sure Tess will have told you about their gossoon that wasn't the full shilling. He went missing too but no one knew what happened. They said he died very young and was buried in Taghsionnod. Others said they'd hear cries around the house in the middle of the night. Some said it was the Banshee but it was years later when your own father, a great man to tell when a cow was due to calf, was passing by when Mulvey called him to check a young heifer that was near her time. Rex gave his verdict that it'd be another day at least and was ready to leave when Fr. Pat pulled up in the very Volkswagen that had chopped the finger of Mulvey a week earlier. He marched in past them without as much as 'how do you do?'

"Your father asked Mulvey if anything was wrong but was as wise going out the gate as going in."

"What do you think happened Brian?" Seamie asked, more by way of keeping him going than anything else now that he had him in full swing.

"Well, it didn't take your father too long to find out. Sure he knows everyone in the parish and is a fair hand at ferreting things out, as you well know. He kept digging and pulling until Oul Mulvey in Ballintubber told him about the gossoon that never died. That put the ferrule on it altogether. It turned out in the long run that the child that was supposed to have died never died at all. He was locked into a small room for years and never got out again as far as anyone around knows. The PP knew of course and called every now when the gossoon was not well or acting up. It's another strange case but sure the place is full of strange cases Seamie as you well know."

Agreeing with him that there were a lot of unanswered questions he wanted to know more about Mulvey's finger and the PP's Volkswagen.

Well a mhic, Fr. Pat was having a bit of bother with his car and got Mulvey to have a look at it. He was too bloody miserable to bring it to a proper mechanic- not that Mulvey wasn't handy enough at an engine, and he having to keep trucks and tractors going day and night. If it wasn't for the new machinery Johnjo and the father kept in to him he'd have to give up altogether. The pull of money that they got from Argentinia didn't last jig time with the abuse they gave it. Some said they got thousands but sure we'll never know. It kept half the parish from going thirsty for a good while. What they didn't drink they invested and like manys the bad investment when it's in the wrong hands it loses its value instead of making it. The machinery kept their slate clean in Mulveys for nearly a year until the well went dry. There was nothing for it then only the old tractor but that soon bit the dust as well. The new tractor they bought wasn't in their names at all as the bloody eejits left Mulvey to organise it for them. What else would he do only put it in one of his own lad's names?

Anyway, wasn't the PP sitting in out of the cold when Mulvey asked him to be ready to turn the engine when he shouted at him. The wind was high and the priest a bit deaf as well so he had to shout at him several times not to turn the key until he told him. Well, they got their messages mixed up and the next thing the top of Mulvey's finger was flying faster than the feckin' fan.

The curses and swears of Mulvey would light candles beyant in Edgeworthstown. Out jumps the PP and orders him into the car and straight over to Doctor McGivney. The doctor took one look at the top of his finger and flung it into the field saying "it wasn't much use before and it wasn't going to be any use from now on either." Maybe he should have checked with the women of the parish first but we'll let that hare sit as Tess says.

Divil the likes of the row that started then Seamie but the PP and the Doctor got into it fairly lively then. Ordering them into the field to find the finger because it'd have to be buried in holy ground, the PP wouldn't budge an inch. McGivney told him if he could jump the quick any better than the excuse of a horse he was after buying then he might come out and help him to find Mulvey's finger. Pat Carrigy was pretending to be topping the quick beside them, but was about as busy as a butcher during Lent. He spotted McGivney picking up a lugworm pretending it was the finger. He took it inside and dressed it up a bit and put it in a tin box where he kept needles and the like. Handing it to Mulvey he told him to take it with him and the priest as well and not to let it out of his sight until it was blessed and buried. Mulvey didn't need to be reminded because he knew their form too well and knew they'd stay at it 'till the cows came home if he didn't sort them out.

They'd be still at it if he hadn't separated the two of them. He had to go up to the North to get butter and stuff that very day and didn't want to waste another minute. Once Carrigy took the wink and verified the find the priest was happy. Carrigy knew how to keep his mouth shut when there was a chance of a shilling. He didn't lie either because all he agreed to was that the doctor had made a find. It didn't matter to him if it were a stick or an onion as that wasn't the question he was asked. Mulvey had the car running anyway so the PP had to jump in or he'd be left standing. They were arguing the toss the whole way to the border but sure the time flew with the way they were planning to hobble the doctor's horse at the upcoming Gymkhana. Two better thieves you wouldn't get if you walked the seven parishes," the Bun told him as he poured boiling water onto the tealeaves in his glass mug. Happy too that he had talked himself better he forgot all about the briar that nearly drained every drop of blood that was in him. Tess told Seamie later that his blood was so thin she had to put him on a feed of nettles and watergrass(watercress) to build him up a bit.

Although anxious to leave as the evening was getting on he still wanted to find out about the cave and where the other Maguire disappeared to. The Bun had enough of it though and was off with the fairies after the tea and the bread and jam. Pulling the door after him as he left he advised the Bun to take it easy for a few days to build up his strength again. There'd be lots of time for the story about the cave now that he had his confidence.

Deep in the cave

He was getting over the Bull field gate a week later when he spotted the Bun standing on the spud stone about to launch himself on his flying machine down the hill towards Tess's palace. Rattling the gate rather than frighten him he smiled as the old man stepped off the stone.

"There you are, the very man I was looking for!" the Bun said as he composed himself by leaning over the handlebars. "Do you mind the time you saved me bacon beyant in the fairy fort?" he asked.

"I do indeed Brian," he replied as he sat on the spud stone hoping he was going to hear more about the Bun's forefathers.

"As I was about to tell you that time before I fell asleep, the secret of the second cave was passed down through the generations. That's all they knew about it, that there was a second cave. They said the first person into it would die a bad dog's death so that kept people from going near it. As well as that the memory of the zigzag path that led over the marsh to the fort was lost. A couple of the Cummins's made a half-hearted shot at it but soon gave up as they began to sink in the marsh; 'quagmire' I heard Munis calling it because he was an edumecated man and knew big words like that. All Munis ever wanted was a good feed above in Wynns Hotel and an armful of wimmen and shure, mebbe he was right. He had a way with wimmen and a way with money, and shure one beggers the other if you know what I mean," he winked conspiratorially.

"Anyway, wasn't I adin with Tess one time when we were younger when I upped and told her about the whole damn thing."

"Why didn't you say that to me long ago?" she said. "Well, the upshot of it all was that she had heard it said that there was a stone with a map engraved on it somewhere not far from the fort. It took me ages to find it because moss had grown on it over the years. I kinda thought as much because I had inspected nearly every fair sized stone in the fields around the fort. I was of the opinion it might be a flat stone as them boys were no eejits way back then. Bit by bit I worked my way back to a flat stone just inside the little Boreen leading past the fort and there it was. No sooner had I peeled off the moss and cleaned it as well as I could than I started to see signs and lines. I took my time at it mind because you can't be rushing these things as you well know; you being the kinda gossoon you are and all that. Tess wasn't far off when she said you'd mind mice at the crossroads and I'm not being a bit disrespectful either. Well, there it was and there I was and what do you think I did then? Not an easy one I know but didn't I look for another flat stone and put it on top of it in case anyone would be passing the boreen and spot it. Sure I don't think anyone went that way but meself but you never know these days a mhic. There's hoors as is going the road day and night and you mightn't be asking them their business because it's said they'd stick a knife in you as quick as look at you. Didn't Sandy lose a bundle just a short while ago and he out the back in the wagon filling a few drums of oil. They were watching him for sure. Well, in they went and lifted his wallet out of his coat pocket and cleaned the till as well. Tis said it was the Blue Door hoor but they might as well be idle as they cut straight across the fields without a sinner seeing them.

As I was saying before you stopped me. No, you didn't stop me, I stopped meself. Sorry about that. I took me time at it and before that summer was out I had it figured. Up I went to Tess and showed her the map I had drawn. I was shocking careful not to make a dog's dinner of it and drew it as good as any man could, not leaving out a dot. Now Tess as you know is a fierce clivir woman and hadn't she it all figured out in a flash. I felt like the Gawk when I saw what she was after doing. Didn't she turn the map upside down and by joining the dots and lines wasn't it as clear as daylight even to an amadaun like meself. We agreed to meet soon after to explore whatever there was to explore and left it at that."

A few days later as the dawn chorus broke, she slipped out the front door, rounded the corner of the house and checked the coast was clear before easing through the tubular bars at Jordan's cross-roads. At the slightest sound of a bike or a tractor she faded into the hedges as only she could. As hard found as a robin's nest she melted into nature because she was part of it. Along by the deep drain she could move rapidly because the few houses in Ballynamanagh were hidden from view. She heard Mad Maggie rousing the Cuddy but knew there was no chance she'd be heard or seen as she hurried past the Buck's and on past Maguire's Lane until she stood in the Bun's yard. A wisp of smoke told her he was up and about and ready for her.

"Come in girl the kittle's boiling. We'll have a mouthful before we set off."

"Alright so Brian, we might as well. God knows when we might drink another sup," she said as she blessed herself at the thought of the strange adventure that lay in front of them. Close as she was to nature her experience of the Underworld was limited to the odd encounter with the fairies and Leprechauns as she wandered far and wide through the countryside. There weren't many she'd bother with but there were a few good men that'd stop for a chat once in a while and if the day was good and no one was in any particular hurry they'd sit on the bridge until the tales were told and it was time for tea. They knew and she too, that to rush away after a decent chat wasn't the right thing to do. Manners being manners they'd time it so the tea was part of the overall visit. They often talked about the Other World and of the few who got there, more by chance than anything else. Yes, she was aware of people living long past their natural but whether they knew they'd passed through the Portal or not was a different story. She had a feeling she was close to that point too because her dreams were full of it of late.

"A grand bit of toast Brian."

"Aye, you can't beat Flynn's bread, or McNamee's either. It's lovely with a bit of jam or marmalade."

"Well, I suppose we'd better be going so before the rest of the world is out and about."

"We could do worse girl. What they don't know won't trouble them."

"What have you in the bag?" she asked as he closed the door behind them.

"Just a few things we might need if we get into any bother. I brought the small billhook, a rope, a good Bord na Móna torch and a few bits and pieces."

"Better sure nor sorry Brian. You did right. I brought a few sandwiches in case we're detained longer than we expect."

"Come on round the house for a minute Tess 'till I show you something," he said as he led her along a path he had recently cut through a thicket of nettles, thistles and bushes. Using the billhook he cleared a section around a flat stone and then with the sharp blade he removed the moss and fungus until a hexagonal symbol was clearly visible. His uncle Pat was the first to engrave the stone so that the secret wouldn't be lost completely. And hid it in a way it wouldn't be easily uncovered. That happened after an exceptionally dry summer exposed the stone path that seemed to wander aimlessly from Billy to Jack. It was far from that. The lines were formal and connected at criss-cross angles, an obvious ruse to confuse the curious. As soon as he came across the stone he covered it with another flat one so as it wouldn't be too obvious. Some time later when he felt the time was right he hoisted it into his wheelbarrow and half-hid it in brambles behind the house where he lived now.

"We slipped over the fields to the Rath before there was a thrush stirring. She had it all in her mind and we hadn't to look at the map wonst. She skipped across that hidden pathway like a fecking fairy and me doing me best to keep in to her. I barely mind but she could pick the best of them and she only a girleen-'a pure hoor to go'-as the fella said. I fancied her meself but sure I wasn't at the races with all those dandies around. She told me later she wouldn't lift her head never mind her skirt for the most of them. She knew what she wanted and got it. That was the way with her but you know that yerself gossoon. Anyway, there we were inside the Rath and before you could say 'kiss me arse' wasn't she after slipping inside the twin rocks and gone on me. Divil the likes of it you ever saw. She left me stewing for a few minutes before she eased the rock back the same as if it was a door. Sitting on an axis it was and easier to move than a well-oiled door if you knew how to do it. Well, in we went and she having the lamp lit and all. There wasn't a bit of fear on her even when a few bats flew past us. It was lucky we had that lamp or we wouldn't have seen the drop and would have ended up in a heap with bones broken as well. Didn't the passageway drop under the river and up again the other side! It would have swept all before it in winter if you didn't know where you were going. Several hollowed out ledges led up and down and by putting your feet in them and leaning over to the other side you could stay bone dry. Clever hawks those that even thought of it never mind built it. On we went a bit more until it opened out into a bigger room like a cave, as dry as my mouth was just then. There were ould ship boxes all around the place and weapons standing up against the side walls too. I never saw the likes before but those were pikes for fighting with, the same as they used long ago in Ballinamuck and Wexford too I heard. There were ould blunderbusses and traps that'd catch a bear never mind a man. The strange thing was, there were fairly new guns and rounds of ammo as well which we decided must have been left there by the RA. There's not much those boys don't know and a better hiding place couldn't be got in a month's march. Tess told me to keep me mouth shut but she needn't have bothered as me mouth is like a clamp when it's no business of me own. The lamp was nearly out so we high tailed it back as fast as we could and just in time too as it gave out as we reached the swinging stone."

Either way, it was a huge mystery and one that needed more thought and careful planning she told the Bun as they decided they had gone far enough for now. She'd have to have a chat with the fairies herself before venturing into their secret world. She knew exactly who she was going to talk to before she'd take another step into this holy of holies; the one and only Fr. McCabe of course.

He often wanted to go back he said but he was afraid the Boys might be there and make him pay for his curiosity. He did go back soon after the brother dying because he had to hide a few things belonging to him.

Gobsmacked by the story, and even more so by the thought that a man that seemed to be a miser to the world was exactly the opposite, he could only admire his attitude to life and the hereafter. The more he thought of it the more he realised how little an influence the Church had on its so-called devotees. People like Tess, the Bun, the Nugget, Babs and their peers knew how to live and make their peace with their own god. Though they attended the sacraments it was more for a peaceful life than anything else. They had seen far too much hypocrisy from the powers that be to pass the slightest bit of heed on them. It was their way and who was to question that he thought to himself as the Bun poured another mouthful into his jam jar. Though anxious to get home he didn't wish to offend him, especially after all he had just heard.

"There's more to it Seamie," he said suddenly as he poked at the dying ambers in the fireplace.

Asking him to hold on a minute Seamie ran out to the lean-to by the house and got an armful of sticks that would keep the fire going for the evening and into the night if it turned cold. Stacking them neatly in the corner by the hearth he threw a few on the still-lit coals.

It wasn't long until flames were leaping merrily and sparks were spitting like wildcats. The Bun's house wouldn't hold a candle to Tess's in terms of heat retention because the roof was of galvanised iron with no insulation underneath. The rafters were of untreated timber that had a short shelf life due to the insects that'd make mincemeal out of it while you'd be saying the trimmings.

"Sorry Brian, go on with your story," he said knowing there was more and probably better to come.

"Right so," he grinned as he eased himself back into his old armchair which groaned like a bad ass under his weight. Reminding himself to give that chair a miss, Seamie put a board on top of the big pot and sat back against the hob.

"As I was saying," he went on, "the biggest surprise was when I was looking for a spot to hide the brother's few bob."

He then proceeded to tell Seamie, that when tapping for a weak spot in the wall, he nearly fell out of his standing when it suddenly caved in exposing another finely worked tunnel leading away into the darkness. Fearing he might be caught he decided to shore it up until he had a chat with Tess and maybe explore it another time with her. He took great care to move the pikes before propping them up to conceal his handiwork. That done, he smoothed everything over making sure there were no obvious footprints. Satisfied that it would hold up, he beat a path home as fast as possible lest anyone should be out counting or hunting.

Doing the Rounds

Babs brought more kids into the parish than ten women and brought the lot of them up in the 'Hut' a two-roomed cabin that had been used as a County Council waggon years before.

"It was better than the Work House adin in Ballymahon," was her answer when asked about the meagre comforts of the Hut.

"There was water a mhic and sure the views would lift your heart when you'd be hungry," she roared laughing as she thought of the nonsense of her last remark.

"They had to learn how to survive as soon as they were able to walk Seamie."

Out after rabbits and pheasants bigger than themselves and nothing only hunger to bring them home was what they'd be at. The lassies as well as the lads could skin and clean a rabbit while you'd be admiring the views' she laughed as she thought of the times. Ah sure we were hardly ever hungry child. You won't go hungry if you weren't waiting for the table to be set. That's the holy all of it now. The lads brought home salmon and trout that'd keep two families going for a week. The Bailiff never got them either and they lifting fish from under his nose and pretending to be fishing for pinkeens. He was after bigger fish though. He knew there was nothing to be got from my crew so he left them alone. May he never have to say an act of contrition" she remarked as she finally pulled her purse from the depths of her ample bosom. Relieved that she hadn't asked him to retrieve it for her he breathed an inward sigh of relief.

His mother had warned him against taking much from the decent woman because she hadn't got it for herself. He reluctantly took a two shilling bit rather than embarrass her as she gave him her blessing and bid him farewell. A promise to apply himself to his studies and to keep her in his prayers was all she wanted in return.

Resting in Peace

There was still one farewell to make. So, parking Betsy behind the tree he crossed the stile near the mass well.

It would be months before he'd see her last resting place and he wanted to be sure she'd not feel her eye was wiped.

He needn't have worried. No sooner had he touched the sacred ground than he felt a warm glow beside him.

"Is it yourself Tess?" he asked, a smile lighting the area as if it was dark.

"Indeed it is a mhic," she replied as her shadow fell across him and warmed him to the depths of his soul.

"You've been beyant at the Lough I see," she said softly.

"You don't mind I hope," he half asked, half sought her permission.

"Divil a bit I mind Seamie. Why would I? I know you'll never forget her or how close ye came to leaving us. It helps to go over these things and these places. Sure I spent half me life doing that until you came along and gave me something to live for. You'll miss her for sure but she'll live on through other people in your life. Get on with your life now and if you have time to think of us well and good. Thanking her, he told her he had to do the rounds over the coming days. Though not really looking forward to it the few bob would come in handy between now and the Christmas."

"And what else would you do? You're the light of the Parish's eye so you'll clean up for sure. Aren't there more misers with money in the mattress than mice at the crossroads and you might as well be having it than the PP's friends and family and they with more than the lot of us put together? Off you go now and mind yourself. I'll be around if you need me."

The warmth of her shadow passed through him as he felt her moving away. It was a sensation he'd only ever feel with Annabel no matter who he was with. His thoughts flew back to the evening she spirited her to him and the way they bonded under her benign gaze.

It was some days later before she felt it was safe to rescue him from the ecstasy that flooded through every fibre of his body.

"A joy like that only hits you the wanst," was how she started to explain his 'crossing.' "You're caught now me boy and no matter who you're with or where you wander, the person you're with at that time of 'crossing' will turn out to be Annabel. And let it not stop you either a mhic because you will hit on others and they'll hit on you but for the two of you know there will never be any other."

It was to be some time before the wisdom of her words hit him and drove it home to the depths of his inner being. Relief and happiness flooded through his very soul as he threw his leg over the bar and took the road to Abbeyshrule.

Taking Leave

His departure imminent, a mere week away, he decided to pay a last visit to his dear departed friend before leaving for Baldoyle, a college by the sea on the outskirts of Dublin. Electing to join the brother in his great adventure away from the daily diet of rural Ireland he settled for the same college. It seemed the best way to escape and he didn't need to be cajoled into going.

Leaving his bike by Sinneach's well he crossed the stile into the old graveyard. There wasn't a sinner around. Ned had already done the rounds of his mearing and, content that all was in order, had gone on about his business.

Checking that the surrounding fields were empty he climbed the Mount to survey the hinterland. Content that he was alone he went back inside the graveyard and went down on one knee by her grave. A simple, wooden cross was all that marked the spot. Nothing else told the world of her passing. He looked around for something more permanent but nothing stood out. He remembered a stone he had seen close to the Limekiln at Lough Sheedon and decided to go look for it. Crossing the fields above the well he left the Lough to one side and descended by the Limekiln. Sure enough it was still where he had seen it. It resembled a face with a hint of a smile- a bit like the Mona Lisa as he remembered seeing it. It seemed a perfect marker for the grave of one who possessed a permanent smile and a unique attitude to life. Mounting it on the carrier he went back to the graveyard and placed it firmly by the head of the grave where it seemed so at ease with its new location. Happy now, he gave it a knowing wink and headed home.

It was time to go. There was nothing left to keep him about the place now. The school pals were getting ready to follow their fathers into the fields or the raised bogs near Kenagh or Mount Dillon where they would commence their formal apprentice-ship. Such courses were integral to a secure future and highly re-garded around Abbeyshrule. Not for Seamie though. The escape hatch was as wide as a haggard gate and he grabbed it with both hands after consulting Tess. Though now with her daughter in another sphere she still hovered close. He felt her presence as that of a Guardian Angel, only much more real and finite. She knew that he could forge his own way now but she poked occasionally to remind him of her presence. How could he forget her? She had opened his mind to other worlds, some long gone, other's to come; trained him for battle as Setanta had trained Cuchulainn, only less for fighting and more for living. With such mental re-sources he could walk where angels feared to tread and rest after battle by the hob where they often broke potato bread and drank mugs of tea by the light of the fire. Possessed of a photographic memory by dint of her constant encouragement, and comfortable in the knowledge that he could recount her tales verbatim, he sought the outlet to display them. It was within arm's reach, just a few days march away or a couple of hours by train from Mullingar or Longford.

The initial sequence of events would closely follow that of his brother Mikey who had already progressed from the college near Moate to a more refined educational outlet in Sutton on the North Dublin coast.

Mikey's stories were almost as good as Tess's. Such goings-on were difficult to comprehend at first but gradually gained credence as one observed the link in the chain. And, why not! They answered most of his questions and provided an opening to a new way of life. Mounting Betsy he set out to bid adieu to his neighbors and friends in the sure knowledge that whatever lay ahead could hardly better that which had already transpired.

"So you're off to join your brother a mhic. If you learn half as much as him we won't be able to keep in with you at all at all," Mammy Egan chuckled through her two remaining teeth as she pressed a ten bob note into the youngster's half-clenched fist.

"Go on, take it Seamie. It'll come in handy for the things you'll need above in the 'Big Smoke'," she advised as she paid little heed to his attempts at refusing her kind offering.

The pattern repeated itself at every other door. Though poorer than church mice, they always had a little held in reserve for a special cause. The Stag and Cowboy were supping tea when he entered. Pulling the stool from under the table the Cowboy told him to sit and join them. Tess told him never to refuse tea in a humble house because it would be considered a slight. The conversation swung to their sister somehow. He didn't quite catch the inference but felt her disappearance had something to do with his father. They beat around the bush a bit before it dawned on them that he had no idea where they were coming from so they let the hare sit. It was years later before he met Violet, a charming older lady still full of life and stories of her youth. But that's another story!

Home Late

Just like a petrol tank when she's reading low" was The Cuddy's way of telling it even though the only tank he knew was the barrel of water at the side of his shanty!

Seamie's cause fitted the bill nicely. The poor of the parish were sick to death of giving alms to Africa for so-called orphaned blacks that would see little of it after the self-appointed dictators like Lamumba and his murderous military had siphoned it away for their nefarious purposes. The Congo was a case in point. Not only did Ireland pour millions in aid she could ill afford but lost many of her finest in defending the indefensible in the killing fields around Leopoldville and Brazzaville.

"We'll never learn," he remembered Tess saying as she spoke of the squandered sums the poor of Ireland threw into The Dark Continent.

No point in worrying about that now he thought as he hurried from house to house as slowly as decency demanded.

It was dark as he turned into the yard but his arrival didn't go unnoticed by Shep who, trained not to give the game away, showed his delight at his master's return by a furious tail wagging as he hared round in circles.

Rex missed nothing either. The soft glow of a Sweet Afton caught Seamie's eye as he wheeled his bike into the turf shed.

"You've been gone a while young man," he half chided as he put his hand on the boy's shoulder.

"I can hardly stand straight with the weight of the halfpennies," he joked as he held out a fistful of silver.

"Bedad, you did do well. I just said that to your mother a few minutes ago. I told her you'd line your pockets if anyone ever could. Ah, you're no daw either I see. The jute bag came in handy too. No better man for holding anything heavy. Go on in and have your dinner or it'll not be worth eating. There's an elephant of a trout on your plate that'll make a man out of you before you know it. I'll be in shortly to hear all the news of your travels. I want to set the snares before I get caught in one myself," he laughed as he headed out the fields, Shep close at his heels.

Sleep came easy after the counting. Though his mother didn't want to take what he insisted she should, he was happy she did so as money was hard to come by. A yardful of turkeys needed lots of good feeding to be ready for the Christmas, but that was a while off yet and bills had to be paid or the neighbours would soon spot the obvious. She wasn't having any of that. Her pride in her housekeeping would not allow that.

They had counted out nearly fifty pound between notes and coins, 'a small fortune in times of need,' as the fella said.

"That will keep the hoors from the haggard for a while," Mike grinned at Nora as she gave Seamie a warm hug before he climbed the thirteen to dreamland.

Fairies and phantoms followed Tess and her besom across the Commons as Annabel and he circled the Glebe for a secure hiding spot.

"Your cave Seamie," she giggled as he gave the knowing wink.

"Right so," he said as he took her arm and led her over the boreen in the direction of the Turlough and their cave of tranquility. Her tartan school skirt felt like a warm blanket as it brushed against him. The tall bulrushes around the lake swayed in the warm breeze as they lay on the soft lichen by the Lime Kiln and hugged each other tightly. Pressure points swelled to maximum as they grey into each other in an ecstasy of wonderment and delight. Though still in the early stages of adulthood they were well prepared by Tess and Allison. Not for them the fear of the Church, or an early pregnancy either. Nature blessed them Tess told him as they drank mugs of tea and ate rasp by the fireplace in her humble but homely abode. They had only been together a few weeks when she invited them both to sup with her. Though wary of his soul mate's response he was delighted when her bright blue eyes lit up with delight at the thought of a visit to Tess whom she knew to be his favorite person. There was little she didn't know about the old lady now. Tess was a break from the mundane, a walk on the wild sideanda glimpse into another world. Her father Tim had studied in Trinity and applied it to his daily life around his sprawling farm. Her mother Allison had met and married Tim while they were both studying there.

"Where there's muck there's money," Tim would laugh as Annabel showed him her farmerette's hands, hair and nails religiously short to keep them strong and undamaged as she helped around the farm. It didn't take from her fine figure or fair face as she grey into puberty in the same form as her mother; strong good looks, clear complexions, fair hair and deep blue eyes.

"The Viking influence," she maintained when queried on her people's past.

"That fecking cock," was his first thought as the rooster ended his dream and propelled him back on terra firma.

It seemed so unfair. How could such an earthy yet saintly soul pass away so quietly?

It was just at that precise moment he decided that she'd never be forgotten. He wasn't sure yet how he was going to achieve that but the thought was already formulating of writing a book of her verses or a book of her life. Or maybe both!

Time flew now as he prepared for his imminent departure to the College in the city. His days were full as he helped at home or went fishing with his father or anyone else who was so disposed. There wasn't much time for that either but he made the most of it as he honed his skills at fly-fishing under the benevolent gaze of Bill Kilmurray, a master of the art. He wished he had more time to devote to it, but as Bill said, "There's always another summer."

Shep was by his side most of the time and lay under the tree for a rest while his young master scanned the horizon for his grandfather who would be on the way home from Knockagh. Realizing he had time to spare, he took advantage of the time lapse to scan the Glebe in the fond hope of catching a glimpse of his fair love. It was not to be. She was gone. Their time together, though limited, was pure joy. He shivered with excitement at the thoughts of their secret hiding places around the Glebe and floated into a deep reverie of delight as he lay beside her in the long grass or swam with her in the Turlough or over by Bosque. The warm sun dried them off as they cuddled and kissed far from prying eyes.

"The Fox dad, the fox is about. I'm sure I heard him. Listen to Shep will you. He's scratching the door like mad," he whispered as his father slipped on his trousers and pullover.

"That dog would talk to you," Rex whispered as he grabbed his shotgun from over the mantelpiece. Watching from the window he saw his father slip out into the dark night. It was hard to follow his progress but a spot of light from the partially hid moon showed him standing beside the old elm. Peering into the darkness he saw him taking aim as the fox approached downwind.

He jumped as the shot rang out. The fox fell like a stone.

"Nice one dad," he nodded as his father strode into the scullery with the fox by the tail.

"I'll leave the rest to you Seamie. Head over to the Barracks in Abbeyshrule tomorrow if you have time and collect the bounty. How did you hear him anyway? I thought my hearing was good but it wouldn't hold a candle to yours. Your mother will be delighted. Off to bed with you now, you can tell me all about it tomorrow."

Hewart was waiting at the haggard gate when Seamie returned from checking on the sheep in the Four Acre. He had a telegram for Jack of the Lock that needed to be delivered but couldn't leave the shop until Miss Nelly returned from the town.

Jack of the Lock was the keeper of the swing gates on the Royal Canal at Tenelick. His neat little cottage beside Lock's bridge was owned by the Royal Canal Authority and was set back beautifully into the side of the hill, more like a cave house than anything else. Apart from the flowers around the front door and windows there was little indication of a house there at all. Theirs was a difficult subsistence on the meagre pay that Jack received from the canal authority, but they managed to make ends meet by selling home-made produce to the bargemen ferrying barrels of stout from Guinness's Brewery to the various licensed establishments around the Midlands.

Jack's wife Mona sold home-made country butter, big fresh hen and duck eggs, all kinds of vegetables and a rich array of jams and tarts to the bargemen as they dallied while Jack operated the heavy mechanism of the big lock gates. Their return trip provided a double whammy for Mona as the bargemen loaded up with the much sought after black Midland peat for their return trip to the Capital. Though Jack was a teetotaller, the odd barrel of porter invariably ended up in the lock house where it could be dispensed at a reduced rate to the locals thereby turning the house into a popular little Shebeen. Likewise, many's the bottle of his fine peat-distilled poteen found its way to the parlours around Portobello in the Rathmines area of the city. Jack often said that if it wasn't for 'the Long Acre' there'd be nothing to feed his few cows on. There were many who were worse off than him but they got on with life instead of complaining about it.

As he returned home he saw his mother chatting at the front gate. It was Biddy, one of his favourite people in the entire area. He often dropped in on her on the way home from serving at the devotions and loved her ribald chats as well as her lovely daughter, though in a more platonic way because he didn't want to offend her or his soul mate Annabel. Nevertheless, it was another learning curve for him as mother and daughter were equally interesting in a very physical way. Tess had told him about Biddy's hospitable ways and how she often invited people in for a cup of tea and a sandwich or whatever they'd fancy. He was amused at the list of names that Tess mentioned by way of explanation but didn't give it much thought until one day he was passing their house after dark when he spotted 'Johnny-no-better-buckalero's' bike hidden behind the azalea bush. Wondering why the bike was there he walked round the house to investigate. Spotting him standing by the back window with his tool in his hand and a face like a beetroot made him even more curious, especially as he appeared to be getting it hard to breath. He thought he might have been attending to nature but it was a strange place to be doing that. Despite the delicacy of the situation he decided to ask him if he was alright or should he go in and get Biddy for him.

You'd think he was after getting a root up the arse the way he jumped back with fright.

"What the fuck!" was all he could say until he got his breath back. "Were you spying on me or what?" he asked as the sweat bubbled on his forehead.

"Not at all, I thought you were checking if the girls were ok or something but sure you might have gone in and ask them seeing you came this far," he answered.

"I'll do that straight away," he replied as he made for the door. "Don't say I was having a piss under their window or they'll make a laugh of me," he half pleaded as Seamie walked out towards the front gate.

"Strange place to have a pee," he thought.

Leaving Abbeyshrule Behind

Free from the glare of finger-held curtains he relaxed at last as he bade farewell to his father and the hackney man at Mullingar Railway Station. There was a while to wait before the train was due so after enquiring about the cost of the ticket he left his case in with the lassie saying he'd be back in a few minutes. A full-scale argument was going on between two hackney drivers as he hung around outside. It seemed one was taking fares from the other and true to their calling they argued like a haggard of turkeys until he politely asked if they'd have the change of a twenty pound note. Distracted and smelling a potential fare they reached for their wallets in the glove compartments Meanwhile Seamie palmed the twenty and handed over a tenner. 'The speed of the hand deceives the eye' Tess told him when she was showing him the three-card-trick and how to hide the dice. Returning to their argument they failed to spot the sleight of hand. Hearing the train approaching Seamie beat a hasty retreat.

Hueston Station become Westland Row, then Raheny before the Baldoyle stop just short of Sutton and Howth as the train passed out from the city and into the suburbs by the sea. A refined area mostly, it boasted big houses with even bigger gardens where palm trees waved in the wind blowing in across the bay from Lambay Island and Irelands Eye, a stone's throw from Howth Harbour.

Mikey had mentioned many of the great walks he and his crew got stuck into at least once every month. The Hill of Howth was reckoned to be one of the greats, both for scenic grandeur and opportunity. Seamie fell around the place laughing as Mikey told him of the many scams they perpetrated on the locals as they played puck with convention and the walk organizer, Gabby, also known as 'Mighty Mouse' due to his diminutive size.

It was easy to pull the wool over their eyes due to the number of walkers and the close relationship between most of them, but Barney was a different kettle of fish altogether. Those who weren't in one of the cliques knew better than open their mouths or they'd find it full of their own shite within jig time. It was rough justice but effective and rarely needed to be repeated. Mikey was a couple of years ahead of Seamie and knew the ropes well. Though different in many respects, the two brothers had a close bond and looked after each other, especially on the playing field or if a row broke out between the Townies and the Culchies. Apart from that, they went their own way, formed their own cliques or became an integral part of a more popular one. In a college of several hundred young men it was easy to keep a low profile and many did. Not Seamie or Mikey though! They were natural leaders and drew others around them 'like flies around a shite' as Griffin used to say when he couldn't get into the group due to his gauche mannerisms. The brothers rarely spoke to each other and never commented on their lives around Abbeyshrule. What happened at home stayed at home and belonged to another life.

All of this flooded through his mind as he walked behind Barney who had been waiting impatiently at the station. He made no attempt to help with the luggage as he watched Seamie struggle with his cases. Unperturbed, he fell in behind the fast striding prefect. Nor did Seamie bother with the other dozen or so youths who seemed to be heading in the same direction as he. There would be time to meet them later he thought as he coped manly with the weight of his cases packed tightly with home-made provisions his dear mother had prepared for him. There were a few other suspect items within but he'd find a safe storage place for them later. Mikey had warned him of the mean whores who'd home in on the raw recruits knowing they were carrying all kinds of goodies from the country.

"Over my dead body," was the warning he gave the first lad that grabbed his case at the main door.

"But we're supposed to help you unpack," was met with an icy stare that brooked no interference.

Barney handed them a room number as they crossed the threshold.

"Fucking 13A," was the first thought that entered his head as he threw his cases on the bed and lay back for a moment to get his breath back. Still, it could be worse he thought as he searched for a safe hiding spot. It didn't take him long as his eagle eye spotted a break in the wooden floor under his bed. Making sure his room was locked he quietly shifted the bed and prised the floorboard lose. It had been done before but whoever had done so hadn't time to withdraw his loot as, to his amazement, it was still there. A pot of jam long past its sell by date showed how long it was since the previous occupant had passed on. Five years seemed a long time but the bottle of Crested

Ten would now be a Crested 15 at least and would provide interior heating through the coming winter.

"Perfect," he thought as he carefully replaced the jam and other objects with his own. A quick root through the items revealed a small treasure throve. A heap of coins, a Stanley knife, a hunting knife, several pens and pencils, a slightly rusted torch and a box of Johnnies carefully wrapped in a muslin bag. That brought a wry smile to his face as he wondered who the previous occupant might be, and more importantly, how he planned to use them.

Someone like himself no doubt! Someone who had something to hide from jealous or prying eyes perhaps?

It mattered little now as he wrapped his belongings carefully before replacing the floorboard. He certainly didn't want anyone coming across his stash or the love letters Annabel had written him over the past two years. They were for the long days and hard nights when he'd take comfort in their warm words.

"A meaner man never lived," Seamie thought as he stood in line with the hundred condemned youths. A few of the Belfast brigade showed indifference but it was not enough to hide their inner fears as Barney swept up and down the line with a cor that'd turn a funeral.

"I'll have to watch that cunt," Seamie swore inwardly as he scanned the line for potential allies. It was far too early to judge but the Templeboy buachaill held promise. A hint of a wink drew an instant response. He relaxed a little. Ben was a big lad for a 14 year old. A farmer's son, he'd be used to hard work and Nature's whimsical ways. The slightest nod of the head reassured him he'd just made a real friend. He didn't need two when one good one would do. Fuck Barney. The game was on and he was no longer on his own. Thanks again Tess. You never lost it.

The inspection parade over Barney ordered all to the refectory.

"Not a word until Grace is over," he barked as the boys shot out the Big Room door and down the stairs as if they weren't there. The Big Mike stood squarely in front of them as they screeched to a full stop and a comma in front of him.

"You big Mikes," he roared as he visualized the college falling around his ears. "Get caught again and you'll all be like wallflowers for the next week," he threatened as he listed sideways to let the tsunami of hungry youngsters into the dining hall.

The older lads were helping the waitresses bring the food to the tables. It was piping hot and smelled like a turkey.

"Hunger is a great sauce," he whispered out of the side of his mouth as Ben left a dent in Gallogly's ribs.

"Fuck off and find a place for yourself," he growled, barely moving his lips. The pecking order was already in situ as alliances built up rapidly.

Grace over, the decibel level rose like a murder of crows as the early hunger pangs subsided and hilarity swept into full flow.

"You fairly sorted that cunt out," Seamie laughed as he winked back.

"They'll not take it kindly though," he said as he shook his head as he spotted the Northern Irish lads glaring across at them.

"We'll sort them out at the football anyway," Seamie advised as he passed the empty plates to the ends of the tables.

A roar from Barney followed a clatter of plates hitting the floor. Looking up Seamie saw the cause of the rumpus. Gallogly had deliberately tripped young Mulligan who was loading the plates onto the big trolley.

"I'll break his friggin' ribs this time," Ben swore as he tried to get up to sort him out. Seamie had a vice-like grip on his belt by now and kept him anchored against his will.

"Stay quiet you eejit," he growled at him as Ben tried to break free.

"Do you want us all to be hung? Leave it and we'll sort the hoor out later. No point in giving ourselves away now and falling into their trap. Can't you see they're testing the waters to see who's who?"

"You're right," Ben answered as he eased back into the seat. "Barney will sort it for now and show us who's who instead. Up there for dancing and down there for thinking," he laughed as he nearly took the skin of his knuckles as a sign of fraternity.

The day shot past in a blur as the new recruits attempted to settle in. Seamie saw no more of Ben until teatime at seven. About to sit down, his two legs were swept from under him. Falling back he hit his head off the bench as he fell. As he lay dazed Ben exploded off the bench like a prizefighter and caught Gallogly fair-and-square with an uppercut. All hell broke loose. In seconds they were surrounded by an eclectic group of Southern followers who swung like maniacs as the Northern contingent sought to pull Gallogly from the fray. It was saothar in aisce(labour in vain) though as Ben towered over them.

"Cover me!" he shouted as he drove into the middle of them flinging bodies left and right as if they were mere stacks of barley. Though bleeding, Seamie was stuck into Gallogly as if his life depended on it. Barney's whistle went off like a machine gun forcing most of the combatants apart.

"Hold it right there young man," Barney spoke in a voice that left no doubt as to who was in charge. Ben was fuming but knew the upper ground had been gained and quickly simmered down.

"That's better," Barney winked as he ushered him back to his seat.

"I saw every bit of that and the culprits will pay dearly," he shouted as they shook themselves down and sorted themselves out.

Calling out a list of names, he ordered them to the Principal's office immediately.

"Over here Séamus," he directed as he saw the young man being held erect by Ben.

"Go get the nurse," he ordered as he examined the cut.

"Ah, it's not as bad as it looks," he smiled as he sat the injured warrior down.

"You covered yourself well young man, and were covered well by Ben but you'll have to take some punishment for getting involved," he added.

"But…" was all Seamie got to say as Barney ordered him to the Principal's office after the nurse was finished cleaning the cut.

"There now, you'll be grand," she said as she cut and tied the loose end of the bandage.

The shouting from the Principal's office was reaching deafening point as he walked the long corridor to the office. Frightened faces shot past him as he joined Ben outside the door.

"Come in you two big Mikes," he ordered as he spotted them.

"Do you think I have nothing better to do than waste my time with you two big hooligans?" he asked as they stood in front of him.

They were about to speak when he silenced them with a winning smile.

"I hadn't planned a regional game for some time yet lads but it seems to me that you're well matched so we'll have it on Sunday instead of the Portrane walk. Now Ben, as captain of the Southerners you have little time to get organized but I think you have a team to match the lads from the North. Would you agree?" he added with a knowing smile. "Now get out of here," he roared so as not to give the impression of favoritism. He zipped his lips by way of telling them not to utter a word or pretend that anything was other than what it should be in light of the fracas in the dining room.

Like seasoned soldiers they strode into the study hall with not a hint of a smile. Ripples of acclamation spread round the room as they took their seats. Barney stood tall as they sat down.

"Now the next time the likes of this bravado breaks out here it will be over my dead body," he spoke fiercely as he thumped the rostrum. But just in case any of you brave hearts should even contemplate it I'm about to put all of you in your places. As he spoke he produced a list of names he was promoting to prefects. Calling out Ben's name first he followed it closely with those of Gallogly, Gibson, Murphy, MacAteer, Molloy, Best and Seamie.

'Evenly balanced' was the first thought to hit him though he wasn't too happy to be pushed into the limelight that early.

Outlining their duties Barney spared nothing as he lay down the law.

"One step out of line and you'll answer to your prefects before answering to me," he cautioned.

I couldn't have done better myself Ben smirked as they were ordered to sit down.

"Now for the good news," Barney smiled. "As you all know we are accustomed to having provincial games from time to time. We hadn't planned on one for another couple of months but the principal has decided there is no time like the present so we're going to have it next Sunday. The two captains will pick their team tomorrow after recreation and post them on the notice board for all to see. We need to put players in their respective categories so this will be as good a time as any to see where each player fits. I'll ref it myself so you know what to expect," he warned. A burst of applause greeted the news and early redemption.

Another round of applause greeted the respective captains Ben and Gallogly as they strode gallantly across the divide to shake hands.

The gesture was warmly received in light of the potentially disastrous opening of the season.

Used to the trimmings after the rosary, Seamie thought of the folks back home as he fell into bed. His mind rambled back to his favorite places as tiredness swept over him.

Tess was leaning over the half door as he ran down the back of the hedge towards her. A warm smile lit up her angelic face as she spotted him. With one bound he was across the stream and waltzing up to her without a care in the world.

"You'll land in the middle of it yet a mhic she laughed as he laid his arm gently on her frail shoulders."

"Is the kettle boiling Tess?" he fired back as she stood aside to let him in. He nearly dropped with shock as a wondrous figure stood up from the hearth and came to greet him.

"How in God's name…?" was all he could say as they fell into each other's arms.

"Tess told me you'd be here so I cycled over," Annabel answered with a mischievous grin.

"But you're in college somewhere. How did you get here?" he blurted out as they surfaced for air.

"And you too Seamie but there's no doubting Tess's power. We're here for now and I know she'll get us back before we're missed," she said as she glanced anxiously at the old lady.

"Don't worry your young heads about a thing," she said as she busied herself with a pan of potato bread.

"Just enjoy the while and leave the travel arrangements to me. Let ye rest on the settle bed there. You'll have a lot to say to each other no doubt," she suggested as she fussed about the fire preparing a bite for them. That done and all happy, she lay back in her sugán chair and fell fast sleep.

The bell startled him. He looked to where Annabel lay and saw only rumpled sheets. She was gone. Glancing quickly around he was amazed to see he was in his cubicle and not in Tess's palace. He wondered if he had been dreaming but knew it couldn't be so as his last act before falling into a deep sleep was a long, lovely kiss. Why, he could still feel her arms around him as they fell asleep together. What kind of magic had Tess worked this time he thought as he threw back the sheets and jumped onto the cold floorboards?

Barney was already doing the rounds as he washed himself with cold water. About to put on his shirt he stood naked as Barney pulled the door open quickly and stepped into the cubicle.

"Not bad young man," was all he said as he smiled and continued his rounds. Though a little shocked at the intrusion he was nonetheless pleased at the Brother's parting remark.

The pattern of each day was very similar but never boring. A seven thirty call led them to the chapel for Matins followed by breakfast and the first classes that ranged across a broad spectrum of learning and study. It didn't bother Seamie as he had come through the hard school of knocks with Quigley. Although a slow learner initially he had listened to Tess's advice and knuckled down to learning from one of the best. Quigley was a tough taskmaster but only because he loved teaching and wanted to bring the best out of all his pupils not just the clever clogs.

In this he had few peers. His pupils headed the list in the Primary Certificate year after year. His proud boast was that the ones who failed would make great farmers and in this he was absolutely right. He didn't mean that to be derogatory in any way as he farmed himself and loved the freedom it gave him. He meant that it was a different type of intelligence more suited to the outdoor life. Being able to read nature, plan good crop rotation and tillage as well as managing animal husbandry was time-consuming and demanding. He equated it to his many stories of the hunter/gatherers who roamed the Midlands many moons ago. The ancient Celts who hunted along the fish-filled Inny used a subliminal intelligence to support their growing clans. They learned from experience initially but soon self-appointed Quigleys taught the young around the campfires after the rigors of a long day's hunting. Many of the farmer's sons whom the Master taught went on to be successful in their own right and owed a lot to his sally rod. The rod soon sang the truth as he often said. It sorted the men from the boys and the farmers from the intellectuals. Few fitted either frame but it was enough to go on. There was no time for leniency or complacency he often told the doctor as they sipped a half one in the snug in Abbeyshrule. He wasn't a social animal but there were a few who got reasonably close to him. Neither was he selective in his companions. He'd enjoy the company of the irascible Clarke as much as Fr. Pat or Hewart even though he was of the other persuasion. His neighbors, Guard Fay and Ned Geoghegan, were close allies too as they aided and abetted each other in keeping the peace, providing basic sustenance to the poor and free boots to the poor of the parish. Religion was paramount and had pride of place in his school. A fervent catholic he never missed Sunday Mass and had little respect for anyone doing so. Not only did he prepare his pupils well, he also provided a string of mass servers for every occasion. There were only a few who could handle the thurible but Mikey and Seamie along with Mullin and Cahill did the honours when necessary.

It was after May devotions when a knock came on the sacristy door. Father Lynch was called to Maria's deathbed. Leaving the two brothers in charge of locking up he hurried away. Although anxious to join the Colehill gang for a bit of excitement on the way home their attention was drawn to the bottle of wine which the priest had forgotten to put away in his haste. Checking the church was empty Mikey ran to the front door and locked it. He did the same on the short aisles because they'd be exiting by the sacristy door and would drop the key off at the priest's house by the airfield. Seamie had already started on the wine knowing that was the game plan.

"It tastes like cat's piss," he grinned as Mikey put the bottle to his head and swallowed half of it nearly choking as he did so. It could be worse he spluttered as he handed it over. It didn't take them long to finish it either. Hiding the empty bottle in their bag they locked up and headed home as high as kites. Yahooing and singing they flew along the road to catch up on their gang who were pairing off by the new time as they approached Belton's 'plantin' a suitably secluded copse of young firs that would allow them to enjoy the pleasures of a shift. Little realizing they were half cut the girls shifted allegiances in order to capitalize on their exuberance. They had the full of their hands before they knew it as the lads threw caution to the winds and went places they'd never been before.

Back at class it was easy to keep up one's interest as new subjects added flesh to the bone. Chemistry and physics became a fascination to the youths as Professors Cuthbert and Mad Mike vied with each other in outrageous experimentsengagingthe students as few of the other teachers could. Minor explosions, loud bangs and even louder guffaws welcomed each successful venture into the realms of the unknown. Their showman style was so unusual that it totally absorbed their classes and opened the eyes and minds to the wonders of the world. Mixing small quantities of ammonium nitrate with sugar provoked a mini-blast combined with a cloud of smoke that woke the lads up with a bang. Enda Mc Menemin was the first to react as to great amusement he held an old chair aloft as if the arse had just been blown off it.

"You did that yourself," Seamie laughed as order replaced chaos.

As the day wore on there seemed to be less and less time to attend to one's personal interests. A buzz of activity ran through the place like a storm brewing. If not at class they were studying, eating, tidying up or preparing for football, handball or cross-country running. And that was only after a few days.

"A bloody fine start," Seamie thought as he could only conjecture what might unfold as the weeks progressed.

The odd chance they got to chat was like manna from heaven to Ben and Seamie. They relished the moment to compare notes, talk of their homes, families, girlfriends and life's experiences up to that point. Ben couldn't get enough of Seamie's stories about Annabel. Though a big lad and reasonably aware of the birds and the bees he was a novice as far as the fair sex was concerned. Though no professional himself Seamie could see the warning signs that Tess had alerted him to when he told her he was off to a male-only boarding college.

She always picked her moment to advise him on what he might encounter along the way of life. She had seen it all on her travels she informed him one evening as they tore into a pan of potato cake and a few heels left over from Flynn's loaf. Her protégé was by now wide to the ways of the world but she knew also that alone was not enough to safeguard him from the praying mantis that would surely hit on him. His unruly mop of blonde curls and good looks were sure to attract attention from male and female so she took him on a tour of the parish to show him who to look out for. As they hovered over barn and stable and swept along the tree-lined banks of the Inny she pointed out the secret lives and wild shenanigans of the so-called good living folk of the parish. He could hardly believe it until safe back beside the fireplace she showed him how hypocritical people could be. The ones who danced their merry way to the front pew at Sunday mass were as likely to be whoring the night away as paying homage to a blind-eyed pulpit.

And it wasn't always the attraction of the opposite sex that held sway. Some pillars of society sought solace in their own kind behind the Blue Doors or in the quarry at Carrickboy where their preferences were satisfied and people kept their mouths shut. It was a closeted society where pretenses were paramount and money could buy anything simply because ninety per cent of the money was in the hands of the ten per cent. There was no arguing that and few did. Those who attempted to do that soon found themselves out of work and in danger of something unfortunate happening to their families or themselves.

"A shut mouth catches no flies," Tess told Seamie as she steered him through the seedier side of life rather than have him victimized later through ignorance.

He quickly saw where Ben's power lay and kept a firm but polite distance rather than hurt his feelings. Nevertheless, a strong curiosity tempted him at times. He decided to let the hare sit for now and see how Ben would seek to satiate his physical urges. It soon became clear that football was to be his savior.

The eagerly awaited challenge between the North and South was nigh. Ben called his charges together at games time after evening tea. The tennis tables normally in high demand soon fell silent as the teams prepared their plan of action for the following Sunday. Though keener than most, Seamie couldn't help casting a wan look at the abandoned bats and silent snooker tables. He'd take on all challengers win or lose. It was the thrill of winning that drove him onwards. Skills honed at home gave him an eagle eye and peripheral vision. His grandfather often remarked on how wide his eyes stood in his head and said it would be a godsend one day. Though puzzled by the observation at first he accepted the old man's wisdom and waited for an explanation. No use rushing his fences he thought. After all, he was supposed to have learned well at Tess's fireside.

The explanation arrived sooner than expected and in a strange form as the renowned guerrilla fighter told him of his heroes who appeared to have eyes in the back of their heads.

"Not at all a mhic," the old man continued. Their eyes were so wide-set they'd spot a midge on the Mountain without moving their heads.

"You'd need that," he continued, "or a knife would be sunk in your back before you knew where you were."

The old man's wisdom stood him in good stead as everyone piled out of the games room. In charge of locking up, he was invariably the last one out. As he turned the key, he thought he saw something move. Gallogly and Gibson were waiting for him.

"Something up lads?" he enquired showing no trace of the fear he suddenly felt.

"There will be tomorrow if you win the game!"

"Would you like to qualify that or are you as cowardly as before?" Seamie asked apparently nonchalantly. The truth was he had spotted Ben materializing out of the darkness behind them.

Like a red rag to a bull they fell for the bait and into the trap.

"Aren't you right cocky for a Culchie," Gallogly sneered as Gibson pinned Seamie to the wall.

"See if this'll get the message across," he said as he drew back to sink a blow into his stomach. That was as far as he got before he almost passed out with pain as Ben drove his arm up his back to breaking point. Gibson let go as if he had been speared.

"Cheeses Ben we meant no harm, just a bit of fun before the game tomorrow," he pleaded as he got caught in the ribs with a haymaker. Gallogly tried to burst past but got caught by a sucker of a head butt by Seamie who was primed like a pistol.

"You fuckers never learn," Ben growled as he banged their two heads together.

Though protesting they were only trying to intimidate and not to threaten they took their punishment knowing they were outmaneuvered, outsmarted and in a blind alley.

"Hold this Seamie," he winked as he threw him his jacket. It was enough to distract them and keep his pal out of the impending fray.

They dropped to their knees as he sank punches where they'd hurt but wouldn't show. There was no place to run.

"That'll do for now Ben. Fuck off the two of you if you know what's good for you."

"Perfect timing dear boy, where did you spring from?"

"I spotted them lurking under the stairs and pretended not to see them. Once they thought I was gone they headed back to the hall. I knew they were up to no good but wasn't expecting that kind of shite. I gave them enough rope to hang themselves and the rest you know," he grinned as he threw a protective arm around Seamie's shoulders.

"That'll take the wind out of their sails for a while," he whispered as they sat down to their supper. They nudged each other as their pale-faced victims slipped quietly onto their benches without a glance in either direction. Seamie kept a wary eye on Barney to see if he smelt a rat but there was no obvious sign of such. They'd have to be careful he knew as he was wide-awake to the wiles of young men and it wasn't that long since he had trod the same floorboards himself. Precious little escaped his beady eye.

A pissy morning promised little as they took part in the Sunday mass. The priest offered a prayer for better weather but 'it was down for the day' according to Ben who knew how to read the signs from minding sheep in the foothills of the Curlew Mountains.

"It's as good for the goose as for the gander," Seamie reminded him as they went about their morning chores.

Known as 'The Hardy Hewers' in the underground language that invariably permeates such institutions, Ben, Seamie and company were quite happy to tone up muscles by cleaning and polishing the floors of the long corridors as well as the dining and recreation areas. Due to their rustic background, Mad Mike, ably abetted by his protégé Barney, usually gave the heavier duties to those better able for them, knowing it was the best way to keep the whole crew happy.

Roughly half of the lads from the South were from rural areas whereas the majority of the lads from the Wee North were townies. The less taxing duties of the laundry rooms, the haircutting, the library and the chapel were assigned to them. This enabled a good balance to be kept both on and off the playing field, which, apart from the odd flare up, kept things interesting. Generally speaking, strong bonds grew across the board irrespective of birthplace, unless of course, they were influenced by the likes of Gallogly and his cronies. It was too early to call it yet but most felt sure the big game would soon sort things out.

Barney mounted the rostrum after breakfast to inform them that the match was being brought forward to midday due to an unexpected but very welcome visit from the bishop. It was well known that the bishop of Dublin had a healthy respect for the CBS colleges and the quality of teachers that graduated from them. The fact that he and Mad Mike had soldiered together through university was another important factor in the relationship, which, some said, went deeper than the surface.

Every table in the recreation hall was occupied as Seamie strode in after a quick visit to the girls in the kitchen. He had already built up a good relationship with the two cooks and found favour with the girls from the Mercy Convent laundries who had been 'lent' by the bishop. Mostly from rural communities they came to be there by gist of either, an unfortunate pregnancy, abuse, a clandestine relationship or any of the many mishaps one encounters in a quiet backwater in rural Ireland.

Reports of these abuses invariably found their way to the Parochial House through rumor, innuendo or, more likely, the housekeeper. The PP loved nothing better than to conduct his own enquiry into the rumor, thus affording him an opportunity to pry into the secret lives of his flock. That the bishop could also be distracted by such juicy tit bits at their poker games in the Palace was well known.

There was also the problem of Curates straying, so, rather than risk them being caught in the marriage bed they were assigned an accommodating housekeeper who'd be only too happy to oblige for such privileged work. It mattered little to the poor girls because hard work in a secure environment was far better than the awful situations they often sprung from. Money didn't matter that much but clean accommodation, food and friends meant everything after the drudgery and desolation of the Mercy Laundries.

Many of those country girls found a haven of happiness in the boarding colleges around the country. Their escape brought relief to themselves and their families and often saved them from worse fates.

Some of these girls were recruited to help out in the kitchens of the colleges and it was one of these that caught Seamie's eye as he entered with a tray full of cutlery. Kate turned towards him and let out a gasp as she dropped a plate.

"It can't be," they said in unison as they hugged each other oblivious of those around them.

"Well, well, well," Maisie the cook said as she tapped Kate on the shoulder warning her someone was coming. They were all back at their posts as Barney entered.

"These cost money," he snapped as he saw Kate picking up the broken pieces. Blushing deeply, she apologized as he dismissed her and turned on Seamie. "We don't have all day boy. Get on with your job and back to your studies". A sigh of relief signaled their narrow escape. Maisie told them she'd organize it so they'd have time to have a proper chat but to leave it for now.

"You won't believe what's after happening," he said to Ben as he joined him for a game of snooker later. Normally they'd be settling for a game of table tennis as it was their favourite, but being as cute as a pet fox, Ben reckoned there was something in the wind and snooker was much more opportune for a quiet chat especially if Barney was supervising. As they set them up Seamie acquainted his pal with the astonishing news that, not only was his old pal from Ballymahon working in the kitchen, but was also the Cook's second in command. Ben was as flabbergasted as his comrade in arms but listened attentively as he outlined his plan of action. He'd have to have a chat with her of course but he was in no doubt as to her loyalty or compliance.

"You're as jammy," Ben grinned as he listened to what his pal had to say.

"They'll be dishing out the goodies at the game today so play your heart out and I'll see what we can arrange later," was enough to motivate an army. It was enough for Ben too.

"Cheeses, I'll pull it out of the clouds if you can set something up," he winked as he sank a red, black and another red but failed to follow up.

"Thought you might," Seamie laughed as he grabbed his opportunity with both hands to take a sizeable lead. Watching the line of shot while stalking each other left them ample time to discuss various possibilities. Ben was like a young bull in a field of heifers. Realising his heightened excitement might give the game away Seamie advised him to get a hold on himself or they'd all be bucked. Bowing to his obvious experience Ben decided on a cold shower to cool off and wrapped up the game in minutes.

Tidying up after supper Seamie seized the moment and slipped into the kitchen when he spotted Barney taking a group of lads for a stroll around the gardens. The Cook was expecting him and sent him into the laundry room where Kate was busy organizing the ironing for a couple of her girls. Dismissing them immediately she ran to hug him as the door closed behind them.

"I bet you weren't expecting me to be here," she smiled as they stood at arm's length to admire each other after such a long time apart.

"Indeed I wasn't but sure nothing is surprising with you," he giggled as she gave him a playful dig. Knowing they hadn't all evening she quickly explained how she came to be in the college. Although normally reserved for those less fortunate than her she told him she had been recommended by a good friend who happened to be in the know. Like him she grasped the chance of escape with both hands and the rest was history.

"You'll have to meet Ben so," he said as he prepared to leave.

"I've seen him with you several times and so has Louise," she giggled as she saw the surprise in his eyes. "She'd love to meet him if you could set it up," she said without the slightest hint of embarrassment.

"Leave it with me," was his parting words as he blew her a kiss before darting out to the kitchen. The Cook was keeping an eagle eye for Barney as he emerged and slipped him a note, which he stuffed deep in his pocket.

"Don't be afraid of anything," she whispered as she laid a maternal hand on his shoulder. Rather than rush away he walked round the tables pretending to check everything was ready for breakfast the following morning. He didn't dare look at the note until lights out but when he did it was like reading Annabel's last letter before she disappeared out of his life.

Dear Seamie

I know you were heartbroken when Annabel disappeared out of your life and left all of us shocked as well. We all knew how much you meant to each other but I knew that some day you'd get over it enough to start again. You always meant the world to me, and though I was quietly destroyed when the two of you paired up I said nothing and did nothing except cry my eyes out at night for ages. You and I were the very best of friends and likely to be even more so but the minute she joined us I knew you were hers and no one else's. I wasn't jealous either because you just couldn't be that way with her. Though you were often rambling with us you only had eyes for each other. In truth we worried a lot about how close you were because we feared the worst but could say nothing. We might have known Tess wouldn't let that happen but it was a real worry at the same time. I often saw you around the place especially at the football matches, which I never missed once I heard what the team was, but it was obvious you had no interest in anyone after Annabel left. I hadn't the courage to approach you if I saw you at

Mass or at the market but I kept hoping we'd meet again one day. Imagine my surprise and delight when Sister María told me you had left for Baldoyle and that if I really wanted she'd recommend me to Sister Superior if an opportunity arose to work in the college. True to her word she approached me one day several months later to say the priests were looking for someone to help the Chef in that same college. I didn't need to be asked twice so here I am. If it's alright with you I'd be happy to be a special friend and promise to look after you any way I can.

Yours affectionately,

Kate

Ps Louise is from Longford and a great friend. She'd love to get to know Ben better.

Barney threw the ball in as soon as the Angelus bell struck its final note. Though Ben rose higher, Gallogly flicked it away from him to McAllister who chipped it over the helpless corner back and on to Gibson who buried it in the back of the net. The Northern crew went manic as the hapless Southern lads hung their heads in despair. Ben let out a roar you'd hear in Connaught as he rallied his troops.

"Sorry lads, it won't happen again," he promised as he ran to field the kick out. His dander up now, he'd go through a brick wall to redeem himself. Gallogly didn't get a smell of it after that as he drove his team forward like a man possessed. The Northern defense held firm however, shouting taunts of 'Remember Derry' and 'The Battle of the Boyne' which was a little unsettling until McEntee silenced them with 'The Siege of Athlone.'

Despite their best efforts a lead of only four points divided the teams at the break.

Dressed in their neat aprons and Sunday bonnets the girls were busily pretending to be disinterested as the Cook led them along the sideline. Gabby summoned all the players to the sideline for oranges and fizzy drinks as Barney blew the half time whistle.

"Feck that," Seamie growled to Kate.

"You're doing fine. Tell Ben that Louise is here. That'll spur him on," she winked.

"Any chance of us meeting after midnight?" he asked as he pretended to be helping her with the basket of oranges.

"We'll be in the garden shed," was all she said as she went to help the other girls who by now were surrounded by about forty virile young men. He couldn't wait to tell Ben but hemightn't have worried because he could see him chatting to Louise.

"Brilliant," he thought as he joined them.

"Catch you later so," he winked at her as he pulled Ben to one side telling him to concentrate because there was lots of fight left in the other lads still.

Barney was already whistling to get the game going so Ben issued orders on the new tactics and lineout.

"They have all their big lads in a line straight down the field so we'll have to use the wings better. Send the ball out to McGoey or Ganly on the wings and they'll move it through to Seamie or Fahey on either side. If they're able to slip it to Spud or myself running in we'll tie this game up in a hurry," he shouted as he banged one fist into the other to show steely determination. "Come on lads. We can do this. We don't want to be laughed off the pitch," he urged as the lads cheered and clapped in unison.

They had reckoned without Gallogly's survival skills though. He too had switched players all over the place causing Ben to adapt his plans immediately. He was afraid of this because he knew it'd unsettle the team. He was right. Three points went over in quick succession as the ploy worked to immediate effect.

Realizing he was being outwitted Ben barked orders right and left as he redeployed his forces. He needed time though. Rising high he took the ball over Carter's head before falling heavily. Seamie was at his side in a minute and just in time to catch the wink. But, it was Tess he saw and not Ben, telling him to play cute. Calling for water, he signaled to Barney that Ben was hurt. The big lad lay supine for long enough to get his wind back, slowly limping to the full forward line. Shouts of glee went up from the Northerners as they thought Ben was finished. Seamie's brother Mikey joined John Ganley at centre field. A St. Sinneach's combination, it was tried and thrusted. The Northern lads felt it was a rash decision as Gallogly and McAteer would lord the centre with Ben out of the way. It was the rock they were to perish on.

"Take your points," Gallogly ordered his forwards. He knew they'd win that way as goals wouldn't be necessary. It might have worked if they were dealing with lesser men. It was a while since Ganley and Mikey had played centre with St. Sinneachs but their intuitive understanding was more than their counterparts could cope with. Straight from the restart Mikey flicked the ball to John who drove it high and hard to Ben who, gathering it in with one hand, turned on a sixpence, sidestepped big Pat Grant and buriedMcAlinden and the ball in the back of the net. Barney wouldn't allow it as it wasn't in the spirit of the game according to him, but the die had been cast. Too late the lads from the wee North realised they had been beaten at their own game. Though they fought on valiantly their bubble had burst and there was no stopping Ben and his men now.

The final whistle signalled wild celebrations. Several of the players including Seamie were hoisted on to broad shoulders. Barney blew full time knowing it was a lost cause for the Ulster boys. The two pals made a beeline to where the opposition was lying around completely deflated.

Complimenting them on a hard fought game they shook hands and left them to lick their wounds.

Though keen to see what they'd have to say for themselves it wasn't the time or place. Like Ben, he was surprised at the warmth of the handshakes and felt the whole story had been put to bed at last. Gallogly even walked to the dressing rooms with them chatting openly. They felt it was a good omen but decided to be cautious nonetheless. The aftermath of the big match was a bit subdued on account of Barney who felt that it was enough to win without rubbing salt into the wound. None of the Southerners could give a fiddler's fuck one way or the other. Pride was in the winning and nothing else mattered to them.

Midnight Escapade

The evening being free on account of the game the lads wandered around the gardens after lunch. It wasn't often they were to be found there but it served two purposes. They could chat in peace and discreetly find out exactly where the garden shed was located. Stopping to chat with old Father Jarlath they stood talking about the game while checking the creature comforts of the shed. Thinking the lads were interested in horticulture he gave them the full tour chatting about the game he enjoyed and the garden he loved. Just retired, he was appointed head gardener as he was about the only cleric who knew flowers well enough to impress the bishop and visitors. It was an enlightened decision for all as the poor man dreaded retirement having given a lifetime to teaching and the service of God. The gardens saved him from imploding. He got stuck in as if his life depended on it, and it did. Happy that Kate had chosen well, Seamie bid adieu to the old man and headed back to the games room.

Some were playing cards, some chess or one of the board games available, while others were trying their skills at snooker, pool or table tennis. Some even went for a game of handball as if they hadn't enough for one day.

The soft rain didn't bother them as they happily vied with each other in the outdoor alleys. An eagle eye was kept on the walkway between the main college and the alleyways because Barney was known to pounce when least expected. Not many smoked but the few who did relied on their friends to keep them informed of potential hazards such as a sudden swoop by Barney's crime squad. As the alley walls were quite high it was difficult to spot the ascending smoke but Barney had a nose like a sommelier and used it to telling effect. It was amazing how he seemed to materialize out of thin air, and even more so that he could pinpoint the culprits. The one saving grace was that he was partial to the odd cigarette himself and usually let the offenders off with a warning while confiscating their illicit booty. It was left at that and tolerated once it didn't feed back to the powers that be. "Even Homer nods," was his out.

A game of chess was perfect for plotting their midnight escapade. It gave them reasonable privacy and kept them focused on their upcoming adventure. If they were found out it would be immediate expulsion of course but the sheer exhilaration and adrenalin flow made it all worthwhile. Seamie had everything under control, or at least felt he had, but 'there was no knowing what a woman might do,' he said knowingly to his companion who readily agreed even though he was as wise to a woman's wiles as he was to the secret life of a woodland fairy. Nevertheless, they continued planning as if all was in order. Satisfied that Kate would come good they finished their rounds and headed back to their cubicles for a nap as the night promised to be long and adventurous.

Seamie slipped into the kitchen just before teatime on the pretence of checking that Kate had everything ready for tea. It proved to be a ready excuse and not even the Cook passed any heed on them as they went about their duties. However, they were a little taken-aback when she gave them a knowing wink as she danced around them.

As he lay awake after lights out Seamie pondered on the possible outcome of his next actions. If he were to be caught it would lead to immediate expulsion and the embarrassment it would cause him and his family. It didn't bear thinking about so he dismissed it knowing it would only make him more nervous.

No sooner had he heard the first sounds of snoring than he eased himself out the already open window. Ben, waiting directly underneath, easily took his weight as he jumped to the ground.

"Good man, did you fix the bed?"

"Don't be stupid. Of course I did. I didn't come down in the last shower you know," brought a smile of relief to both of them.

The dense shrubbery at the back of the college provided good cover as they slipped into the undergrowth. It wasn't long before two forms materialized from the other side of the garden.

"They're here," Ben whispered.

"I brought Louise," she giggled as she hugged Seamie.

Ben needed no coaxing and slipped his arm around Louise's waist as naturally as an actor.

"Years of experience," he said later when he was asked how he had managed to remain so calm.

Seeing they were happy together Seamie and Kate took their cue to break away for themselves.

"You'll be alright here," he told them as he led Kate towards the laundry room.

The pinpoint beam of his torch led them to a heap of discarded jute and flour bags.

"Will these be alright," he asked as he turned to his smiling companion.

"If they're ok for you they're ok for me," she responded as she led him firmly onto them.

A sharp tap on the window brought them to their feet in an instant. Looking at his watch he was amazed to see that it was near dawn. Ben and Louise were already on the move and joined them at the corner.

"We'll have to move fast or we're bucked," he told them. Apologising to the girls for putting them at risk he was surprised by Kate's answer.

"Don't worry about us because the cook knows we're with you," she said to his utter amazement.

"I'll fill you later, go on back now and grab an hour before the bell." They were gone as quietly as they had arrived hours earlier.

Ben was like the cat that got the cream as they made their way back to their cubicles.

They mightn't have worried because there wasn't a sinner in sight as they slipped back into their respective cubicles and into a deep sleep.

Though tired the following day they kept up pretences as best they could. Nor did they seek each other's company in case it might arouse Barney's suspicions. He couldn't be trusted, even having spies lined up so he could put pressure on some of the more vulnerable of the groups. It would be a while before the lads were to find out why, but for now they just needed to protect themselves and their immediate friends. It didn't take long to figure out whom to trust after seeing Rynne having his hole kicked soon after attaching to the group. This was done to send a clear message to anyone close to the group. The inner circle became just that, as tight as the lid on a pot of Lamb's jam as the Bun used to say. Despite that, great care was needed to keep Barney at bay if their next plan was to reach fruition.

Now that the stage was set Seamie was rarin' to go. Kate slipped goodies like there was no tomorrow. And it wasn't only food! Now accepted as part of the Kitchen Circle run by the Cook and Kate, he knew he was made. Favours could easily be bought with an extra portion here and there and Kate made sure he got the best. Not alone that! She soon had the rest of the girls in on the act as she led their initiation from girl to woman. The kitchen became more like Fagin's Den than a college. Maisie ruled her kitchen like Queen Meabh her armies. A set of warning signals kept her in tune with every move that Barney and his cohorts made. A cough being far too obvious the tap of a spoon or the clink of a glass worked wonders and kept her charges on their toes. Her girls were largely from farming stock but surplus to requirements when times were hard. With more mouths to feed than was physically possible it only needed one mistake to ensure a girl was dismissed from her service in the big Protestant houses and sent home to be either treated as a slave or worse. Sometimes they had to take their chances in the city where their naivety could make or break them. The lucky ones found tolerable work in the college kitchens. By keeping on top of her job Maisie made sure her staff were looked after.

A college full of red-blooded lads needed an escape valve, an outlet, and she had the wherewithal to meet the demand. With Seamie and Ben as willing helpers she soon had the girls on overtime. Her roster took on a new meaning as the late shift carried a couple of meanings. Working the 'shift' or getting a 'shift' could mean one-and-the-same thing, or not. It depended who was saying it and what they meant by it.

It was after a long walk to the Hill of Howth on one of the finest days of early autumn when Seamie suspected something was wrong. Patrolling the periphery of the large group of walkers he felt a tug at his jacket. It was none other than Gallogly.

"We need to talk," he whispered as the group made way for Seamie. A maneuver the military would be proud of, it meant each group of three had to drop one so that it wouldn't be obvious to Barney's eagle eye. Failing to do so meant a spell in the Stink Bin, a claustrophobic cupboard of a room with a tiny window high up on the wall. It was used to store all kinds of brushes and mops as well as wax and polish for the long corridors.

Handing him a note Gallogly warned him not to let a sinner see it. Pretending it was a sweet he made nothing of it. All he was worried about was Barney. Some said he had a pact with the devil and would sacrifice anything in order to maintain absolute control over his flock.

It was sometime later before he could risk reading the note. It froze him to the spot.

"Either you lose the game on Sunday or your little operation is history and so are you." Nothing more. He knew the bastard wasn't messing but he also knew he couldn't give in to the threat or all he stood for was over.

Answering the tap on his window Ben held it open as his pal entered.

"We're fucked," Seamie said as he proceeded to relate the encounter with Gallogly.

"Will you settle sonny for crying out loud," Ben advised as he sat his worried friend on the bed. He listened a little more before dismissing the whole thing out of hand.

"Look Seamie. I have that cunt over a barrel, and he's fucked not us. Didn't I see him and his gang in the Broadmeadow pool only yesterday. I heard them laughing and crept up on them as they were acting the bollocks. You wouldn't see women carrying on like that. They're a gang of queers the fecking lot of them. They were hugging and holding and more as well. After the shift with Louise I'm fairly sure I'm not gay but that'd give an erection to a donkey. Feck the likes of it I ever saw and I know how animals act in the wild."

"I know what you mean and I've been close to that myself. The time Smullin joined me fishing on the island on the Inny in Tenelick I had no idea what he was up to for ages. He was joking and laughing, giving me sweets and talking about girls he went with and all that. I was surprised because Tess told me he was a queer. The next thing he was showing me his lad and asking to see mine. I told him to fuck off quick or I'd tell my father on him. He left but I was amazed I had an erection afterwards. Maybe there's a bit of both in all of us. I'd far prefer the fairer sex though because they're built differently as I've found out."

"Well, stop worrying about that cunt Gallogly. I have him by the hasp of the arse over his poker of queens."

"Thanks Ben. We needed something like that. We'll sicken him at 11's tomorrow." With that he was gone happy in the knowledge their other little game was sound too.

Tempus Fugit

The first three years slipped by at a rapid rate. There was so much happening it was hard to keep up with it. Kate kept him from missing Annabel in her own fashion and there were the hours of serious study, long walks, football, outings and the exams. Apart from helping with the turf, timber, hay and so on during the holidays there was little to keep him occupied at home. Fishing became a lifeline and introduced him to many an interesting personality and location as he went further afield from the Inny. From Barley Harbour to Banagher and back he joined lake and river fishermen as they vied with each other for a biggie. It was on one of these expeditions on Loch Ree that he first bumped into the legendry boatman and fisherman per excellánce, Johnny Moran, who took him under his wing and taught him where to look for a big trout and how best to land it. A unique individual, Johnny spent more hours on the lake than most and put it to good stead when the wealthy alickadoos came on a good day to be photographed with a big one they had supposedly caught. Clever as a jailor Johnny knew how to string them along as he took them to his special spots where a catch was virtually guaranteed. His special relationship with the families recently relocated by the ESB kept him posted on all that happened around the lake from Lanesboro to Athlone where he often took chances rowing home in the dead of night after a fair few pints in 'The Point.'

Not wanting to waste another year hanging around, he persuaded Kate to join him in Red Island Holiday Camp in Skerries where there was good money to be made and an escape from boredom as well. He had heard from Cummins that all he needed to do was turn up and he'd get an interview because his father was the security manager there. They had a chat with Maisie just in case Kate was tied up in any way. She had no problem with her leaving and gave an excellent reference to ease her way.

The interview was short and sweet. Once vetted, they were asked if they could start immediately. Put in charge of the entertainment section at first meant organizing the fun and games for the adults over from The British Isles. Although bingo and dancing was the most popular initially the after-dinner-sing-along was also a huge hit. Old Man Quinn was quick to spot their potential and gave them free rein to organize it as they wished. It soon developed a mind of its own leading to a series of talent competitions which Eugene Lambert and family got involved in. Eugene Junior, being drafted, quickly-left his mark through his organizational skills. As their fame spread so did the bookings. People flocked in from all over the UK with the prize money rising accordingly. Sponsorship attracted big names and brought its own problems as the average punter gave way to the semi-professionals. Feeling this would kill the golden goose Seamie and Kate went to Quinn to outline their fears. A sharp businessman, he listened attentively and promised an early answer. Calling them to his office the following day he told them he agreed with them and that he wanted them to look after the bar and buffet. No easy task, they nevertheless accepted and left the entertainment to young Lambert who had the pedigree for it coming from a family of entertainers. Completely unselfish, he involved them in the live arts as much as he could. They revelled in it as Seamie was no mean singer and Kate could draw more than her breath. She loved sketching people and landscapes and it was this that drew Eugene's attention. Even Mr. Quinn expressed surprise at the life-like pictures and thought the world of a special one she painted of a scene of the older customers in The Harbour Bar. Offering her a fair price for it he hung it over his desk because it caught the sunlight streaming in the window.

Before long they were making a real go of it and coining it with tips. The English were great at tipping especially if they got a ready smile and advice on where to go and what to do. Seamie had another angle. He organized a kind of dating service for the visitors, many of them escaping from difficult relationships across the water. As there were about fifty fellow workers he had no difficulty fixing them up with a date but the visitors had to pay a fee for the service. Few complained as they often got more than they bargained for as the lusty Irish males and females rose to the occasion.

One evening as they were gearing up for a busy night of music and song, the owner dropped in, requested a coffee and sat down for a chat. He asked if they were happy working in the complex and if there was anything special they needed.

"A bit of privacy would be huge," Seamie replied without batting an eyebrow.

"Done," he replied without quibble. "Pick your rooms before the new batch comes in on Friday and no more about it."

"Could we have one room instead?" Kate piped up.

He looked a bit askance for a moment, then replied: "Why not? You're old enough to look after yourselves and it'll save me using two rooms. Take the big room facing the Little Harbour and you'll have great views as well as privacy." Thanking them for their dedication he finished his coffee and left.

"Cheeses Kate you went for gold there," Seamie said as hugged her to celebrate their good luck.

"If you don't ask you won't receive," she laughed as they kissed just before the crowds started pouring in.

It was a long hot summer full of surprises and hard work. Whenever they had time off they went rock fishing, a sport they both loved. It was dangerous enough because it meant timing the tides and getting through the rocks as fast as possible before the next wave broke over them. A few good drownings taught them quicker than any Old Moore's Almanac. It didn't stop them because with a little knowledge, a lot of patience and no shortage of courage they were sure of a good catch in the pools left by the retreating tides. Bass, crab, pollock and mackerel often got stranded in the pools and were easy enough caught with an improvised net and broom handle. But it was the element of danger, the fight against nature and the excitement that drove them on.

Although only a short distance offshore and only reachable at low tide, Saint Patrick's Island often beckoned, especially if they had a few free days. That wasn't often but it did happen from time to time. Making a point of retiring as early as possible one Friday night they decided to have a go at visiting the island over the weekend.

'Pierpoint Joe' known as 'Piers' for short (a part-time fisherman with the "Queen of Skerries") often popped into the bar for a chat. Seamie ribbed Kate that it was because of her he showed up so often. Joe Mays had been his haunt for years but he loved chatting with the two of them and kept them posted on all kinds of local gossip. His favourite chair stood at the end of the bar where he could keep an eye on the harbour as well as everyone who came and went. It was he who gave them the lowdown on the tidal situation and even asked to join them as it had been years since he had risked it. Thanking him for his interest they politely declined. It would be a handful for themselves never mind taking on someone of limited mobility. His throwaway expression of 'risking it' didn't help his cause either.

Rising early, they hoisted their rucksacks and started out after the receding tide. It was slow going but there was no hurry and the sun was already taking the bite out of the cold east wind. Taking off their boots and socks and rolling up their pants they waded through the last channel. It was nearly the undoing of them as the pull was much stronger than they expected and would have swept them off their feet had they not held hands and dug deep with their long poles, a precaution the old man had strongly advised, not only because of the tide but also because badgers were said to have moved onto the now deserted island. They were grateful for his advice as they clambered over the sands and up the rocks to safer ground.

Being early yet, they searched for a sheltered spot on the landward side to erect their tent. It didn't take them long to find a suitable spot to set up camp prior to exploring the island. Many of the old cottages had fallen into lamentable decay and were overgrown with ferocious looking brambles, whins and whitethorn.

"No bucking way," Seamie answered when Kate suggested they attempt tramping them down to get a good look inside the houses. Explaining he had seen the 'Bun' come undone by the same bastarding bucky briars he had no trouble convincing her to give it a miss. Nevertheless, she was keen to get into at least one of them as rumour had it, and Piers assured her it was true, several of the cottages had been abandoned almost overnight for some strange reason. Seeing three semi-ruins huddled under a cluster of rocks they decided to investigate further. The few stunted briars were kept in check by the fast-growing rhododendron allowing them easier access here than to the others.

"Look out," he shouted as he leaped back through the open doorway. She had already taken to her heels and was clambering up to the safety of the rocks above them.

"A fecking badger," he swore as he wiped the perspiration from his brow.

"Damnit," she cursed, "we were so close."

Not wanting to give up he did a quick reconnoitre of the buildings from the top before calling her over. The badger got as big a fright as them and had hightailed it through the undergrowth to the other side of the island. As there was no sign of a sett he felt sure the animal was just grubbing around for insects and was no longer a threat. Just so, they proceeded cautiously, beating the flagstones as they checked out the rooms. It was easy as none of the three cottages had more than two good-sized rooms.

"Look at this?" she said as she cautiously opened an old chest. It was full of family heirlooms which the owners had obviously hoped to recover way back then. They had either passed away or considered it unsafe or unlucky to return. The goods had remained untouched for some considerable time.

"What'll we do?" she asked. Telling her to pick out whatever she wished he was already exploring another sea chest in the adjoining room.

"This stuff is valuable," he said as he examined some silver plate, ornaments and beautifully crafted religious ware, including what appeared to be goblets and chalices. "They're gold," he called as he rubbed them with his sleeve.

"Seamie," she called. Her tone of voice warned him something was amiss. Replacing them instantly and covering the chest with a dust-covered coat from the back of the door he went to join her. Spotting someone approaching she drew him out of the cottage as quickly as possible. "It's Piers!" he said as he recognized their old friend who was climbing slowly towards them. Running to help he asked what had brought him.

"Curiosity gossoon," he replied dryly. "I see you were in my old place. Did you find anything interesting?"

"Divil the much," he answered. "There's a couple of old wooden boxes but I doubt there's much in them."

"There should be," Piers declared. "It's years since I was here or anyone else for that matter," he added. He told them he had kept a close eye from a distance and his old fishing mates would have told him if strangers had set foot on the island. It was known that a few botanists and the like had been there but they'd have no interest in the interior of the houses, he continued as he lifted the lid of the chest Kate had been investigating. "Not a thing missing," he said happily as he proceeded to fill them in on where the goods had come from. Piracy and shipwrecks for the most part, he told them. Many a passing boat ran aground during heavy squalls with anyone surviving either dispatched forthwith or drowned trying to gain land. 'Savage times' he said but there was no alternative. The bailiffs were stuck everywhere trying to extract every last penny for the absentee landlords. With barely enough to feed their own people never mind the stranger, mercy went out the window. He shook visibly as he recalled the sacrifices his forefathers had to make to stay alive.

The booty borne from the shipwrecks was hidden away in tunnels for generations he reminisced. Pirating was also rife way back then and Islanders pretending to be fishing often pulled in at Portrane and further afield to raid the monasteries and cells.

It was impossible to dispose of all the booty but even the British had their fences who traded with the pirates, often paying handsomely for quality goods that eventually found their way to traders in London and the Continent. As always, some families did well while others suffered. Eventually forced to leave with the little they had, they took their chances in Argentina and America where many had gone before and after the famine.

'That didn't boil the kettle,' according to Piers. What to do now was the obvious question? Saying it was up to him as they were only exploring, Seamie made as if to go.

"You're as cute as a pet fox lad," the old man grinned. "You've found the treasure and you have my blessing to do with it as you wish as long as you deal me in on some of the profits."

"Done," said Seamie as they shook hands before preparing to conceal their find. Telling them to follow him he soon led them to a circle of boulders on an elevated point where, to their amazement, a heavy rock pivoted as soon as he put his shoulder to an oval-shaped depression on it. Not waiting on ceremony they followed his torchlight as he led them into a man-size tunnel which was bone dry and seemingly devoid of furniture or fittings.

"This will be perfect for storing everything until you have time to organise yourselves," he told them. Delighted with the amazing turn of events they thanked him profusely promising to honour the bargain made with him.

"D'ya think I didn't know that when I followed you?"

"I've been waiting for ages for the right person to come along and now I have two. It's true what they say 'all things come to those who wait.' Sure it might be my last chance to save what my people had fought and died for," he added as he looked away in case they'd spot a tear in his eye.

Inviting him to join him for sandwiches and minerals he reluctantly agreed when Kate told him they had brought enough for the two days and there was no way they were letting him go without celebrating with them. Without further ado they set about moving what they could as Kate prepared the picnic.

"Glory days," Seamie thought as he carried the heavier items rather than 'hoist the cliamh(wicker basket) on the old man's shoulders' as his grandfather would say. It took the two of them to manhandle the old sea chests and, even then, they had to lighten the load to do so. Although he'd have loved to examine everything there was no time to waste if they were to transfer everything before they got too tired or night fell on them. Happy to hear her calling them to lunch his heart skipped a beat as he saw her sitting cross-legged on a tartan cloth laid out invitingly with sambos and goodies. It was then he remembered why they had come to the island; to get away by themselves and to savour a special relationship that started innocently in the college kitchen.

They had been so busy working together they hardly had time to speak of anything except the business they were running. Likewise, when they retired to their room they were so spun-out they fell into a coma in each other's arms. That was fine too but they knew they had to escape to rekindle what had been too good to lose. Piers, being anxious to get back to the mainland, Seamie accompanied him as far as the channel to make sure he was safely across. Waving goodbye he headed back to Kate as they had planned on staying overnight and returning when the tide was low the following day.

Tidying up after their wholesome snack, courtesy of the cook who always gave them the best, they readied their nest for a feel good night. This is what they came for but there had been a few hitches along the way while getting organized. There was the crossing, the badger, the lost treasure and, not least, the unexpected but not unwelcome visit by Piers. There was a lot to think about and a lot to do but it could wait they agreed. Hours later as they lay in a coma in each other's arms they were suddenly awakened by strong winds and heavy rain beating on the tent. Peering out,they were dismayed to see waves lashing the island just below them. Putting plan B into action immediately they gathered up as much as possible and made a beeline for the dry tunnel. As soon as the rain eased a little they dismantled the tent before it was ripped to shreds or blown across the island. Thrilled to find the tunnel so spacious and almost airtight despite the storm they lay out their bedsheets and sleeping bags and made it as comfortable as possible.

There was little respite as the morning progressed making it difficult to plan a crossing with the channel still being full despite the tide being on the turn. Realising they'd be stranded if they didn't soon make a burst for it they strapped on their backpacks, grabbed their long poles and dashed to the narrowest point. Despite the driving rain and fierce gusts they could see a group of people hurrying towards them with what appeared to be ropes and poles. Piers had obviously called out the troops knowing how difficult the crossing was even in fine weather. Wading in deep, the rescue team was attempting to form a human chain in the fast rushing channel. Gallantly, the two youngsters ploughed in and struck out towards them. Despite their long poles the going was extremely difficult. Suddenly their feet were swept from under them with the swell and they were caught up in the dangerous current. As he rose to the surface he saw Kate being swept away. The men were running frantically to reach her but it was too late. As he battled to swim towards her he found himself being restrained by strong arms.

Kate was out of sight and gone.

THIS BOOK
WAS EDITED IN CERCEDILLA
IN AUTUMN 2015